RELIGION AND PUBLIC LIFE
IN THE SOUTH:
IN THE EVANGELICAL MODE

RELIGION BY REGION

Religion by Region Series
Co-published with the Leonard E. Greenberg Center for the
Study of Religion in Public Life at Trinity College
Mark Silk and Andrew Walsh, Series Editors

The United States is a nation of many distinct regions. But until now, no literature has looked at these regional differences in terms of religion. The Religion by Region Series describes, both quantitatively and qualitatively, the religious character of contemporary America, region by region. Each of the eight regional volumes includes overviews and demographic information to allow comparisons between regions. But at the same time, each volume strives to show what makes its region unique. A concluding volume looks at what these regional variations mean for American religion as a whole.

1. Religion and Public Life in the Pacific Northwest: *The None Zone*
   Edited by Patricia O'Connell Killen (Pacific Lutheran University) and Mark Silk

2. Religion and Public Life in the Mountain West: *Sacred Landscapes in Tension*
   Edited by Jan Shipps (Indiana University–Purdue University, Indianapolis) and Mark Silk

3. Religion and Public Life in New England: *Steady Habits, Changing Slowly*
   Edited by Andrew Walsh and Mark Silk

4. Religion and Public Life in the Midwest: *America's Common Denominator?*
   Edited by Philip Barlow (Hanover College) and Mark Silk

5. Religion and Public Life in the Southern Crossroads Region: *Showdown States*
   Edited by William Lindsey (Philander Smith College) and Mark Silk

6. Religion and Public Life in the South: *In the Evangelical Mode*
   Edited by Charles Reagan Wilson (University of Mississippi) and Mark Silk

7. Religion and Public Life in the Middle Atlantic Region: *The Fount of Diversity*
   Edited by Randall Balmer (Columbia University) and Mark Silk

8. Religion and Public Life in the Pacific Region: *Fluid Identities*
   Edited by Wade Clark Roof (University of California, Santa Barbara) and Mark Silk

9. Religion by Region: *Religion and Public Life in The United States*
   By Mark Silk and Andrew Walsh

RELIGION AND PUBLIC LIFE IN THE SOUTH: IN THE EVANGELICAL MODE

Edited by

Charles Reagan Wilson

and

Mark Silk

Published in cooperation with the Leonard E. Greenberg
Center for the Study of Religion in Public Life at
Trinity College, Hartford, Connecticut

ALTA MIRA
P R E S S

A Division of
ROWMAN & LITTLEFIELD PUBLISHERS, INC.
Walnut Creek • Lanham • New York • Toronto • Oxford

Published in cooperation with the Leonard E. Greenberg Center for the Study of Religion in Public Life at Trinity College, Hartford, Connecticut

ALTAMIRA PRESS

A division of Rowman & Littlefield Publishers, Inc.
1630 North Main Street, #367
Walnut Creek, CA 94596
www.altamirapress.com

Rowman & Littlefield Publishers, Inc.
A wholly owned subsidary of The Rowman & Littlefield Publishing Group, Inc.
4501 Forbes Boulevard, Suite 200
Lanham, MD 20706

PO Box 317
Oxford
OX2 9RU, UK

British Library Cataloguing in Publication Information Available

Library of Congress Cataloging-in-Publication Data

TK

Printed in the United States of America

The paper used in this publication meets the minimum requirements of American National Standard for Information Sciences—Permanence of Paper for Printed Library Materials, ANSI/NISO Z39.48–1992.

CONTENTS

PREFACE

Geographical diversity is the hallmark of religion in the United States. There are Catholic zones and evangelical Bible Belts, a Lutheran domain and a Mormon fastness, metropolitan concentrations of Jews and Muslims, and (in a different dimension) parts of the country where religious affiliation of whatever kind is very high and parts where it is far below the norm. This religious heterogeneity is inextricably linked to the character of American places. From Boston to Birmingham, from Salt Lake City to Santa Barbara, even the casual observer perceives public cultures that are intimately connected to the religious identities and habits of the local population.

Yet when the story of religion in American public life gets told, the country's variegated religious landscape tends to be reduced to a series of monochrome portraits of the spiritual state of the union, of piety along the Potomac, of great events or swings of mood that raise or lower the collective religious temperature. Whatever the virtues of compiling such a unified national narrative—and I believe they are considerable—they obscure a great deal. As the famous red-and-blue maps of the past two presidential votes make clear, region has not ceased to matter in national politics. Indeed, in this era of increasing federalism regions are, state by state, charting ever more distinctive courses.

To understand where each region is headed and why, it is critical to recognize the place of religion in it.

Religion by Region, a project of the Leonard E. Greenberg Center for the Study of Religion in Public Life at Trinity College in Hartford, represents the first comprehensive effort to show how religion shapes, and is being shaped by, regional culture in America. The project has been designed to produce edited volumes (of which this is the sixth) on each of eight regions of the country. A ninth volume will sum up the results in order to draw larger conclusions about the way religion and region combine to affect civic culture and public policy in the United States as a whole.

The purpose of the project is not to decompose a national storyline into eight separate narratives. Rather, it is to bring regional realities to bear, in a systematic way, on how American culture is understood at the beginning of the twenty-first century. In line with the Greenberg Center's commitment to enhance public understanding of religion, these volumes are intended for a general audience, with a particular eye towards helping working journalists make better sense of the part religion plays in the public life—local, statewide, regional, and national—that they cover. At the same time, I am persuaded that the accounts and analyses provided in these volumes will make a significant contribution to the academic study of religion in contemporary America.

The project's division of the country into regions will be generally familiar, with the exception of what we are calling the Southern Crossroads—a region roughly equivalent to what American historians know as the Old Southwest, comprising Louisiana, Texas, Arkansas, Oklahoma, and Missouri. Since we are committed to covering every state in the Union (though not the territories—e.g. Puerto Rico), Hawaii has been included in a Pacific region with California and Nevada, and Alaska in the Pacific Northwest.

Cultural geographers may be surprised to discover a few states out of their customary places. Idaho, which is usually considered part of the Pacific Northwest, has been assigned to the Mountain West. In our view, the fact that the bulk of Idaho's population lives in the heavily Mormon southern part of the state links it more closely to Utah than to Oregon and Washington. To be sure, we might have chosen to parcel out certain states between regions, assigning northern Idaho and western Montana to the Pacific Northwest or, to take another example, creating a Catholic band running from southern Louisiana through south Texas and across the lower tiers of New Mexico and Arizona on into southern California. The purpose of the project, however, is not to map the country religiously but to explore the ways that politics, public policies, and civil society relate—or fail to relate—to the religion that is on the ground. States have had to be kept intact because when American laws are not made in Washington, D.C., they are made in statehouses. To understand what is decided in Baton Rouge, Louisiana's Catholic south and evangelical north must be seen as engaged in a single undertaking.

That is not to say that the details of American religious demography are unimportant to our purpose. That demography has undergone notable shifts in recent years, and these have affected public life in any number of ways. To reckon with them, it has been essential to assemble the best data available on the religious identities of Americans and how they correlate with voting patterns and views on public issues. As students of American religion know, however, this is far from an easy task. The U.S. Census is prohibited by law from asking questions about religion, and membership reports provided by religious bodies to non-governmental researchers—when they are provided at all—vary greatly in accuracy. Most public opinion polling does not enable us to draw precise correlations between respondents' views on issues and their religious identity and behavior.

In order to secure the best possible empirical grounding, the project has assembled a range of data from three sources, which are described in detail in the Appendix. These have supplied us with, among other things, information from religious bodies on their membership; from individuals on their religious identities; and from voters in specific religious categories on their political preferences and opinions. (For purposes of clarity, people are described as "adherents" or "members" only when reported as such by a religious institution. Otherwise, they are "identifiers.") Putting this information together with 2000 census and other survey data, the project has been able to create both the best available picture of religion in America today and the most comprehensive account of its political significance.

Religion by Region does not argue that religion plays the same kind of role in each region of the country; nor does it mean to advance the proposition that religion is the master key that unlocks all the secrets of American public life. As the tables of contents of the individual volumes make clear, each region has its distinctive religious layout, based not only on the numerical strength of particular religious bodies but also on how those bodies, or groups of them, function on the public stage. In some regions, religion serves as a shaping force; in others it is a subtler conditioning agent. Our objective is simply to show what the picture looks like from place to place, and to provide consistent data and a framework of discussion sufficient to enable useful contrasts and comparisons to be drawn.

A project of such scope and ambition does not come cheap. We are deeply indebted to the Lilly Endowment for making it possible.

Mark Silk
Hartford, Connecticut
January 2005

INTRODUCTION

PREACHIN', PRAYIN', AND SINGIN' ON THE PUBLIC SQUARE

Charles Reagan Wilson

Lester Flatt and Earl Scruggs were one of bluegrass music's most popular duos, and their post-World War II song, "Preachin', Prayin', Singin'," suggests a beginning point for consideration of religion's role in southern public life. The narrator is an outsider in a community, one who is "intent upon my way," but he notices a crowd that turns out to be a religious gathering. He hears "a welcome voice," which in good evangelical Protestant style is "pleading me to come and share the preachin', prayin', singin' down on the public square." It seemed that "all of God's children were together there," as the group shouted God's "love and care." He feels "so much at home amid the nameless throng" that he is able to "lay the burdens down," becoming a redeemed part of "an old-time meeting down on the public square." The narrator urges everyone to continue to "leave the doorbell on, down on the public square."[1]

Religion in the American South has been distinguished by the long cultural hegemony of evangelical Protestants, and the Flatt and Scruggs song was a classic expression of its expectation to be at ease not only in the region's churches but also on its public squares. Evangelical Protestants have been deeply tied to dominant southern cultural styles and traditions, at the very center of a regional context that defined parameters for private selves and public identities. "Preachin', Prayin', Singin'" shows relationships between the individualistic ethos of evangelicalism and its public expression. Evangelicalism is a religion of sin and salvation, deeply influenced by Calvinism's dim view of human nature and yet offering believers free grace toward redemption. The central theme of religion in the South has been the compelling drive toward conversion and the moral life afterwards. Churches orient their resources toward evangelistic and missionary work designed to further the Great Commission that Jesus Christ outlined—going out and converting the world.

The narrator of the Flatt and Scruggs song reveals a lost soul, one "intent upon my way," but hearing God's message on the public square makes all the difference. This public square aspires to be an inclusive setting, as the song says, with "all of God's children" present; and the South's oral culture reveals God's presence through the "preachin', prayin', singin'" that connects the individualistic faith of personal salvation to a public event expressing the community's faith.

The South of Flatt and Scruggs was perhaps the nation's most distinctive region, and religion had long been part and parcel of that distinctiveness. It is still so, despite the past half century of dramatic changes in the region. Observers used to speak confidently of the region's identifiable social, economic, political, and cultural patterns within the United States. The South had a predominantly agricultural economy within an industrialized nation; cotton was king; *de jure* racial segregation, political disfranchisement, and the sharecropping economy defined a near-caste system for black southerners; and the Democratic Party embodied a political solid South. In the 1930s, the sociologist Howard Odum identified hundreds of specific items from social science analysis that made the South distinctive, and the *Encyclopedia of Southern Culture*, half a century later, showed similar numbers of still-persisting cultural markers of regional distinctiveness.

Much has changed since Odum's time, and change has been palpable in the South of the last decade of the twentieth century and the first years of the twenty-first century. The South has more industrialized jobs than any part of the nation, but its textile mills have now fled the region seeking cheaper Third World labor. Cotton has long been dethroned as king of agriculture, and even the once bottom-feeding catfish has been dressed up in pond-fed luxury, often getting as much attention as the fields of white once did. Race relations are no longer so identifiably distinctive, and the region is being enriched by an in-migration of African Americans, making it the country's fastest growing African-American locale.

At the same time, the region's traditionally dominant population groups, who traced their ancestry to Western Europe and West Africa, are meeting new ethnic groups, especially Latinos, who have become a major social group throughout the South since the 1990s. The Republican Party has not just risen from political marginality in the South but has come to dominate, at least in national elections. The South seems politically solid again, but with the GOP now in charge. The South's economy was the nation's fastest growing regional sector in the 1990s, underlying many of the other changes.

Religion has shown some notable continuities in this period of enormous change, especially the continuing influence of denominations that have traditionally dominated the region—black and white Protestants in evangelical denominations. As Ted Ownby shows in his chapter, among the major features that differentiate the South from the rest of the country is the dominant role of evangelicals—Baptists above all. The context for these continuities with the southern past is different, though, from a century ago or even 50 years ago.

In some representations, of course, the South remains fixed, with its image as an enduring, stable, static place. Its recent changes belie such stereotyping, and throughout its history the region has, in fact, faced repeated challenges to its identity. Despite these changes, there still exists an identity that has helped southerners maintain a culture and a distinctive outlook. The historian C. Vann Woodward famously wrote essays on the "burden of southern history" and the "search for southern identity" that located southern distinctiveness in particular regional historical experiences, including the defeat of the Confederacy in the Civil War, guilt over its unjust race relations in a nation dedicated to ideals of liberty and equality, and generations of pervasive poverty in a nation that celebrated material abundance. In addition, religion has been central to the southern identity, and a brief look at the history of the religious basis of the southern identity allows evaluation of continuities and changes in that identity in recent times. The southern identity has offered psychological support functions for southerners undergoing changes and has provided an ideological basis for public life.

The Religious Right today speaks often of protection of the family, with the Southern Baptist Convention even affirming an older patriarchy as a continuing ideal. The Church of England was the first religious establishment in the colonies that would later become the American South, and that church helped stamp the region with a hierarchical English social system that long outlived Anglican religious dominance, with its patriarchal ideal especially noteworthy. The metaphor of "family" provided a justification for white male dominance over the southern household, from upper-class planters through small farmers and the working class. The southern concern for place, for sometimes rigid expectations about where individuals and families fit in the social hierarchy, came from these early religiously based patterns, which took deep root in a slave society that especially had to justify a "place" for its slaves and later freed, if second-class, citizens, but which also defined white women within their submissive "place."

The religion expressed in "Preachin', Prayin', Singin'" was not Anglicanism, but evangelical Protestantism, which emerged in the late eighteenth-century southern colonies among the socially marginal; while not unique to the emerging southern region, it was a form of Christianity that took deep root there. At the turn of the nineteenth century, frontier revivals emerged on the border between Kentucky and Tennessee, spreading evangelicalism's message of the need to be born-again throughout the South's largely unchurched frontier areas.

The South's rural areas and small towns still hark back in memory to the founding images of evangelicalism, with its camp meetings, brush arbors, and family-centered life. Bill Gaither's popular southern white gospel programs still project these images as fundamental ones that nurtured the old-time faith. Baptists, Methodists, and Presbyterians—the first of the South's evangelicals—were all part of this spiritual fervor in the early nineteenth century. Over the next six decades, they spread to become the South's largest religious groups. They made their peace with the dominant social patterns of the region, including slavery, and soon converted much of the elite to this passionate faith. As Donald Mathews has written, evangelical "symbols, style of self-control, and rules of social decorum became dominant in the social system."[2]

These early evangelicals stressed the need for the individual to get right with God through conversion, but they also believed in establishing purified moral communities of the saved. They aspired to influence public life through shaping the moral lives of individuals—the kingdom of God on earth would come through individual moral reform. Evangelicals soon went beyond this model, though, and began identifying their fortunes with the South itself.

The rise to dominance of evangelicals coincided with the emergence of a distinctive southern identity in the years after 1820. The impassioned sectional conflict crystallized southern fears of political vulnerability within the nation, just as the region was acknowledging the slave system as a basis of the southern social system as well as much of its economy. At the beginning of the 1830s, when northern abolitionism began attacking the morality of slavery and the Nat Turner slave rebellion occurred in Virginia, white southerners turned to their religious leaders to articulate a biblical defense of their "peculiar institution." Citing Paul's admonition for servants to obey their masters, they made the claim that chattel slavery had coexisted with Christianity.

Soon, in fact, they made the Bible the fundamental text of southern life in general; it was the good book that could be found from the seats of state government to the backwoods cabins. The inerrantist view of the infallible Scriptures among the contemporary Southern Baptists evolved from these beginnings of southern evangelicalism in a period when the southern faithful were under not just political attack from the North but religious and moral judgment from above the Mason-Dixon Line as well. Evangelicals had come to see themselves as the moral custodians of their culture and now they were becoming its public defenders against outside attack.

Evangelical Protestantism was used by nineteenth-century white southerners to establish boundaries between themselves and northerners, on the one hand, and black southerners, on the other. When Baptists and Methodists from the South split off from their northern brethren to form distinctively southern denominations in the 1840s (and the Presbyterians during the Civil War), they created the first institutions of the southern civil religion, asserting a God-ordained regional identity against northern moralists and against the African Americans within southern society. These institutions long outlasted the Civil War to provide ongoing structures for the southern identity and for mobilizing the southern faithful for public crusades. Today, the Southern Baptist Convention (SBC) preserves its institutional separateness.

The story of race and religion in this formative period was more complicated, though, than the story above. In response to northern attacks on southern religion, the southern denominations launched a newly invigorated mission to the slaves in the 1830s. Missionaries promoted a paternalistic vision of an evangelical biracial community, with religious leaders assuming new responsibilities for the fate of slave souls. Black Baptists and Methodists shaped evolving evangelicalism from the earliest revivals, as black preachers and exhorters were a prominent feature of frontier camp meetings.

Antebellum biracial churches became a space nurturing the cultural interaction of blacks and whites. The generation before the Civil War was part of the one moment in southern religious life when blacks and whites shared the same ritual and spatial setting, listening to the same sermons, partaking of communion together, and sharing church disciplinary procedures. Such settings were segregated, but the interaction within biracial churches represented a foundation for later spiritual commonalities among blacks and whites in the South and provides the historic basis for moral commonalities on some contemporary public issues.

Blacks responded to the evangelical message for different reasons, though, than those advanced by slaveowner-sanctioned preachers who often were as concerned with social control as with anything else. Evangelicalism offered a profound vision of spiritual, and maybe even earthly, equality, and slaves embraced that hope. Nat Turner could use the Bible to imagine a slave rebellion to transform the public order of the South, even though his vision proved to be only that.

Slavery gave African Americans in the South a different sacred history that would forever after be the basis of their own civil religion, as Andrew Manis discusses in his chapter. The spirit-filled religion of the slave quarters harked back to African spirituality, and the folk religion nurtured there became fundamental to a worldview that was itself distinctive, yet a force shaping southern culture in general. The African-American churches that see their faith today as a potentially redemptive force for a nation that has not always lived up to its ideals draw from their own deep sense of mission.

The southern white churches defined a racial ethic that made them supporters of the region's civil order. The southern Presbyterians spoke for other Protestant groups in asserting the doctrine of the "spirituality" of the church, which would long remain a justification for non-involvement of churches and religious leaders in many social issues, yet they always selectively applied it. The eager assertion of the proslavery argument and general defense of southern society provided easy justification by all the leading southern denominations for the Confederate cause in the Civil War.

The war provided the context for the full flowering of the southern identity and the church's increased role in shaping southern public life. Ministers gave moral support through preaching that the South's cause was a holy war against Yankee atheists; they blessed troops marching off to war, cared for soldiers in battle, preached revivals, led prayer groups, and performed mass baptisms. They interpreted battlefield victories as God's blessings and defeats as God's chastisements for their failures. Religious institutions declared days of fasting and thanksgiving to promote understanding of the spiritual nature of the war. Behind the lines, women joined with ministers in staging rallies to support the troops, preaching sacrifice for home and God, feeding those in need, teaching the children of veterans, nursing the sick, and leading missionary societies. The war promoted new public roles for women in southern religious life, as they took over new responsibilities for praying, counseling, and even conducting home services in the absence of ministers off in the war effort.

In the late nineteenth century, evangelicals expanded their influence on the South's public culture. The Methodists, Baptists, and Presbyterians extended an evangelical ethos over the region before the Civil War, but the period of the most rapid growth of those denominations came at the same time as the region struggled to maintain a cultural identity despite the Confederate national failure. The Baptists grew to be the largest and most dynamic southern denomination, an unofficial established church of the region and defender of the status quo. As Nancy Ammerman observes, it was a "peculiar religious establishment," with no official church hierarchy to set legal norms for the region. Nonetheless, "the norms of conversion and pious living became the rule of life."[3] Evangelicals' emphasis on individual redemption, the spirituality of the church, and the world to come restricted efforts toward social reform, but their churches were so central to southern communities that they had considerable authority to sanction individual and community behavior.

The Baptists were the institutional expression of the South's plain folk, developing within the context of a self-conscious regional defensiveness and cultural separatism from the nation. While the Methodists and Presbyterians shared much conservative theology with the Baptists, the latter differentiated themselves from the other two denominations as less likely to support social reform, more rural in outlook, and more assertive of themselves as the voice of white solidarity. The growing Baptist institutional structure in the late nineteenth and early twentieth centuries, with regional associations, schools, and publishing houses, encouraged thinking in South-wide terms, promoting a regional consciousness. For example, at the end of the nineteenth century I. T. Tichenor, secretary of the SBC's Home Mission Board, saw the need for "Southern literature for Southern churches," thereby helping convince the SBC to create its own Sunday School Board.[4] Foreign and home missionary work gave southerners an early global focus for their public outreach beyond local communities, encouraging their confidence that a righteous southern way of life could be exported.

African Americans were both participants in the evangelical culture of the post-Civil War South and yet separate from it. They came to be excluded from influence on the region's public culture, but they created a distinctive public space for themselves that expressed a black sense of civil religion to redeem the flawed South, a vision that led ultimately to the reforms of the Civil Rights Movement.

Blacks had established independent churches after the Civil War, withdrawing their membership from biracial churches of which they had once been members. This separation of Baptists, Methodists, and Presbyterians into separate racial denominations was the great rupture in southern religious life. Black denominations combined evangelical denominational traditions with the distinctive praise worship traditions rooted in the slave quarters and with a notable sense of black spiritual destiny. The black churches became central institutions not just of religion but of African-American culture in general, resources for the restricted public life that was possible under segregation.

Just as the prewar separation of northern and southern evangelical denominations underlay the future development of a southern cultural identity, so the racial separation of churches after the war helped crystallize a self-perception of a white religious and cultural solidarity that would come to be reflected in white religious support for Jim Crow segregation laws and political disenfranchisement. The political scientist John C. Green identifies evangelical and mainline Christian denominations in the South as the "white Protestant alliance" that was linked for the first 70 years of the twentieth century to the Democratic Party and became the "linchpin of the 'solid South.'" The main motivation for white voters to cast their ballots for Democrats was surely race and the need to protect white supremacy, but, as Green notes, "this alliance involved more than racial animosity, states' rights, and bitter memories of the Civil War." It was also about "traditional morality and the maintenance of a corresponding social order." As Green concludes, "For many deeply religious southerners, opposing sin and supporting Jim Crow

were unconsciously bound together."[5] This was especially so for the most observant Protestants, those who regularly attended church services.

By the early twentieth century, white southerners had come to believe they had
a special destiny in redeeming the nation. With the passing of the Confederate
generation, southern soldiers fighting in the Spanish-American War and World
War I, the election of a southern-born president (Woodrow Wilson), and other
changes, the South became more incorporated into the nation by the 1920s, and
grew to see the United States as having sacred meanings that the region's evangelical outlook supported. "Evangelical faith has had here its best chance in the
world to show what it can do for a civilization," wrote the SBC leader Victor
I. Masters in 1918. The South's material deprivation after the Civil War had,
Masters claimed, promoted in the region "a great gentleness of spirit which was
worth more than all the billions we have now gained," and he went on to compare
the spiritual legacy of the South to its relative New South prosperity. Because
of the earlier sufferings and the qualities of spirit it nurtured, the South had a
"peculiar responsibility" to show its moral and spiritual superiority. Embedding
the region's religious tradition in a larger Manifest Destiny, Masters wrote of
spreading the "Anglo-Saxon evangelical faith uniquely preserved in Southern
religion."[6]

Religion in southern public life was thus conceived as a dimension of a special regional destiny. The region had to witness for its faith through preserving
moral strictures not only for individuals but for society as a whole. To be sure,
the churches did not rush into trying to influence legislation. The Baptist commitment to separation of church and state (which had been a foundational belief
from early sectarian days), the concern for the spirituality of the church, and
otherworldly preaching still militated against ready involvement in many public
issues, and the churches never came to see racial segregation as a moral issue
justifying their involvement.

Religious people did see certain issues as necessitating their going beyond
individual conversion to provide legal restrictions on behavior, partly on issues
of personal vice such as gambling, drinking, dancing, and Sabbath observance.
Progressive reformers who came out of evangelical backgrounds justified
reforms to improve society as moral imperatives to assist those in need, including initiatives to improve public life through better schools, improved sanitation,
elimination of child labor, prison reform, and women's suffrage. As Paul Harvey
notes in his chapter, the South harbored many "inside agitators" and most of them
used their faith to spur reform.

Tensions remained, though, between mainline popular southern denominations that wanted to exert their influence on the region's public life as a whole
and the new sectarian groups that emerged from the 1880s to the 1920s, includ-

ing Holiness churches, Pentecostalism, the Churches of Christ, the Seventh-day Adventists, the Church of God (Cleveland, Tennessee), and the Church of God in Christ. Believing the large regional denominations had become too bureaucratic in their organizations and too materialistic in their aspirations, these sectarians reasserted the primacy of purified local congregations that sought to restore early New Testament approaches. Seeking greater spirituality in worship, they often asserted the importance of recognizing the varied gifts of the spirit, and they embraced a sometimes dark millennialism that saw little hope for redemption of the wicked in this world and looked to Christ's second coming in the Apocalypse. These new faiths injected considerable new passion into the southern religious scene, but they seldom engaged the public sphere, seeking instead to carve out their own independence and continuity.

The fundamentalist movement might be classed as a similar new religious impulse in the early twentieth century, but it had surprisingly little direct impact in the South—because there was no need for it. In the words of the historian James Thompson, "[The] establishment of a fundamentalist wing among Southern Baptists was a superfluous act."[7] By the 1920s, though, with more southerners in urban areas, the influence of such popular culture expressions as movies and recordings, and a general sense of modern threats to southern traditional values, religious leaders and institutions became convinced that they could no longer just rely on fire-and-brimstone preaching and church disciplinary procedures to keep their region witnessing for righteousness. The increased availability of text-books in the public schools acquainted the southern public with the teachings of evolutionary science, and Tennessee became the focal point for efforts to legally proscribe the teaching of Darwinian theory.

In June 1925, the Scopes Trial in Dayton, Tennessee, dramatized the conflict between science and religion for the nation and fostered the image of the South as a backward, benighted Bible Belt. H.L. Mencken did more than his fair share to create that image, covering the Scopes Trial and claiming that no local citizen of Dayton doubted "so much as the typographical errors in Holy Writ," and he added that saying someone was a religious skeptic there was tantamount "to accusing him of cannibalism."

Those evangelicals who supported laws restricting the teaching of evolution saw the issue as one of local control of public culture. The fundamentalist leader William Jennings Bryan had been a keen spokesman for "the people" in the Populist and Progressive eras, and he and his followers saw the Scopes Trial as resistance by a local community against the fragmenting, undemocratic tendencies of modernism that Darwinian science symbolized to them. Faced with nationwide ridicule during the trial, and subsequent ineffectiveness in stemming the teaching of evolution in the schools, the fundamentalist forces retreated to such various venues as private secondary schools and colleges, independent associations, and interdenominational groups to keep their views alive.

In the first half of the twentieth century, mainstream evangelical denominations occupied a privileged place in Southern society. National mainline churches, such as the Episcopalians and Lutherans, were present in parts of the South, with the Episcopalians playing an especially significant role in shaping the southern identity through their social leadership and embrace of regional cultural styles, not to mention their economic resources in parts of the region.

They, nonetheless, could not challenge the cultural hegemony of evangelicals when the latter devoted themselves to pressing for legislation to, for example, prohibit the sale and distribution of alcohol—a bit of public policy alien to the Episcopalian lifestyle. States passed blue laws to regulate Sunday conduct, and gaming laws as well as Prohibition gave evangelical moral standards legal force. Public schools were like ancillary evangelical institutions, with local pastors serving as school chaplains and denominational Sunday school teachers leading students during the week in Bible reading and prayer.

An assumed religious consensus governed the day, partly because of the numerical dominance of evangelicalism through most of the South and the assertiveness of missionary-driven evangelical groups. Baptists, Methodists, and Presbyterians occupied the mainstream, serving in effect as The Southern Church. Black Baptists and Methodists functioned similarly for the South's African-American population. The sectarian groups sometimes challenged this cultural establishment at the margins of society, but they typically remained minority groups through most of the region.

The limited numbers of Roman Catholics and Jews in most areas of the South gave a special context for issues of religion and public policy. In a region dominated by racial dichotomies, their histories were tied in with immigration, adding a degree of ethnic complexity to the southern religious picture. Although immigrants came to the South in the late nineteenth and early twentieth centuries, they came in much smaller numbers than in other regions of the country, so the region failed to develop the same pluralistic context of public life as in much of the rest of the nation.

The Catholic Church, recognizing that it was a stranger in a strange land, stressed the preservation of a Catholic identity for its members through recreational organizations, devotional groups, use of southern-born priests, and especially parochial schools. The church adapted to southern society as well, even establishing Jim Crow segregation in parishes and parochial schools. The Catholic writer Flannery O'Connor looked at the southern identity as incisively as any southern writer and was only the most perceptive of other Catholic writers from the region. Despite this accommodation, in the half century after 1890

Catholics suffered increased Nativist harassment, which limited the success of Catholic political aspirants.

Anti-Semitism was similarly at its worst in the decades after 1890, and the lynching of Leo Frank in 1916 dramatized the terror that could affect anyone in the South who did not fit the expectations of what James Silver called the "closed society."[8] Southern Jews practiced their religion, but they especially embraced Reform Judaism, with its less restrictive dietary and ritual requirements than Jewish Orthodoxy, making them stand out less publicly from their Protestant neighbors. They built temples that could sometimes look like Protestant churches and sometimes even had Sunday schools. Southern evangelicals are people of the Bible, and they could see the Jews among them as like Old Testament Hebrews. In *The Provincials*, his memoir of Jews in the South, Eli Evans tells of southern Jews who grew up, like other whites in the region, hearing Uncle Remus tales but also eating kosher grits. Catholics and Jews thus became southerners, albeit with differences from the large number of Protestants around them.

Religion's public role in the South has always depended partly on where the faithful have lived. To be Catholic in south Florida is different than to be Catholic in a small Mississippi town. Ted Ownby and Samuel Hill explore the geography of religion in their chapters, with Ownby's demographic picture of the region drawing distinctions within and among states in the southern region, and Hill assaying the margins of the region in Appalachia and Florida. The Upper South of hill country and mountains, for example, nurtured different experiences and cultural forms from those of the Lower South, including in religion.

Where one worships within the southern region makes a difference in terms of the context of particular denominations and traditions. The Baptists represent, for example, the largest religious denomination in most counties of the South, but their greatest strength reaches from southern Appalachia into the Deep South states of Georgia, Alabama, and Mississippi. Their strength in southern Arkansas, northern Louisiana, east Texas, and southeastern Oklahoma connects the southern region to the Southern Crossroads region (see volume five in this series). The mountains of east Tennessee were an important hearth for white Pentecostalism, giving birth to the Church of God, while the Deep South of Mississippi and nearby Memphis nurtured black Pentecostalism through the Church of God in Christ. The Churches of Christ, a theologically conservative and morally strict group that grew out of the Presbyterians, are often one of the numerically largest and culturally powerful groups in middle Tennessee, down through north Alabama, north Mississippi, Arkansas, and into central and west Texas, but the group is hardly known in other parts of the South.

Religious traditions that are outside predominant evangelical Protestantism have special significance within particular places in the South. Ethnic groups have long planted and sustained religious traditions in particular regions within the South, in enclaves that have been outside the South-wide evangelical hegemony. Roman Catholic dominance in south Louisiana, in the Southern Crossroads, is well known and creates a unique landscape for those many people from the Southeast who regularly visit there. But Catholics also heavily influence life in Cuban areas of south Florida, along the Gulf Coast, and increasingly in the interior South—especially in cities such as Atlanta, Charlotte, Birmingham, Nashville, and Memphis.

Jews have been small in numbers in the South, which, as Charles Lippy recounts in his chapter, has shaped their peculiar patterns of accommodation and resistance to the region's overall culture. The geography of Jews in the region is an urban one, but Jews have been a significant cultural presence in small towns throughout the South as well. That small-town influence has faded considerably in the contemporary period, with Mississippi's Museum of the Southern Jewish Experience preserving sacred artifacts that are left when synagogues close their doors.

Migration has also shaped religion's role in public culture. Blacks and whites left the South seeking opportunities elsewhere in the United States, with the years around World Wars I and II and the Great Depression especially noteworthy in that regard. After 1970 the rise of Sunbelt prosperity and racial changes in the region reversed this migration, bringing non-southerners to the region. Members of mainline American denominations and Roman Catholics became growing members of southern religious life. Baptists and Methodists now faced a changing regional context, with new claims of pluralism and increased secularism. Church membership no longer was essential in many places to becoming an accepted part of local communities. In urban areas, churches were unable to set and control community moral standards. The assumed connections between churches and local government, between evangelicalism and culture, were loosening beyond recognition for older southerners.

Southern evangelicals themselves were changing, as prosperity and increased social and recreational opportunities led to less concern for traditional moral prohibitions. Middle-class values spoke of moderation rather than abstinence, and earlier suspicions of dancing, movies, playing cards, and similar "worldly" activities were diminishing. Such changes tended to diminish connections with local communities, including churches, in favor of individual choice and personal autonomy. The sociologist Philip Hammond has referred to this process as the "third disestablishment"—a disestablishment that is weakening the traditional bonds of the religiously solid South.

Many of these changes were long term, escalating after World War II. The Civil Rights Movement has special meaning in the South as a historical experience on par with the Civil War a century earlier—a moral crisis tied in with broad socioeconomic developments—and it has continuing meaning as the backdrop for continuing efforts of African Americans to achieve social justice in the nation. Civil rights was a moral challenge to the white South, and it drew from the institutional and moral strength of black churches in local communities throughout the region. Its public images of kneeling, praying, and singing protestors fighting segregation with spiritual weapons overturned generations of white delusions about the contented blacks in their midst. Using non-violent protest methods, Christian teachings on social justice, and traditions of the southern black church, the Civil Rights Movement demonstrated how religious leaders, institutions, and lay people could change the region's public culture. It is noteworthy that Martin Luther King Jr. used the rhetoric of the southern identity in appealing to white southerners for change, insisting that racial justice would add to "our cultural health as a region." He spoke of "our beloved Southland," a region that "has some beauty, that has been made ugly by segregation." He lauded the "intimacy of life that can be beautiful," and he predicted that the nature of life in the South "will make it one of the finest sections of our country once we solve this problem of segregation."[9]

The end of segregation enabled southern blacks to embrace the region as their homeland and to use their energies to bring continuing reform. Today, black churches are organizing sites for community activism and for political campaigns. Black ministers join with white ministers in biracial community groups as leaders of racial reconciliation efforts, such as Mission Mississippi, led by the former civil rights activist Dolphus Weary. The group builds its racial reconciliation activities around the shared evangelical outlooks of so many people in that state, using the slogan, "the grace is greater than race." While it is uninvolved formally in politics, its evangelical-based prayer breakfasts and public rallies are typical for such groups across the South that seek a public square that will witness for racial reconciliation.

The Religious Right began its rise in the immediate aftermath of the successes of the Civil Rights Movement and learned from the movement's organizational and ideological successes. It also began in the context of the "third disestablishment." The Moral Majority, the first prominent national Religious Right organization, focused the efforts of evangelicals and fundamentalists in the late 1970s and early 1980s by stressing a specific agenda of moral issues and an assertive patriotism. Significantly, the organization found many followers in the Upper South and the nearby Midwest—befitting the leadership of its founder, the Virginia Baptist Jerry Falwell—but fewer in the Deep South. Even as the Moral Majority attracted supporters throughout the nation, the South was fertile territory for many other Religious Right efforts. And with the collapse of the Moral

Majority at the end of the 1980s, other organizations took its place, including Christian Voice, the Religious Roundtable, the National Christian Political Action Committee, and above all the Christian Coalition.

These parachurch groups advanced a moral agenda that became the guide to public life for their members. Items that had traditionally been prominent issues for southern churches declined in significance after 1970—above all the defense of a white racial ethic and the prohibition of alcoholic beverages. These had virtually defined the churches' active social involvement in many earlier periods. Especially noteworthy was the decline of overt racism in conservative white evangelical Protestantism. Although its style and political outlook do not attract many African Americans, white evangelicalism no longer openly preaches nor practices racism, and white charismatics particularly embrace a spirit-filled biracialism. The Religious Right often finds common cause on social issues with the black churches with whom they share so much moral belief.

Principal areas of concern for the Religious Right have to do with the family and sex, but control of schools, regulation of mass culture, and policies of the federal government are also guiding interests. Prominent specific issues have been abortion, pornography, gay rights, school prayer, and the Equal Rights Amendment. The Religious Right has been adept at forging alliances among Roman Catholics, Mormons, Missouri Synod Lutherans, and Orthodox Jews and even, on specific issues like pornography, with feminists. The agenda has focused on traditional southern evangelicalism's concern for private morality rather than morality writ large in social systems, on individual sin rather than public injustices.

Even as race disappeared as an overt divider in southern religious life, evangelical leaders did not give up their campaign against the political philosophy that had brought Jim Crow down. In a 1988 sermon to the Southern Baptist Convention, W.A. Criswell, the long-time pastor of Dallas' First Baptist Church, who had repented of his segregationist views, argued that because of "the curse of liberalism today," his opponents in the SBC "call themselves moderates," but "a skunk by any other name still stinks." He insisted that "we have lost our nation to the liberals, humanists, and atheists and infidels." The United States was once known as "a Christian nation, but now we are a secular nation." It's important to recognize that when latter-day preachers like Criswell speak of the nation, they draw on earlier images of the South as the evangelical bastion of righteousness. As Carl Kell and L. Raymond Camp point out, the rhetoric of SBC presidents since Criswell "suggests that of a denominational recapture of the lost 'Southern cause.'"[10]

As Paul Harvey makes clear in his chapter, gender issues have become particularly potent items on that agenda, and the Religious Right has easily, if unselfconsciously, adapted earlier racial rhetoric of keeping others "in their place." Recent evangelical leaders have affirmed an updated version of the old patriarchy that had been planted in the antebellum slave society, with women in their place at the base of the envisioned healthy society. Since 1980 SBC resolutions have affirmed that women should forever be subjected to men and have banned them from ordination to church ministry. Still, as Cynthia Lynn Lyerly notes in her chapter, women are becoming notable in numbers as ministers of Episcopal, Lutheran, Methodist, and Presbyterian churches in the South; and even a few bold Baptist congregations have chosen women pastors.

Politics became a battleground for such issues for the Religious Right, which allied in the 1970s with the Republican Party. Richard Nixon's southern strategy foresaw appeal to religion as one way to capture southern white voters, and Ronald Reagan won the observant evangelical Protestant vote in the election of 1980. Jimmy Carter, himself a born-again evangelical, captured some of that vote in the 1976 campaign. But Carter's success also rested on black Protestants, Catholics, secular voters, and less observant white Protestants. It's worth noting that in 1976, Carter enjoyed the support of both Pat Robertson and Jesse Jackson.

In the late 1970s, Republican political operatives saw that the earlier white Protestant alliance could be reconstituted by putting together a coalition of religiously observant evangelicals, based on moral issues, and other white Protestants, based on free-market economic issues. This coalition would be southern based but part of a broader national conservative coalition, and it more or less formally came into being in the 1980 election campaign. With the Reagan presidency, white evangelicals began to turn into the base of the Republican Party in a process that seemed to reach its complete fruition with the reelection of George W. Bush in 2004. In the mid-1980s, Samuel Hill compared southern evangelicals' rallying to Republican moral-based ideology in 1980 with the southern white embrace of the race-based ideology of the Dixiecrats in the late 1940s. The "interjection of new kinds of moral and social issues," at a time of changing southern society, Hill noted, "mark a dramatic change."[11]

The southern identity today resides most clearly among white conservatives and African Americans, with religion at the core of that identity. A Vanderbilt University study concluded that from 1991 to 2001, the number of people living in the South who identified themselves as southerners declined from about 78 percent to 70 percent. The study concluded that the exceptions to this trend were Republicans, political conservatives, and the wealthy, who had the same percentage in 2001 of self-identification as earlier. One newspaper story about the poll quoted a resident of Franklin, Tennessee, saying that being a southerner is "a way of life," and religion remains central to that way of life. Evangelical Protestants witness for its proscriptive moral character through their increasing political role, trying to preserve and extend the southern way to the nation.

An analysis of the Southern Focus Polls conducted at the University of North Carolina at Chapel Hill isolated where that self-identification as "southerner" is more specifically located. Looking at results over the years 1992-1999, the study found that residents of Deep-South states had the highest identification as "southerners." Ninety percent of Mississippians claimed the label, followed by people from Alabama (88 percent), Tennessee (84 percent), South Carolina (82 percent), and Georgia (81 percent). The percentages drop down precipitously, to Virginia (60 percent) and Florida (51 percent), suggesting differences between core and marginal Souths.[12]

The North Carolina poll included blacks as well as whites, indicating the high identification with the South among African Americans, especially in the Deep South where they are located in greatest numbers. As a result of the Civil Rights Movement, newly enfranchised blacks became Democrats, creating a particularly powerful constituency of black Christians in that party, symbolized by Jesse Jackson's active political role in the 1980s. The prominence of the black church has made southern public life more diverse, and yet the movement of blacks into the Democratic Party has strengthened that party's expression of traditional religious beliefs and is emblematic of how African Americans in the South have come to perpetuate the distinctive South. One recent study of party activists in the South found that "African Americans were more likely than whites to have had a born-again experience, believe that the Bible is the word of God, and attend church regularly." These values have long been a core of the religious component of southern culture, and their expression by blacks should be seen as an expression of southern distinctiveness. But it is a regional identity with a re-imagined southern ideology, unlike the religiously sanctioned, white-dominated Jim Crow South. Blacks who claim a southern identity affirm an idealized, biracial South that witnesses for human equality and against injustice.

The role of black churches in the Civil Rights Movement has become a continuing inspiration in the South of religion's ability to draw from the conversion-centered religion of the region, whether white evangelical Protestantism or African-American Protestantism, to change the public culture. The documentary film "Eyes on the Prize" showed the face of a black woman in a civil rights meeting in Albany, Georgia, in the 1960s, singing and fanning herself with one of the cardboard fans once pervasive in southern churches. In a later scene, viewers see the same woman, now kneeling with others in prayer, moving with the spirit, in front of Albany's City Hall and jail. As she rises to be arrested, she is still waving that church fan. As Vincent Harding notes, that scene testified "in that simple motion to the fact that the religion that moved her life was one and the same in the church building and in the public square—and it would remain the same in the city jail."[13] This church mother was kneeling, praying, and singing on the public square, evoking the white evangelicals who, in the song, were "preachin', prayin', singin'."

The Religious Right now looks to the Civil Rights Movement as a model for its reform efforts and forms coalitions with black Protestants to oppose, among other proposals, state recognition of gay marriage in the South. Even though the southern context in which white evangelicals and black Protestants live and worship has changed dramatically, they remain the embodiment of a biracial South that has long been distinctive within the nation and which, in the evangelical mode, is the shaping force of public life in the region.

Endnotes

1   Lester Flatt, Earl Scruggs, and the Foggy Mountain Boys, "Preachin',
    Prayin', Singin'," The Complete Mercury Sessions, Polygram Records,
    1992, 314-512-644-2.

2   Donald G. Mathews, Religion in the Old South (Chicago: University of
    Chicago Press, 1977), 83.

3   Nancy Tatom Ammerman, Baptist Battles: Social Change and Religious
    Conflict in the Southern Baptist Convention (New Brunswick, NJ: Rutgers
    University Press, 1990), 30.

4   Robert A. Baker, The Southern Baptist Convention and Its People, 1607-
    1972 (Nashville, TN: Broadman, 1974), 273-276.

5   John C. Green, "Believers for Bush, Godly for Gore: Religion and the 2000
    Election in the South," in Robert P. Steed and Laurence W. Morland, eds.,
    The 2000 Presidential Election in the South: Partisanship and Southern
    Party Systems in the 21st Century (Westport, CT: Praeger, 2001), 13-15.

6   Quoted in Ammerman, Baptist Battles, 39.

7   James J. Thompson Jr., "Tried as by Fire": Southern Baptists and the
    Religious Controversies of the 1920s (Macon, GA: Mercer University
    Press, 1982).

8   The phrase comes from the subtitle of James W. Silver's book Mississippi:
    The Closed Society (Harcourt Brace and World, 1964).

9   Martin Luther King Jr., The Wisdom of Martin Luther King In His Own
    Words (New York: Lancer Books, 1968), 23, 41, 64, 75.

10 Carl Kell and L. Raymond Camp, In the Name of the Father: The Rhetoric
    of the New Southern Baptist Convention (Carbondale: University of
    Southern Illinois Press, 1999), 122.

11 Samuel Hill, "Religion and Politics in the South," in Charles Reagan
    Wilson, ed., Religion in the South (Jackson: University Press of
    Mississippi, 1985), 149.

12 Amber McDowell, "Influx Diluting 'Southern Ethos," Washington Times,
    August 22, 2004; John Shelton Reed, "South Polls: Where Is the South?",
    (Summer Southern Cultures, 1999): 116-117.

13 Vincent Harding, "Fighting for Freedom with Church Fans: To Know
    What Religion Means," in Larry G. Murphy, ed., Down by the Riverside:
    Readings in African American Religion (New York: New York University
    Press, 2000), 474.

RELIGIOUS AFFILIATION IN THE
SOUTH AND THE NATION

The charts on the following pages compare two measures of religious identification: self-identification by individuals responding to a survey and adherents claimed by religious institutions. The charts compare regional data for the Mountain West and national data for both measures. The sources of the data are described below.

On page 28
Adherents Claimed by Religious Groups

The Polis Center at Indiana University-Purdue University Indianapolis provided the Religion by Region Project with estimates of adherents claimed by religious groups in the Mountain West and the nation at large. These results are identified as the North American Religion Atlas (NARA). NARA combines 2000 Census data with the Glenmary Research Center's 2000 Religious Congregations and Membership Survey (RCMS). Polis Center demographers supplemented the RCMS reports with data from other sources to produce estimates for groups that did not report to Glenmary.

On page 29
Religious Self-Identification

Drawn from the American Religious Identification Survey (ARIS 2001), these charts contrast how Americans in the Mountain West and the nation at large describe their own religious identities. The ARIS study, conducted by Barry A. Kosmin, Egon Mayer, and Ariela Keysar at the Graduate Center of the City University of New York, includes the responses of 50,283 U.S. households gathered in a series of national, random-digit dialing, telephone surveys.

Adherents Claimed by Religious Groups
South

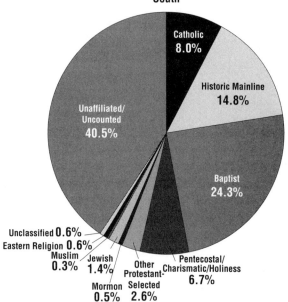

Adherents Claimed by Religious Groups
National

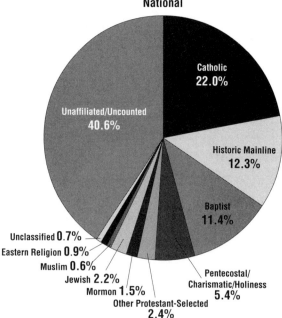

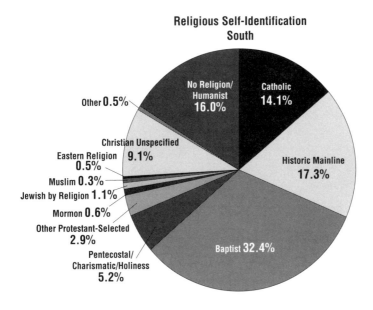

Religious Self-Identification
South

- No Religion/Humanist 16.0%
- Catholic 14.1%
- Other 0.5%
- Christian Unspecified 9.1%
- Eastern Religion 0.5%
- Historic Mainline 17.3%
- Muslim 0.3%
- Jewish by Religion 1.1%
- Mormon 0.6%
- Other Protestant-Selected 2.9%
- Baptist 32.4%
- Pentecostal/Charismatic/Holiness 5.2%

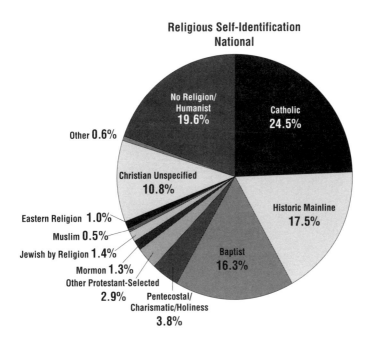

Religious Self-Identification
National

- No Religion/Humanist 19.6%
- Catholic 24.5%
- Other 0.6%
- Christian Unspecified 10.8%
- Eastern Religion 1.0%
- Historic Mainline 17.5%
- Muslim 0.5%
- Jewish by Religion 1.4%
- Baptist 16.3%
- Mormon 1.3%
- Other Protestant-Selected 2.9%
- Pentecostal/Charismatic/Holiness 3.8%

CHAPTER ONE

EVANGELICAL BUT DIFFERENTIATED: RELIGION BY THE NUMBERS

Ted Ownby

In its demography, the South still tends to be a story of black and white, of rural and poor. The region has a considerably higher percentage of African Americans and considerably lower numbers of Latino and foreign-born residents than the national average. Although very few people anywhere in the country identify themselves as being part of more than one race, the South has the lowest number of self-identifying multiple-race people in the United States. (Black Southerners know their mixed-race heritage as well or better than African Americans elsewhere. But they also know that, in the South more than elsewhere, there is no in-between category.)

The statistics in **Figure 1.1** show that the South also has far fewer urban residents than the national average and stands out as the region with the largest rural population. It has somewhat fewer people with high school diplomas and college degrees than other parts of the country. And a higher percentage of households live in poverty in the South than in the country as a whole.

Only two Southern states, Virginia and Georgia, have median household incomes higher than the national average of $41,949. As **Figure 2.2.** makes clear, Virginia is considerably above and Georgia slightly above the national average. North Carolina and Florida are slightly below that average; the poorest states, Mississippi and West Virginia, are far below.

Southern Religious Affiliations in Comparison to other Regions

Looking broadly at the number of church members in the South in comparison to the rest of the country, a few things stand out, some of them not at all surprising.

Figure 1.1   Population Characteristics of the South Compared to the
             Nation, 2000 (2000 U.S. Census)

	Nation	South
Population	281,421,906	62,139,825
	Percentage	Percentage
Caucasian	75.1	74.4
African American	12.3	20.0
Hispanic	12.5	6.8
Asian	3.6	1.6
Other (American Indian, Hawaiian/Pacific Islander, Other Race, Mixed Race)	8.0	3.7
Foreign born	11.0	7.6
Total reporting more than one race	1.5	2.4
Living in urban areas (over 25 years old)	79.0	69.4
- without a High School degree	19.6	22.0
- with at least a Bachelor's degree	24.4	22.0
Living in poverty	12.3	13.3

First, the region leads the nation in the percentage of Protestants. Counting all of the various Protestant groups, 48 percent of all Americans identify themselves as Protestants; 65 percent of all people in the South identify as such. By delving more deeply, it becomes clear which groups give religion in the South its distinctive character. Forty-seven percent of Southerners fit into the broad category of white Protestant, 12 percentage points higher than in the United States as a whole. The only regions comparable to the South in this respect are the Midwest and the Southern Crossroads regions, where 45 percent and 42 percent of the population, respectively, are white Protestants.

The South emerges as even more distinctive when one breaks down white Protestants into evangelical and mainline Protestants. This distinction, much debated by students of American religion, suggests a rough division between evangelical churches, which have historically tended to emphasize personal salvation as the center of religious life, and mainline denominations, which put more emphasis on what the historian Martin Marty has called "the social destinies of men."[1]

Evangelicals have tended to be more concerned with the reality of sin, the need to reform individual behavior, and something close to literal interpretations of the Bible. Mainline groups, on the other hand, concentrate on the need to reform society and on the possibility of reconciling Biblical and human understandings of the world and history. Evangelicals, historically, have felt more of

Figure 1.2   **Median Household Income in the 10 Southern States, 2000 (2000 Census)**

Virginia	$46,677
Georgia	42,433
United States	41,949
North Carolina	39,184
Florida	38,819
South Carolina	37,082
Tennessee	36,360
Alabama	34,135
Kentucky	33,672
Mississippi	31,330
West Virginia	29,696

a defensive estrangement from the broader American culture while mainline groups, broadly speaking, were more at ease, or at least more at home, in their position at the center of American culture.

These terms, no matter how awkward and uncertain in application, are useful at least in comparing American regions. In the Religion by Region series, the mainline Protestants consist of an admittedly wide range of Methodists, Lutherans, Presbyterians, Episcopalians, Congregationalists, Disciples of Christ, and churches in the Reformed tradition. Only 15 percent of Southerners identify with these churches, which places the region at precisely the national average and very close to the percentage of mainline Protestants in New England, the Mid-Atlantic states, the Mountain West, and the Pacific Northwest. White Methodists, long one of the leading and defining groups in the region, claim 7 percent of the South's people; a bare one percentage point higher than the national average.

What makes the South religiously distinctive is the large proportion of evangelical Protestants. They are white and black, Baptist and Pentecostal and Holiness and Seventh-day Adventist and Churches of Christ and, by self-definition, non-denominational. White evangelicals make up 28 percent of the South's population. This is almost twice the national average (16 percent)—considerably higher than in any other region except the Southern Crossroads, where they constitute a quarter of the population.

Indeed, the South and the Southern Crossroads regions stand out for the percentage of Protestants who belong to evangelical rather than mainline groups; 71.5 percent of all Protestants in the South are evangelicals (in the Southern Crossroads they constitute 76.2 percent). Moreover, although Methodists nationally are considered a pillar of mainline Protestantism, in the South many Methodists consider themselves evangelicals, and the same can be said of some southern Presbyterians and Episcopalians. In the South, in short, evangelical Protestantism is the establishment.

Among the evangelicals, no group stands out more than white Baptists, who make up 24 percent of the region's population, as compared to 12 percent nationwide (20 percent of the people in the Southern Crossroads region are white Baptists, while the group makes up less than 10 percent in all other regions of the country). White Baptists are the largest group in every southern state except Florida, and they are the second largest there, behind only Catholics. Most white Baptists in the South are members of churches in the Southern Baptist Convention (SBC). There are other varieties—Independent Baptists, Primitive Baptists, and Regular Baptists, to name a few—but the SBC is by far the largest religious group in the South.

On the other side of the racial divide, 14 percent of the South's population identify with African-American Protestant groups—nearly twice the national average of 8 percent. African-American Protestants make up the second largest statistical category in every southern state except West Virginia, Kentucky, and Florida.

The South also stands out for a smaller proportion of people in certain important religious categories than other parts of the country. Catholics are less of a presence than in any other region, making up less than 15 percent of the South's population, compared to 25 percent of all Americans. Ten percent of Southerners are white Catholics, 3 percent are Latino Catholics, and a little more than 1 percent are African-American Catholics or Catholics of another ethnicity. Some other regions number a similarly low percentage of white Catholics—the Pacific region (10 percent), the Southern Crossroads (10 percent), and the Mountain West (11 percent). But unlike the South, each of those regions boasts a large number of Latino Catholics.

The South is distinctive, as well, for the small percentage of the so-called "Nones," —those who told telephone interviewers from the American Religious Identification Survey (ARIS) that they are either atheist, agnostic, humanist, secular, or simply that they had no religion. Eleven percent of Southerners fall into this category, a figure well below the national average of 14 percent and far below the Mountain West (19 percent), the Pacific (19 percent), and the Pacific Northwest (25 percent).

Finally, the South joins the Midwest and the Southern Crossroads regions in lacking sizable proportions of other religious groups. For example, Mormons make up 11 percent of the population in the Mountain West and 2 or 3 percent in the Pacific and Pacific Northwest regions, but only 1 percent of the southern population. Jews are 4 percent in the Middle Atlantic and 2 percent in the Pacific, but only 1 percent in the South. Two percent of the people in New England and all the western regions belong to "Other Religions," a heterogeneous category that ranges from Unitarian Universalist and Native American to Scientology, New Age, Rastafarian, and Sikh. In the South, only a tiny fraction of the population professes "Other Religions." Likewise there are smaller percentages of Muslims, Buddhists, and Hindus in the South than in a number of other regions.

On the Ground in the South

Where does one find the different groups who make up religious life in the South? White Baptists—primarily members of the SBC but also members of many smaller Baptist groups—are plentiful throughout the region, sometimes in overwhelming numbers. They are the largest or nearly the largest religious groups in almost all areas of the South, excepting only parts of Florida, West Virginia, and a corner of Virginia.

African-American Protestants, whose denominations include the National Baptist Convention, the Missionary Baptists, the African Methodist Episcopal (AME) Church, the African Methodist Episcopal Zion (AMEZ) Church, the Christian Methodist Episcopal (CME) Church, and the Church of God in Christ, are mostly concentrated in the Black Belt—a large sweep of land that runs from southeastern Virginia through large parts of the Carolinas, Georgia, northern Florida, Alabama, southwestern Tennessee, and Mississippi. It is important and tragic to note that the areas with the largest percentages of African-American Protestants are also among the areas with the highest rates of poverty.

Two geographic patterns prevail among the other religious groups. Some are spread widely across the region while others are concentrated in a few areas. The former have a substantial presence but never constitute a majority of religious adherents. The latter sometimes constitute majorities here and there.

The South's third and fourth largest groups, Catholics and United Methodists, dramatize this difference. As **Figures 1.3** and **1.4** demonstrate, United Methodists are spread in significant numbers all over the South, while Catholics cluster in particular areas. Many southern Catholics live in areas where Catholics are the largest single group. But outside some counties in Virginia and a healthy section of West Virginia, United Methodists are never the largest group. United Methodists can be found in significant numbers everywhere in the South except parts of southern Florida and the Mississippi Delta, but almost nowhere do they have over a third of the churchgoers. A national image that Catholics tend to live in urban areas is only partially true in the South. One of the most striking things about southern Catholics is that most live at the geographic edge of the southern states—south Florida (especially along the coasts), coastal Alabama,

Figure 1.3   Concentration of Catholic Adherents in the South

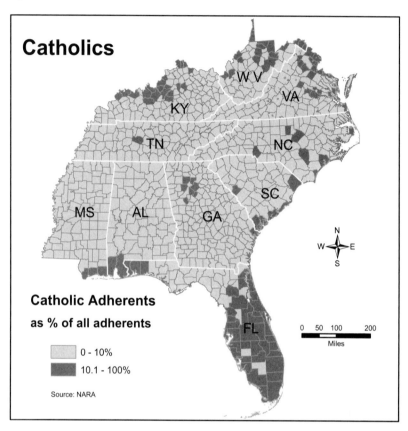

Catholics

Catholic Adherents
as % of all adherents

0 - 10%
10.1 - 100%

Source: NARA

0   50 100   200
Miles

and Mississippi, coastal counties in South Carolina and North Carolina, the northernmost counties in Virginia, West Virginia, and a broad swath of northern Kentucky.

The Upper South is notable for having a range of Protestant groups that goes beyond white Baptists, African-American Protestants, and United Methodists. The highest concentrations of Presbyterians are in Virginia, eastern West Virginia, and North Carolina. Members of the Churches of Christ are especially prominent in Tennessee and Kentucky. A smaller group in the South, the Disciples of Christ, has pockets of popularity in northern Kentucky, while most members of another small group, the Cumberland Presbyterians, live in central and western Tennessee. Lutherans have popularity primarily in Virginia, central North Carolina, and also in central South Carolina.

Church members in the category called Holiness/Wesleyan/Pentecostal belong to a range of churches in the South, especially the Church of

Figure 1.4   Concentration of United Methodist Adherents in the South

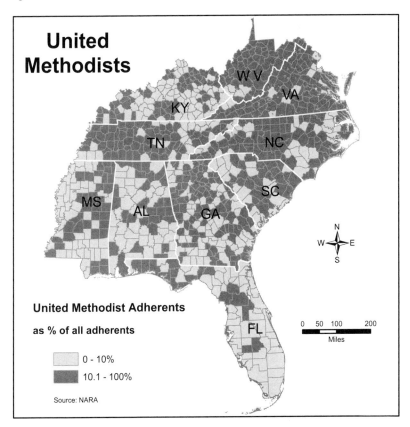

God headquartered in Cleveland, Tennessee, the Assemblies of God, the Pentecostal Holiness Church, and the Church of God of Prophecy. They fit the Methodist model of having popularity all over the South, without dominating anywhere. They are most popular in West Virginia, western Virginia, and eastern Kentucky and Tennessee, but they have members throughout most of the region.

Members of the South's oldest Christian group, the Episcopalians, are spread throughout the South, but the largest number are in Virginia and Florida. One of the newest Christian groups in the South, the Mormons, likewise have spread throughout the region in small numbers, and the largest concentrations are also in Virginia and Florida. The areas with the fewest Mormons are the rural areas of Mississippi and Alabama, the mountain areas of eastern Tennessee and western North Carolina, and the southernmost counties of Florida—those dominated by Catholics and Jews.

What of non-Christian groups? Jews make up over 2 percent of southern religious adherents, and it is clear that the largest concentrations of southern Jews are in two places: Florida, and metropolitan areas such as greater Atlanta. In no counties in Mississippi or Alabama do Jews make up as much as 1 percent of adherents. In fact, in only two counties in those states, Montgomery and Jefferson counties in Alabama, do Jews make up as much as 0.5 percent of all religious adherents. Jews are almost as scarce in Tennessee and Kentucky, where they make up between 1 percent and 2 percent of adherents only in Nashville, Memphis, Louisville, and Lexington. In the Carolinas, Jews make up between 2 percent and 3 percent of religious adherents only in Charleston and Durham. The proportions are higher in greater Atlanta, the South's largest metropolitan area, where county by county Jews range from 3 percent to 8.5 percent of religious adherents. Only in Broward and Palm Beach counties in south Florida are there areas where Jews make up more than 20 percent of religious adherents.

Practitioners of Buddhism, Hinduism, and other Eastern religions constitute a significantly smaller minority of the southern religious population. Like Catholics and Jews, and very much unlike Methodists, Presbyterians, and Mormons, Buddhists and Hindus tend to concentrate in a few areas with considerable populations. A majority of the counties in Mississippi and Alabama, and most counties in southern Georgia, east and west Tennessee, much of Kentucky, and southwestern Virginia have no people who claim to practice Eastern religions. However, substantial groups of people practice Eastern religions in clusters of counties in Virginia, North Carolina, South Carolina, and Florida.

In 20 counties, people practicing Eastern religions make up at least 5 percent of all churchgoers, and in a perhaps surprising nine counties they make up over 10 percent. In six counties in northern Virginia and northern West Virginia, people practicing Eastern religions make up more than 10 percent of all religious adherents, led by Greene County, Virginia (20.7 percent) and Marshall County, West Virginia (19.2 percent), and single counties in North Carolina, Georgia, and Kentucky have similar percentages.[2]

The most striking demographic fact about the Muslim population is how small it appears to be. According to data from the North American Religion Atlas (NARA), most counties in the South have no Muslims at all, and the region has only 22 counties in which Muslims make up at least 1 percent of all religious adherents. Cities such as Atlanta, Durham, and Nashville have small Muslim communities; in each Muslims constitute about 2 percent of all adherents. The only part of the South with a substantial Muslim population are the northern Virginia counties of Alexandria, Arlington, Fairfax, Louden, Prince William, and Spotsylvania—Washington, D.C. suburbs where Muslims make up about 5 percent of all adherents.

Overall, the statistics offer rich confirmation of the image of the South as the country's evangelical heartland. Yet, looked at more closely, they offer some unexpected twists and cautions. The percentage of United Methodists is lower than expected, given that the South has so often been portrayed as the land of Baptists and Methodists. Those who view the Episcopal Church as a rock of southern tradition may be surprised to learn that only about 2 percent of all southerners are Episcopalians. Despite the relative paucity of Catholics in the region, they outnumber United Methodists by a substantial margin and are twice as numerous as all the other mainline Protestants combined. And there are too many Jews, Mormons, Buddhists, Hindus, and Muslims to simply write them off as exceptions.

An interesting twist in the statistics has to do with the category of those professing no religion. In the ARIS telephone survey, only 10.7 percent of all southerners who answered their telephones and talked to the pollsters said they had no religion.* That number, not at all surprisingly, is the lowest of all American regions. On the other hand, NARA counts 40.3 percent of all southerners as unaffiliated with any church or as uncounted. Given the South's Bible Belt identity in almost all national comparisons on religious topics, that is surprisingly close to the national average of 40.6 percent. Unlike all other regions of the country, where the ratio of the ARIS percentage of "Nones" to the NARA percentage of unaffiliated or uncounted ranges from 1:2.5 to 1:2.9; in the South it is 1:3.8. What accounts for this discrepancy?

In the first place, it is important to bear in mind that having a religious identity seems to be more of a cultural requirement in the South than in the rest of the country. Southerners who have little to do with religion may well be less inclined than other Americans to tell a telephone interviewer they have no religion. But it is also the case, as the sociologist John Shelton Reed notes, that "[e]ven those Southerners who don't go to church at least know which one they're not going to."[3]

In addition, religious membership appears to be disproportionately under-counted in the South. The Glenmary survey, on which the NARA data are based, depends on reporting of members by denominational bodies. But a later chapter will discuss at greater length the southern areas with the highest numbers of unaffiliated and uncounted people are in the Appalachian counties of West Virginia, Virginia, and eastern Kentucky—home to countless evangelical Protestant churches that are part of no denomination. As a result, the South may have a higher proportion of "uncounted " in NARA's "unaffiliated and uncounted" category than other regions of the country. Finally, it is worth noting that the other southern area with the highest percentage of unaffiliated and uncounted people is the Gulf Coast of Florida. In this populous, fast-growing part of the state, many newcomers may simply not yet have affiliated with a religious institution.

* In the pie charts on page 29, the "No Religion/Humanist" category includes respondents who refused to answer, or who said they didn't know their religious identity. The percentage of the latter ranged narrowly from 4.9 percent to 6.3 percent across the regions, with the South at 5.3 percent.

Figure 1.5   Demographic characteristics of Alabama and Mississippi,
by percent (2000 U.S. Census)

	Alabama	Mississippi	South	United States
Caucasian	71.1	61.3	74.4	75.1
African American	25.9	36.3	20.0	12.3
Hispanic	1.7	1.3	6.8	12.5
Asian	0.7	0.6	1.6	3.6
Other (American Indian, Hawaiian/Pacific Islander, Other Race, Mixed Race)	2.0	1.5	3.7	8.0
Foreign born	1.9	1.4	7.6	11.0
Living in urban areas (over 25 years old)	55.4	48.7	69.4	79.0
- without a High School degree	24.7	27.1	22.0	19.6
- with at least a BA degree	19.0	16.9	22.0	24.4
Living in poverty	16.1	19.9	13.3	12.3

These considerations point to an important truth: not all parts of the South are religiously the same. Indeed, to have an adequate picture of the region's religious demography, it is important to look at it, as it were, sub-regionally.

Alabama and Mississippi: Southern Baptists and African-American Protestants

Alabama and Mississippi, often considered the deepest states of the Deep South, have several demographic features that give them a distinctive religious profile. By a considerable margin, African Americans make up a higher percentage of the population of Mississippi than any other southern state, and Alabama ranks fourth. These states rank second and third in the region in the size of their rural populations, behind only West Virginia. Mississippi and Alabama, as **Figure 1.5** makes clear, rank below the regional and far behind the national average of people who completed high school and college, and they rank first and third in the region in the percentage of their people who live in poverty.

Mississippi and Alabama also stand out as the most typically southern religious states, if "southern" means the features that differentiate the South from the rest of the country: evangelical dominance, white Baptists, and African-American Protestants. In Mississippi and Alabama white Baptists, United Methodists, and African-American Protestants constitute more than

Figure 1.6   Adherents as percentage of All Adherents, Mississippi
and Alabama (NARA)

	Mississippi	Alabama
Baptist (except historically African American)	40.9	42.2
Historically African American Protestant	34.2	27.8
United Methodist	10.0	9.6

80 percent of all adherents. Both states stand out as distinctive in the South
in that no other group constitutes as much as 5 percent of the states' religious adherents. As **Figure 1.6** shows, white Baptists and African-American
Protestants are by far the largest groups in both states.

One can posit a model of a prototypical county for Deep South religion as one
in which African-American Protestants and white Baptists each make up at least
a quarter of churchgoers. Statewide, Mississippi, Alabama, Georgia, and South
Carolina are the southern states that conform to that standard.

This model is common in almost all counties in Mississippi, except the predominantly white counties in the northeastern corner, the areas in the Mississippi
Delta where African Americans constitute large majorities of the population, and
a few counties on the Gulf Coast. The prototypical Deep South model prevails
in much of Alabama outside the heavily white northern counties, and scattered
counties in the central, especially urban parts of the states. In both states, as
Figure 1.7 shows, either African-American Protestants or white Baptists make
up a majority of all churchgoers.

The greatest concentration of African-American Protestants can be found in a
wide and dramatic sweep of counties stretching from coastal Virginia and North
Carolina through most of the eastern half of South Carolina and most of central
and southwestern Georgia, through the southern half of Alabama and much of
Mississippi, especially its western half, and into the southwestern counties of
Tennessee. In all of these areas, African-American Protestants make up at least a
third of the churchgoing population.

In Mississippi and Alabama, the percentages of African-American Protestants
are especially high. **Figure 1.8** shows that African-American Protestants make
up at least half of all churchgoers in 11 counties in Alabama and 22 counties in Mississippi. In all of the counties in the Mississippi Delta, stretching
along the Mississippi River from Tunica County near the Tennessee border
down to Issaquena and Yazoo counties, over half of the churchgoers are
African-American Protestants. The counties with the highest percentages of
African-American Protestants are Tunica, Mississippi (80 percent), and Macon,
Alabama (83.1 percent).

Figure 1.7   Southern Counties Where Historically African-American
Protestants Constitute 25 Percent of all Adherents

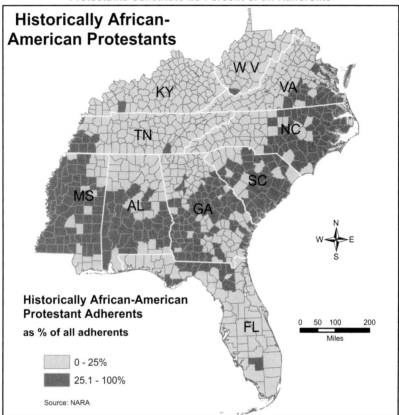

Southern Baptists are all over Mississippi and Alabama, with at least 20 percent of all churchgoers in all but a few counties that are dominated by African-
American Protestants. White Baptists make up more than half of churchgoers
in the hill country of northern Alabama and northeastern Mississippi, and in the
Piney Woods counties of both states. They dominate especially in a hilly stretch
of Alabama along the Georgia border, where white Baptists constitute more than
three quarters of all churchgoers in Cleburne County (82.3 percent), DeKalb
County (76.2 percent), and Cherokee County (76 percent).

As in much of the South, there are substantial numbers of United Methodists,
but they never dominate. In more than half the counties in Mississippi and
Alabama, United Methodists make up more than 10 percent of all churchgoers,
but in no county do they constitute as many as one quarter of the churchgoers.
There are other groups of Methodists as well, in particular the African Methodist
Episcopal (AME) and African Methodist Episcopal Zion (AMEZ) churches

Figure 1.8 Southern Counties Where Historically African-American Protestants Constitute 50 Percent of all Adherents

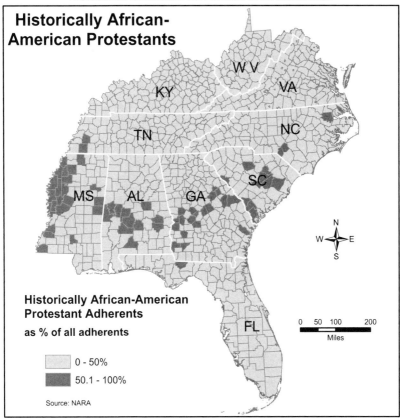

Historically African-American Protestants

Historically African-American Protestant Adherents

as % of all adherents

☐ 0 - 50%

■ 50.1 - 100%

Source: NARA

included in the category of "Historically African-American Protestant" denominations. And a number of independent white Methodist churches began in the civil rights era in opposition to a merger of national groups that was intended, among other things, to support racial integration.

The only other groups of statistical consequence are Catholics, historically white Holiness and Pentecostal bodies, and the group of Other Conservative Christians. All of these are considerably smaller than in most parts of the South. Catholics in Mississippi and Alabama are located primarily along the Gulf Coast—the only areas in both states where more than 10 percent of churchgoers are Catholic. Hancock County, Mississippi, where 56.8 percent of all churchgoers are Catholics, stands out as exceptional. It is one of only five counties in the entire South in which Catholics make up more than half of churchgoers. The other notable feature about Catholics in Mississippi and Alabama are the places where they have little presence at all. In 33 counties in Alabama and 44

Figure 1.9   Adherents as percentage of All Adherents, Mississippi
and Alabama (NARA)

	Mississippi	Alabama
Catholics	4.8	4.4
Holiness/Wesleyan/Pentecostal	2.5	4.9
Other Conservative Christian	3.1	5.0

counties in Mississippi, Catholics make up 1 percent or less of the churchgoing population.

Most of the Holiness and Pentecostal groups are in northern Alabama, near the Appalachian roots of many of those churches. The "Other Conservative Christian" churches are primarily from the Churches of Christ denomination, and similarly tend to be located in northern Mississippi and Alabama. Because no other groups have as much as 2 percent of all church adherents in either state, it is clear that the great majority of Mississippi and Alabama churchgoers are either white Baptists, African-American Protestants, or United Methodists. Here the religious significance of the low number of foreign-born residents seems especially dramatic; no large groups of new people with different religions have moved in to alter or add to the nature of Deep South religious life.

Overall, Mississippi and Alabama stand out as having the highest percentage of evangelicals among their Protestants: Only 20.3 percent of those in Mississippi and 19.5 percent of the Protestants in Alabama belong to mainline groups.

Georgia, South Carolina, and North Carolina: Southern Baptists, African-American Protestants, and Pockets of Religious Diversity

In many ways, Georgia, South Carolina, and North Carolina are much closer to southern regional averages than Mississippi and Alabama. Like those two states, Georgia and the Carolinas have high percentages of African Americans, but unlike them they have Latino communities and substantial foreign-born populations. With the region's largest urban center, Georgia has an urban population above the regional average, and the Carolinas have far more urbanites than Mississippi and Alabama. As **Figure 1.10** shows, poverty levels and educational levels in these states are at about the regional levels.

Georgia, South Carolina, and North Carolina conform to the broader southern model in which white Baptists and African-American Protestants claim far more members than any other groups. Among Protestants, evangelicals are clearly in the majority, although not as dramatically as in Mississippi and Alabama. Mainline Protestants make up 26.2 percent of all Protestants in Georgia, 30.8 percent in South Carolina, and 35.3 percent in North Carolina—the highest

Figure 1.10   Demographic characteristics of Georgia, South Carolina and
North Carolina, by percent (2000 U.S. Census)

	GA	SC	NC	South	United States
Caucasian	65.0	67.1	72.1	74.4	75.1
African American	28.7	29.5	21.5	20.0	12.3
Hispanic	5.3	2.3	4.7	6.8	12.5
Asian	2.1	0.8	1.4	1.6	3.6
Other (American Indian, Hawaiian/Pacific Islander, Other Race, Mixed Race)	3.8	2.1	4.7	3.7	8.0
Foreign born	7.0	2.8	5.3	7.6	11.0
Living in urban areas (over 25 years old)	71.6	60.4	60.2	69.4	79.0
- without a High School degree	21.4	23.6	21.8	22.0	19.6
- with at least a BA degree	24.3	20.4	22.4	22.0	24.4
Living in poverty	12.9	14.1	12.2	13.3	12.3

proportion in the South outside Virginia and West Virginia. White Baptists, as **Figure 1.11** shows, are the largest single religious group, but they do not make up as large a share of the church-going population as their counterparts in Alabama and Mississippi.

If the religious prototype of a county in the Deep South is one where at least 25 percent of all religious adherents are white Baptists and at least 25 percent are African-American Protestants, Georgia is far more prototypical than the Carolinas. Much of the southern half of Georgia conforms to this model, but in South Carolina only a few western counties near the Georgia border do so, as do a few North Carolina counties along the Georgia border and a number in the east.

White Baptists, as **Figure 1.12** demonstrates, are prominent throughout virtually all counties in Georgia, but they blanket north Georgia and western North Carolina. Georgia has a startling 58 counties in which Southern Baptists are a majority of all churchgoers. In fact, in 18 of those counties, over two-thirds of all churchgoers are Southern Baptists. North Carolina's Baptists have their largest numbers in the mountainous counties along the Tennessee border. Twenty-three North Carolina counties have Southern Baptist majorities. Southern Baptists are less prominent in eastern and central parts of the Carolinas. Southern Baptists are the majority in only seven South Carolina counties, all of them in the state's northwestern upcountry.

Figure 1.11   Adherents as percentage of All Adherents, Georgia, South Carolina, and North Carolina (NARA)

	Georgia	South Carolina	North Carolina
Baptist (except historically African American)	35.5	34.9	33.8
Historically African American Protestant	26.1	28.3	22.8
United Methodist	11.1	11.2	13.1

African-American Protestants are a large presence along the eastern coast of North Carolina, and they have their largest number of adherents in coastal and central South Carolina and central and southwestern Georgia. In six counties in South Carolina and four in North Carolina, African-American Protestants make up more than half of all churchgoers. The numbers are more dramatic in Georgia, where there are 19 such counties, most in the state's central and southwestern sections.

United Methodists are mostly found in central North Carolina, coastal South Carolina, and scattered throughout Georgia. As in Mississippi and Alabama, United Methodists seem to be present almost everywhere, but dominate nowhere. They make up at least a third of adherents in only two counties: coastal Dare County, North Carolina (38.9 percent) and Heard County, Georgia (33.8 percent).

Each of these states, as **Figure 1.13** helps to demonstrate, has a distinctive element. Atlanta and the ever-expanding area around it stand out as being particularly religiously diverse. In Fulton and Rockdale counties, Jews make up 8.5 percent and 6.9 percent of religious adherents respectively; these are two of only 13 counties in the South where Jews make up more than 3 percent of adherents. Catholics constitute between 10 and 20 percent of adherents in the seven metro-Atlanta counties. In DeKalb County, Georgia, which includes a small part of Atlanta and suburbs on its east side—including Emory University and the Centers for Disease Control—practitioners of Eastern religions are 4.3 percent of religious adherents.

Outside the Atlanta area, Catholics congregate in especially large numbers only in a few areas. In South Carolina, Catholics constitute between 10 percent and 16 percent of churchgoers in several counties along the coast near Charleston. In Georgia and the Carolinas, as in Alabama and Mississippi, there are large areas with only tiny numbers of Catholics. There are 76 Georgia counties, most of them in the southern half of the state, where Catholics constitute 1 percent or less of religious adherents. North Carolina has 20 such counties; South Carolina has 16.

Figure 1.12   Southern Counties Where White Baptist Adherents Constitute A Majority of all Adherents

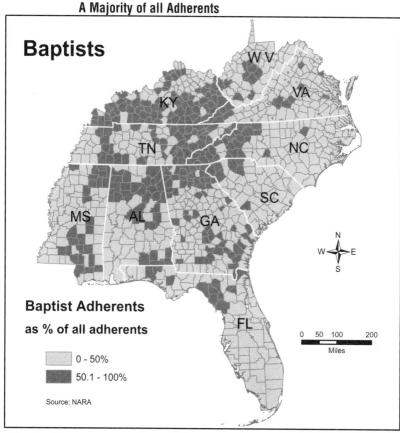

The Lutheran presence is small in most of the South, but a few counties in the upcountry areas of North and South Carolina have substantial Lutheran populations. Lutherans make up more than 10 percent of churchgoers in three counties in North Carolina—Alexander, Catawba, and Rowan—and two counties in South Carolina—Lexington and Newberry. In Newberry County, Lutherans make up 26.5 percent of church adherents—the highest percentage in the South.

The Presbyterian Church USA (PCUSA) likewise has a small membership throughout much of the South. But the PCUSA has some substantial popularity in the Carolinas and Georgia, where members make up more than 5 percent of churchgoers in 22 counties. At 4.2 percent, North Carolina has the highest percentage of PCUSA adherents in the South, with West Virginia second and South Carolina third. In two North Carolina counties, Avery and Moore, PCUSA members account for more than 10 percent of all adherents.

Figure 1.13   Adherents as percentage of All Adherents, Georgia, South
               Carolina, and North Carolina (NARA)

	Georgia	South Carolina	North Carolina
Catholics	7.3	5.0	6.5
Other Conservative Christian	4.2	2.4	3.7
Holiness/Wesleyan/Pentecostal	5.6	5.8	5.6
Presbyterian USA	2.1	3.8	4.2
Lutheran (ELCA)	0.7	2.3	1.8

Georgia and the Carolinas have greater numbers of white Holiness and Pentecostal adherents than Mississippi and Alabama, although fewer than in other parts of the South. Those groups make up over 10 percent of churchgoers in scattered counties in western and central North Carolina, two counties in western South Carolina, and a large number of counties in both northern and southeastern Georgia.

Tennessee and Kentucky: Southern Baptists, Other Conservative Protestants, and Kentucky Catholics

Tennessee and Kentucky, the two states of the Upper South, have their own distinctiveness. Both, but Kentucky in particular, have smaller African-American populations than the Deep South, fewer Latinos than Georgia and North Carolina, and quite small numbers of foreign-born residents. By regional standards, as **Figure 1.14** makes clear, they remain rural and poorly educated, although Tennessee is considerably more urban and better educated than Kentucky.

Like the states of the Deep South, Tennessee and Kentucky are, as **Figure 1.15** demonstrates, rich in white Baptists, and the United Methodists are important there as well. Among Protestants, both states are as evangelical as any other southern state; 80.1 percent of Protestants in Kentucky and 79.5 percent of those in Tennessee belong to evangelical denominations. But the smaller numbers of African-American Protestants in both states, the significance of conservative Christian groups such as the Churches of Christ, and the large numbers of Catholics in northern Kentucky, all help distinguish the area from other parts of the South.

There are more Southern Baptists in Tennessee and Kentucky—32 percent—than the southern average. They are spread throughout both states, but have large, often extraordinarily large, numbers in the eastern parts of both states. Tennessee has only one county (Jackson) and Kentucky has only three (Jessamine, Bath, and Fleming) in which white Baptists make up less than 20 percent of religious

Figure 1.14 Demographic characteristics of Tennessee and Kentucky, by percent (2000 U.S. Census)

	Tennessee	Kentucky	South	United States
Caucasian	80.2	90.0	74.4	75.1
African American	16.3	7.3	20.0	12.3
Hispanic	2.1	1.4	6.8	12.5
Asian	0.9	0.7	1.6	3.6
Other (American Indian, Hawaiian/Pacific Islander, Other Race, Mixed Race)	2.2	1.7	3.7	8.0
Foreign born	2.7	1.9	7.6	11.0
Living in urban areas (over 25 years old)	63.6	55.7	69.4	79.0
- without a High School degree	24.0	25.8	22.0	19.6
- with at least a BA degree	19.5	17.1	22.0	24.4
Living in poverty	13.4	15.8	13.3	12.3

adherents. Kentucky leads the South with 78 counties in which Southern Baptists make up more than 50 percent of adherents; in 36, Southern Baptists make up more than two-thirds of adherents. As for Tennessee, there are 47 counties where Southern Baptists make up more than half of the adherents; in 13 of them, they make up more than two thirds. The most heavily Southern Baptist places in the South (and probably the world) are in Tennessee and Kentucky. In Hancock County in upper east Tennessee, 97 percent of all adherents are Southern Baptists, and white Baptists make up more than 90 percent of adherents in three other counties: Grainger and Scott in upper east Tennessee and Edmondson in central Kentucky.

Tennessee has about as many United Methodists as the southern average of 10.1 percent; Kentucky is just slightly below. As in other parts of the South, they do not constitute a majority in any county. In eight counties in Kentucky and one county in Tennessee, United Methodists make up at least a quarter of churchgoers. The highest percentage is in Cumberland and Clinton counties in Tennessee, where about a third of churchgoers are United Methodists.

Because of the relatively low number of African Americans in the two states, Tennessee and Kentucky have few counties that exemplify the prototypical Deep South religious model. That prototype fits only one county (Christian) in Kentucky and only eight Tennessee counties, all but one (Hamilton, home of Chattanooga) in the southwestern corner of the state near Memphis. Unlike most southern states, Kentucky has only one county in which African-American

Figure 1.15 Adherents as percentage of All Adherents, Tennessee and Kentucky (NARA)		
	Tennessee	Kentucky
Baptists (not African American)	40.8	44.9
Historically African American Protestants	18.9	8.0
United Methodists	10.6	8.5
Catholics	4.9	16.6

Protestants make up a quarter of adherents, and only 15 counties in which African-American Protestants are 10 percent of adherents. In Tennessee, African-American Protestants make up a quarter of the adherents in nine counties, and only in Haywood do they constitute a majority, at 51.2 percent. In 25 Tennessee counties in the central and western parts of the state, African-American Protestants constitute at least 10 percent of adherents.

Kentucky has the second highest percentage of Catholics in the South, behind only Florida. Settled along the southern edge of the "German triangle" (the area of high German immigration bounded by Cincinnati, St. Louis, and Milwaukee), Catholics in Kentucky dominate several counties in the central and north-central section of the state, bordering Indiana and Ohio. In 12 Kentucky counties, Catholics make up at least 20 percent of adherents; in the South only Florida and Virginia can boast more. They make up more than half of all religious adherents in two Kentucky counties: Marion (54.4 percent) and Campbell (52.2 percent). Only four other counties in the South—three in Florida and one on the coast of Mississippi—have such high percentages. Altogether, there are more Catholics in Kentucky than United Methodists or African-American Protestants. More typical of most of the South, Tennessee has only one county—Williamson—in which Catholics make up as much as 20 percent of religious adherents. Most Catholics in Tennessee are scattered through the central part of the state and in Memphis. As in other parts of the South, some sections have virtually no Catholics. In 32 Tennessee counties, especially in the northeastern and southwestern part of the state, and in 20 Kentucky counties, especially in the southeast, Catholics make up less than 1 percent of all adherents.

The statistics in **Figure 1.16** reveal the continuing effects of some of the distinctive moments in the religious history of the upper South. Tennessee and Kentucky were the site of a series of Protestant schisms in the nineteenth and early twentieth centuries that led to the formation of the Christian Church, the Disciples of Christ, and the Churches of Christ. The Disciples of Christ has its greatest number of adherents in a stretch of eight contiguous counties in north central Kentucky.[4] In each county, between 10 and 19 percent of churchgoers

Figure 1.16   Adherents as percentage of All Adherents, Tennessee and Kentucky (NARA)

	Tennessee	Kentucky
Other Conservative Christian	10.0	8.2
Holiness/Wesleyan/Pentecostal	4.7	5.0
Disciples of Christ	0.8	2.8
Confessional/Reformed	2.6	0.8

belong to the Disciples of Christ. Henry County, with 19 percent, has the highest percentage of Disciples in the South.

"Other Conservative Christians," who comprise 5 percent of adherents in the South, are particularly plentiful in Tennessee and Kentucky. There, most belong to the Churches of Christ, a group that developed as part of the Stone-Campbell restorationist movement in the early 1800s. By the early twentieth century, it had become clear that this group was different enough from the Disciples of Christ to be considered a separate denomination. Altogether, 15 of the 37 counties in the South in which "Other Conservative Christians" make up at least 20 percent of adherents are in Kentucky and 14 percent are in Tennessee. In Kentucky they are concentrated in the northeastern and south-central parts of the state, and a wall of Churches of Christ runs through middle and parts of west Tennessee. In middle Tennessee, in Clay and Jackson counties, "Other Conservative Christians" dominate, constituting 69.9 percent and 63.4 percent of adherents respectively.

Tennessee also has the South's largest percentage of people in the "Confessional/ Reformed/Non-UCC Congregational" category—basically representing those in the Calvinist tradition outside the mainline Protestant United Church of Christ. In Tennessee, the largest group in this category are the Cumberland Presbyterians, who split off from the main body of Presbyterians around 1800. Cumberland Presbyterians are scattered in substantial numbers in central and northwestern Tennessee; in Houston County they make up 10 percent of all adherents.

Holiness and Pentecostal groups are about as common in Tennessee and Kentucky as in most of the South. Roughly 5 percent of all adherents in the two states belong to such groups, concentrated in a line of counties in mountainous or at least hilly areas in the eastern parts of both states. Kentucky, with six counties with rates over 20 percent, and Tennessee, with three, have some of the areas with the heaviest concentrations of such churches in the entire South.[5] Many of these churchgoers belong to the Churches of God (both those headquartered in Cleveland, Tennessee and in Anderson, Indiana) and the Assemblies of God, with others in Church of the Nazarene and Pentecostal Holiness Church congregations. But the category includes many other churches, including independent congregations.

Virginia and West Virginia: Fewer Southern Baptists, More Mainline Protestants, Considerable Religious Diversity

On the edge of the South, Virginia and West Virginia pose a set of contrasts dramatized by the statistics in **Figures 1.17** and **1.18**. West Virginia has the least ethnically diverse population in the region, with few African Americans, Latinos, or foreign-born residents. Virginia, in contrast, has about the regional average of African Americans, and it has substantial Latino and foreign-born populations. Virginia has the South's lowest percentage of poor people and highest percentage of people with a college education, while West Virginia has a high poverty rate and ranks with Alabama and Mississippi in the number of its poorly educated residents. Significantly for considering issues of religious diversity, Virginia has the South's second largest urban population.

The two states have considerably fewer African-American Protestants than most of the South. West Virginia's 5.9 percent is the lowest in the region and Virginia's 17.6 percent is comparable to Tennessee. Only a handful of counties in southeastern Virginia—and no county in West Virginia—fit the Deep South prototype of at least 25 percent white Baptists and 25 percent African-American Protestants. Finally, Virginia and West Virginia stand out as areas with greater religious diversity than in much of the South. Each state has a wider range of groups with substantial numbers than in most of the region.

Although white Baptists constitute a smaller percentage of adherents in Virginia and West Virginia than in all other southern states except Florida, they nevertheless are the largest single religious group in both states. In Virginia, white Baptists are located in substantial numbers almost everywhere except the Shenandoah Valley counties. In most of northern and eastern West Virginia, they make up less than 25 percent of churchgoers; those counties of West Virginia, along with the coastal counties of south Florida, make up the South's least Baptist sections. West Virginia has seven counties in which Baptists make up less than 10 percent of churchgoers, led by Tucker County, the only county in the entire South where Baptists make up less than 1 percent of churchgoers. On the other hand, Baptists constitute more than half of all adherents in a few areas. In Virginia, Baptists are a majority in 14 counties, primarily in the southwestern corner near Tennessee and Kentucky and in a circle in the center of the state. In two Virginia counties, Dickenson and Lee, white Baptists make up about three quarters of all churchgoers. West Virginia has only two counties, Braxton and Calhoun, with white Baptist majorities.

As in most of the South, United Methodists have a presence throughout West Virginia and Virginia, making up 10 percent of churchgoers in virtually every county in each state. West Virginia is the only southern state where United

Figure 1.17   Demographic characteristics of Virgina and West Virgina,
by percent (2000 U.S. Census)

	Virgina	West Virginia	South	United States
Caucasian	72.3	95.0	74.4	75.1
African American	19.6	3.1	20.0	12.3
Hispanic	4.6	0.6	6.8	12.5
Asian	3.6	0.5	1.6	3.6
Other (American Indian, Hawaiian/Pacific Islander, Other Race, Mixed Race)	4.1	1.0	3.7	8.0
Foreign born	8.0	1.0	7.6	11.0
Living in urban areas (over 25 years old)	73.0	46.0	69.4	79.0
- without a High School degree	18.5	24.7	22.0	19.6
- with at least a BA degree	29.4	14.8	22.0	24.4
Living in poverty	9.5	17.9	13.3	12.3

Methodists (20.8 percent) are almost as numerous as white Baptists, and Virginia (12.8 percent) ranks second in the region. The eastern and northern sections of West Virginia are the most heavily United Methodist area of the South. Of the 24 counties in the entire South where United Methodists constitute a third of all churchgoers, West Virginia has 13 and Virginia seven. Highland County, Virginia, located on the West Virginia border, is the only county in the South where United Methodists constitute a majority of adherents. In large part because of the number of Methodists, the two states are a land of mainline Protestants. West Virginia in particular seems closer to the Midwest than the South inasmuch as 60.4 percent of its religious adherents belong to mainline Protestant groups, according to NARA data.

Along with Kentucky, Virginia and West Virginia have the highest percentage of Catholics in the South outside Florida—16.5 percent and 14.5 percent respectively. As in Kentucky, Catholics are concentrated in two places—in cities and along the northern borders of both states. The area around Washington, D.C. has an especially high number of Catholics, as does Brooke County, which is located in the thin West Virginia panhandle that separates Pennsylvania and Ohio—coal, iron, and steel country—where Eastern European Catholics came to work in the mines and mills. Like most southern states, Virginia has numerous counties with the smallest of Catholic populations; Catholics make up less than 1 percent of churchgoers in 33 counties in southern and mountainous parts

Figure 1.18   Adherents as percentage of All Adherents, Virginia
and West Virginia (NARA)

	Virginia	West Virginia
Baptists (except African Americans)	23.6	24.3
United Methodists	12.8	20.8
Catholics	16.5	14.5
Historically African American Protestants	17.6	5.9

of the state. By contrast, West Virginia has no counties where Catholics are such tiny minorities.

The variation in the African-American population accounts for a large part of the difference in the religious profiles of Virginia and West Virginia. In a large swath of southeastern Virginia, African-American Protestants are the largest single religious group. In most of Virginia's southeastern coastal counties—tobacco counties where the English established their first permanent North American settlements and began importing slaves in the early 1600s—African-American Protestants make up more than 40 percent of religious adherents. In West Virginia, African-American Protestants make up as much as 10 percent in only a handful of counties in the southern part of the state. In most parts of that state, and especially through the mountain counties of Virginia, African-American Protestants make up less than 5 percent of adherents.

West Virginia, as **Figure 1.19** makes clear, also stands out for its high concentrations of Pentecostal and Holiness churchgoers. At 11.5 percent, these folks constitute a far higher proportion of adherents than in other southern states. Here, as elsewhere in the South, most of these churchgoers belong to the Church of God (Cleveland, Tennessee), the Assemblies of God, or Pentecostal Holiness churches. The area with the greatest concentration of such churches is in the coal-producing region of West Virginia. In five counties in mountainous southeastern West Virginia and four counties in mountainous southwestern Virginia, as **Figure 1.20** shows, these groups make up over 20 percent of all adherents.[6] The leader is Logan County, West Virginia, with 30.9 percent.

West Virginia also ranks high in the South, second only to Tennessee, for its number of "Other Conservative Christians." In northern and southwestern West Virginia, and also scattered in several parts of Virginia, especially near the West Virginia line, several counties have substantial Church of Christ and Christian Church populations. In Craig County, Virginia, Christian Church and Church of Christ adherents make up almost 60 percent of all church adherents, the highest percentage outside a few areas in Tennessee.

Figure 1.19 Adherents as percentage of All Adherents, Virginia and West Virginia (NARA)

	Virginia	West Virginia
Holiness/Wesleyan/Pentecostal	5.4	11.5
Other Conservative Christian	4.2	8.4
Presbyterian USA	3.7	3.9
Episcopalian	3.4	1.6
Lutheran	1.8	1.9
Pietist/Anabaptist	1.4	1.3
Mormon	1.4	1.4
Jewish	2.1	0.3

These two states have the second and fourth highest percentages of Presbyterians in the South, but Virginia is home to the most Presbyterian area in the region. Eight of the 13 counties in the South in which members of the Presbyterian Church USA make up at least 10 percent of church adherents are in Virginia, most of them in a mountainous stretch in the western part of the state. At 34.7 percent, Rockbridge County has the highest percentage of Presbyterians in the South, and in three other Virginia mountain counties—Allegheny, Augusta, and Bath—Presbyterians make up more than 20 percent of religious adherents. In West Virginia, Presbyterians are concentrated in the state's eastern section.

The South's first official Christian churches were Anglican churches in colonial Virginia. The descendents of the Anglicans, the Episcopalians, have far more members in Virginia than any other part of the South. Eight of the nine counties in the South in which Episcopalians constitute at least 10 percent of all adherents are in Virginia, and even the names of those counties—Powhatan, James City, Albemarle, Goochland—recall the colonial South. Goochland County is the most Episcopalian county in the South, with 22.8 percent of adherents belonging to that denomination. Most of Virginia's Episcopalians live in the northern half of the state, especially along the east coast. West Virginia, like most southern states, has no area with large concentrations of Episcopalians.

Like the Carolinas, Virginia has a few pockets of Lutherans. Shenandoah County (25.5 percent) and Page County (15.8 percent) are two of six counties in the South where Lutherans constitute more than 10 percent of adherents; in several other Virginia counties and one county in West Virginia, Lutherans make up at least 5 percent.

Both states are also distinguished for having more adherents of Pietist or Anabaptist traditions—especially Churches of the Brethren but also some

Figure 1.20   Concentration of Holiness/Wesleyan and Pentecostal
Adherents in the South

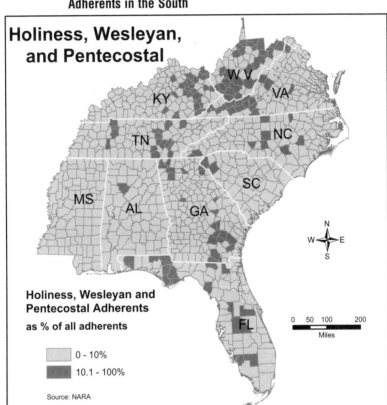

Mennonites—than any other part of the South. While the numbers of these
groups are small, Brethren and Mennonite groups living in the mountains on
the border of the two states make up a significant part of religious life in a
unique part of the South. Eleven of the 12 southern counties in which over
10 percent of churchgoers are part of Pietist and Anabaptist churches are in
Virginia, especially in the mountains.[7] Pietist/Anabaptist adherents make up
over a third of the churchgoers in Virginia's Floyd and Rockingham counties,
and in Hardy County, West Virginia. (The only other Pietist/Anabaptist pockets in the South are in Noxubee County, Mississippi—7.1 percent of adherents—where there is a substantial Mennonite population, and Alleghany—7.3
percent—and Forsyth—6.6 percent—counties in North Carolina, home of
some Church of the Brethren groups.)

At 2.1 percent of adherents, Virginia has the highest percentage of Jews of any
southern state outside of Florida. Virginia's Jewish population is concentrated
primarily in cities. Richmond, Norfolk, Fairfax, Alexandria, and Charlottesville

make up the third primary area of the southern Jewish population, along with south Florida and metropolitan Atlanta.

Mormons are a tiny percentage of southern churchgoers, with their largest numbers in Virginia and West Virginia. Most counties have some Latter-day Saints, but few areas have large numbers. Nine of the 20 southern counties in which Mormons make up at least 5 percent of all churchgoers are in Virginia or West Virginia, led by mountainous Highland County, Virginia, at 15.7 percent.

Florida: Catholics, Protestants, Jews, and Religious Diversity

In demography, Florida differs so much from most of the South that many people do not consider it part of southern history or southern society. Florida represents a fascinating blend of people and experiences that are long central to southern history, and those who have other histories. Three characteristics, as **Figure 1.21** shows, distinguish Florida from the rest of the South. Almost 90 percent of the state's people live in urban areas—a percentage far higher than any other southern state. Second, 16.7 percent of the state's people are Latino, a figure more than 10 percentage points higher than anywhere else in the region. Closely related, 16.7 percent of the state's people are foreign-born.

In southern religion, Florida stands alone. Its religious demographics differ from all other southern states—perhaps a combination of the Caribbean, the urban Northeast, and the Deep South. In every other southern state, white Baptists are the largest group, but in Florida, as **Figure 1.22** demonstrates, Catholics lead the way. In the twentieth century, Florida has been a place where people come from other places, and with that immigration its religious life has become more diverse and less like the rest of the South.

Catholics make up at least 10 percent of churchgoers in most Florida counties, and Florida has most of the South's counties in which Catholics constitute at least a quarter of all religious adherents. In a ring extending from Flagler County on the Atlantic coast to the southern tip of the state and reaching back up to Citrus County on the Gulf Coast, Catholics make up between 25 and 59 percent of churchgoers. The most heavily Catholic counties in the South are Hernando, at 59 percent, and Flagler, at 57.2 percent; Catholics make up about half of all adherents in nine other Florida counties, including the highly populated areas of Miami-Dade, Broward, and Palm Beach counties.

Most, but far from all, of Florida's Catholics are Latino, some of them recent immigrants and some with roots deep in the state's history. About a third of the state's Latinos are of Cuban origin, and Florida has substantial populations with roots in Puerto Rico, Mexico, South America, Central America, and the Dominican Republic. Also, as a state whose climate and opportunities attract people from all over the United States, Florida has many Catholics who have moved from outside the South.

Figure 1.21 Florida demographics, by percent (2000 U.S. Census)

	Florida	South	United States
Caucasian	77.9	74.4	75.1
African American	14.6	20.0	12.3
Hispanic	16.7	6.8	12.5
Asian	1.6	1.6	3.6
Other (American Indian, Hawaiian/Pacific Islander, Other Race, Mixed Race)	5.5	3.7	8.0
Foreign born	16.7	7.6	11.0
Living in urban areas (over 25 years old)	89.2	69.4	79.0
- without a High School degree	20.0	22.0	19.6
- with at least a Bachelor's degree	22.3	22.0	24.4
Living in poverty	12.5	13.3	12.3

Historians, geographers, and Florida residents themselves have distinguished Florida's northwestern Panhandle from the rest of the state. As the "Deep South" part of Florida, it has few Catholics—less than 1 percent in six Panhandle counties. Catholics are concentrated along the Panhandle coastal counties: Escambia (14.8 percent), Santa Rosa (11.2 percent), and Okaloosa (12.5 percent).

With its Catholic plurality, Florida has only seven counties that fit the 25 percent white Baptist/25 percent African-American Protestant prototype of Deep South religious life. All are located in northern Florida, all but one on the Georgia border.[8] Still, the Sunshine State does not lack for white Baptists and African-American Protestants. White Baptists make up at least a quarter of churchgoers throughout northern Florida and in most of the inland areas in southern Florida as well. Indeed, they constitute over half of all adherents in 11 counties, led by Gilchrist (76.9 percent) and Lafayette (76.3 percent), adjacent north Florida counties inland from the Gulf Coast between Tallahassee and Tampa. In much of Florida, either Baptists or Catholics dominate numerically.

African-American Protestants are proportionately smaller in Florida than in any southern state but Kentucky and West Virginia. Still, they make up between 25 percent and 40 percent of adherents in most of north Florida; in Gadsden County in the Panhandle, a typical Black Belt area, they reach 68 percent. By contrast, in Catholic-dominated south Florida, African-American Protestants range from as low as 2 percent in Hernando and Hardee counties to 16 percent in Miami-Dade and 18 percent in Okeechobee.

South Florida also stands out as the most Jewish part of the South. Jews, as **Figure 1.23** shows, make up 7.9 percent of all religious adherents in Florida. The

Figure 1.22 Adherents as percentage of All Adherents, Florida	
	Florida
Catholics	32.6
Baptists (except historically African American)	17.0
Historically African-American Protestant	14.1

state has 12 counties—more than anywhere else in the region—in which Jews make up more than 3 percent of the religious adherents. All are coastal counties around the southern tip of the state. In three of them Jews make up more than 10 percent of adherents: Palm Beach (11.2 percent), Miami-Dade (23.6 percent), and Broward (24.2 percent). In the latter two, they are outnumbered only by Catholics.

Florida has about as many Holiness/Wesleyan/Pentecostal churchgoers as most parts of the South, but some of the heaviest concentrations are in the state—over 10 percent in 15 Florida counties, led by the Panhandle counties of Franklin (25 percent) and Holmes (20 percent). In Santa Rosa County, where one of the largest and longest series of revival meetings in recent history took place at the Brownsville Assembly of God Church in Pensacola, 12.8 percent of churchgoers are Holiness and Pentecostal adherents. Such groups are also popular in peninsular Florida, where Sumter County, northeast of Tampa, boasts 17.1 percent Holiness/Pentacostal churchgoers; Lee and Henry counties, in South Florida, count 11.8 percent and 14.6 percent respectively, as seen in **Figure 1.23**.

One of the most striking aspects of religion in Florida is the low proportion of United Methodists. To use sporting language, through most of the South the United Methodists run a solid third or fourth, behind Southern Baptists, African-American Protestants, and, in some places, Catholics. But in Florida they exist in significant numbers only in the north-central part of the state across the state's northern tier. At 16.9 percent, Santa Rosa County has the highest percentage of United Methodists in the state; by contrast, in south Florida, in Miami-Dade, Broward, and Palm Beach counties, they make up less than 3 percent of adherents.

It is, finally, important to note the diversity of Florida's Christians relative to the rest of the South. Christian Churches and Churches of Christ are spread throughout much of the state. Presbyterians are too, though they are somewhat more concentrated in central and south Florida. With 1.9 percent of the adherents, Episcopalians have a higher percentage of adherents than any state in the South other than Virginia. St. Johns County (10.1 percent), home of St. Augustine, is the only southern county outside Virginia in which Episcopalians make up 10 percent of churchgoers. The 1.8 percent of the state's churchgoers who belong to the cat-

Figure 1.23 Adherents as percentage of All Adherents, Florida	
	Florida
Jewish	7.9
Holiness/Wesleyan/Pentecostal	5.9
United Methodist	5.8
Other Conservative Christian	4.9
Presbyterian USA	2.0
Episcopalian	1.9
Confessional/Reformed/non-UCC	1.8

egory called "Confessional/Reformed" are primarily Missouri Synod Lutherans and members of the Presbyterian Church in America; their greatest popularity is in south-central Florida. And although Mormons make up only a tiny percentage of Florida's churchgoers, the small Panhandle county of Liberty has, at 22.4 percent, the highest proportion of Mormons in any southern county.

Religion in the South is changing most quickly in those parts of the region that are changing most dramatically in other ways. For a lot of people, especially old-timers, "the South" means what they imagine it has long been. In their eyes, it is a place with downtown areas with several large white Protestant churches, and with thousands of small Protestant churches in the rural countryside, attended by a few dozen people—either black or white but never both—who were family members and close friends. That South still exists, but it is changing as the South changes. One of the most significant conclusions of this demographic survey is that cities, especially metropolitan Atlanta and the urban areas in Florida and Virginia, are a burgeoning archipelago of religious diversity. This may help account for how so much religious diversity exists in a region that too often takes little notice of it.

Still, the image of the South as a region numerically dominated by Southern Baptists and a range of African-American Protestant groups is absolutely correct. Catholics and United Methodists run a distant third and fourth, and many smaller groups, most of them evangelical in style and belief, make up a broad panorama of Protestants. For that reason, understanding religion in the public life of the South requires understanding how the evangelical Protestant world works—by race, by gender, by subregion, and by ideology. Whether or not they belong to them, like them, or understand them, everyone in the South has to deal with evangelical Protestants.

Endnotes

1 Martin E. Marty, *Righteous Empire: The Protestant Experience in America* (New York: Dial Press, 1970), 139.

2 Rabun County, Georgia (15.3), Powell County, Kentucky (18.4), Yancey County, North Carolina (14.8), Buckingham County, Virginia (16), Warren County, Virginia (10.7), Hampshire County, West Virginia (10.4), and Roane County, West Virginia (16.4).

3 John Shelton Reed, *My Tears Spoiled My Aim, and Other Reflections on Southern Culture* (San Diego: Harcourt Brace, 1994), 141.

4 Anderson, Bath, Bourbon, Fleming, Franklin, Henry, Montgomery, and Scott counties, Kentucky.

5 Wolfe, Menifee, Powell, McCreary, Leslie, and Lee counties, Kentucky, and Houston, Bradley, and Bledsoe counties, Tennessee.

6 Mingo, McDowell, Grant, and Boone counties, West Virginia, and Bath, Pulaski, Tazewell, and Wythe counties, Virginia.

7 Augusta, Botetourt, Floyd, Franklin, Page, Rockingham, Shenandoah counties, Virginia, and Grant, Hardy, Mineral, and Pendleton counties, West Virginia.

8 Baker, Bradford, Columba, Gulf, Hamilton, Jefferson, Madison counties, Florida.

CHAPTER TWO

AT EASE IN ZION, UNEASY IN BABYLON: WHITE EVANGELICALS

Paul Harvey

In Thomasville, Georgia, in the mid-1990s, a young white woman named Jaime L. Wireman gave birth to a child she named Whitney, after the contemporary black singer Whitney Houston. Wireman's husband, an African-American man named Jeffrey Johnson, worked odd jobs locally, and the two lived together in a trailer just outside the southwest Georgia town. The child, born with a skull not fully formed, died after just 19 hours. Jaime Wireman wanted the baby to be buried with her maternal grandfather in the cemetery of the Barnetts Creek Baptist Church. After her burial, however, deacons of the church, who had not known previously that the father was black, asked the family to remove the child from the historically all-white cemetery. When the embarrassing incident came to light, church members criticized the deacons' action and permitted the child to remain in the cemetery. With some prodding from Whitney's maternal grandmother, the deacons and the pastor of the church met the family, apologized for their actions, and asked for forgiveness. "Our church family humbly asks you to accept our apology," the chairman of the deacon board told the family. "I believe people are sorry," the child's grandmother concluded. "She was just a baby."[1]

This story of race and religion in the contemporary South retells familiar themes of southern history: racial separation, sin, forgiveness, and an ambiguous healing. Racial division runs headlong into biracial sex and an innocent childhood disrupted by the intrusion of an unjust social world. The culmination, on the face of it, brings healing. Just as importantly, the story puts into relief a paradox of southern, and American, religious history: namely, the deep contradiction between human spiritual equality in the eyes of God and divinely ordained social inequality in the everyday world.

For better or worse, and despite increasing immigration from all parts of the world to the region, the South is still the Bible Belt—or, to be more precise, the Evangelical Belt. As the previous chapter makes clear, evangelicals dominate the South in a way they do not in any other region of the country. Using the data from the American Religious Identification Survey (ARIS)—which offers the best picture available of how people see themselves religiously—Baptists (white and black) constitute one-third of all Southerners, outnumbering Catholics in the region by three-to-one. Nowhere else in the country is there anything approaching such a ratio. And in the South there are many more evangelicals than Baptists alone: Holiness folks and Pentecostals of various stripes, a large portion of the members of mainline dominations (above all United Methodists), and an ever-increasing number of those who belong to non-denominational megachurches.

To be sure, by some numerical indicia, the Evangelical Belt is, at best, holding its own. The 40 percent of Southerners who show up in the North American Religion Atlas (NARA) data as religiously unaffiliated or uncounted seems startlingly high in a region that prides itself on church membership. The Southern Baptist Convention (SBC), the denomination that dominates the South, has ceased growing at a pace to keep up with the growth in Southern population. By other measures, however, the Evangelical Belt is nearly as potent as ever.

In a 1998 poll, 20 percent of Southerners said they attended church services more than once a week—twice the rate of non-Southerners. Forty-two percent of Southerners (as opposed to 33 percent of non-Southerners) agreed with the statement that religion was "extremely important" in their lives. Six of 10 Southerners said they accepted the account of creation in Genesis over that of Darwin. Even a large proportion of the unchurched in the region still believes in God and afterlife.

The predominance of southern preachers on the airwaves provides the kind of oral soundtrack that many Americans associate with conservative Protestant Christianity more generally. "Several of my Christian friends had asked me why I seemed to slip into a Southern accent when praying or praising the Lord," one woman recently ruminated. "It dawned on me one night that I had been learning about prayer and ministry from several television ministers."[2] In other words, the religiosity of Southerners is better indicated by the 11 percent who told ARIS surveyors that they have no religion than by NARA's 40 percent unaffiliated/uncounted.

The evangelical influence makes itself felt no less forcibly in Pew survey data compiled by John Green of the Bliss Center at the University of Akron. Among all regions of the country the South has, after the Southern Crossroads, the fewest supporters of gay rights (51.1 percent) and the most pro-lifers (48.9 percent). In the Pew survey taken at the time of the 2000 election, the South as a whole topped all other regions in the proportion of people who endorsed some variant of the statement that the Bible is the inspired Word of God: 68 percent, as opposed, for example, to only 47 percent of people living in the Pacific region. Strikingly, all religious groups in the South—evangelical, mainline, black, Catholic, "Other Christian," Jewish, and (most interestingly of all) those self-identified as "secular"—are more likely (usually considerably more) to claim such a "high view" of biblical authority. Eighty-five percent of southern evangelicals take this view, as do 62 percent of mainline Protestants and 30 percent of secularists. The corresponding figures for each group in the Pacific region are 78 percent, 50 percent, and 9 percent. The South is, in short, the country's most solidly evangelical region, and the South's evangelicals are the most conservative in terms of voting patterns, views of biblical authority, and attitudes towards significant social issues.

Evangelical Protestantism does not exert its dominance uniformly across the region. Evangelicals as a percentage of population are heavily concentrated in particular sub-regions and counties, most thickly spread in a broad swath that cuts directly through the historic cotton country and some upcountry regions of the Old South. Indeed, "Evangelical Belt" is apt, for when mapped by county, the area of evangelical dominance looks just like a belt (albeit with a considerable belly overhang in parts of the Upper South). For whites, it almost exactly parallels the historic Black Belt. Together, these belts cut a wide arc through the Deep South until, nearing the coastline and reaching into the northern half of Virginia or the lower half of Florida, they fade from view almost entirely. This is the "God-haunted" South of myth, legend, and some of the best fiction ever written in America.

Scholarship in southern religious history—including titles such as *At Ease in Zion* and *Churches in Cultural Captivity*—tends to support this apparently timeless image. The prevalence of southern accents on the televangelical airwaves cements it in the public mind. Southern religious culture is personalized by the Grahams (Billy and his more outspokenly partisan son Franklin), Pat Robertson, and Jerry Falwell (notwithstanding the considerable differences among them in their conception of the relationship of religion and public life). To study the relationship of religion and public life in the historic South is to examine the influence of a dominant evangelical culture that has shaped the region's social mores and political life.

That does not mean, of course, that the South is morally purer than the rest of the nation. Its homicide rate is high, and it has the highest divorce rate of any region in the country. Southerners also consume alcohol in large quantities—and, increasingly, methamphetamines and Oxycontin. Mississippi is one of the most solidly evangelical states in the nation, but it now sports a "casino belt" in its historically impoverished northwest corner as well as along its Gulf Coast. Jobs are jobs, and tax dollars are tax dollars, a point that evangelicals who work in those "sin" industries realize.

Moreover, if the Bible Belt image gives the South the aura of repression and intolerance, the southern arts, high and low, are anything but. The region boasts some of the nation's most inventive (and, at times, raunchiest) writers, artists, intellectuals, and musicians. If southern evangelicalism seems dominated by spare and plain meeting houses, fundamentalist fire-and-brimstone sermons, and repressive behavioral restrictions, the southern artistic imagination has been infused with rich biblical imagery that has exploded in word, sound, and visual imagery. This is evidenced by the rich literary tradition of such writers as Flannery O'Connor, William Faulkner, Alice Walker, and Walker Percy; in the musical world of shape-note singing, black spirituals, quartets, and gospel music in both white and black communities; and in the visionary work of self-taught artists like Howard Finster and McKendree Robbins Long.

In fact, southern evangelicals are not nearly as self-confident as they let on. As suggested by the title of another recent work, *Uneasy in Babylon: Southern Baptist Conservatives and American Culture*, evangelicals have always seen themselves at war with temptations and corruptions that lie in wait around every corner, regionally as well as nationally; indeed, the South has never been Zion. Significantly, since the civil rights revolution rendered the South less alien from the rest of America, conservative southern evangelicals have increasingly felt impelled to seek out allies with those of like minds in other parts of the country, forming cross-regional, religio-political alliances that would have been unthinkable, even heretical, in previous generations.

The Evangelical Belt in Historical Perspective

The Bible Belt of early America was New England, not the South. The South was known for deism among intellectuals like Thomas Jefferson, high-church Anglicanism among white planters, rabble-rousing in the backcountry among Scots-Irish folk famously indifferent or hostile to organized religion, and a huge body of enslaved people whose religious views appeared to whites to be inscrutable and unknowable. It was the great accomplishment of nineteenth- and twentieth-century southern evangelicals to radically change the South's religiosity—a feat of proselytization analyzed by such historians as John Boles, Donald Mathews, Randy Sparks, Lynn Lyerly, Rhys Isaac, and Christine Heyrman. The story these scholars tell is bound up with the rise of a slaveholding Republic, the national Second Great Awakening, the coming of "civilization" to the rustic southern backcountry and newly opening states of the Deep South, the innovative methods (such as circuit-riding preachers and mass-produced pamphlet literature) employed by the newly rising evangelical denominations, and the concerted (and partially successful) effort to evangelize among slaves. But, as other historians have argued, the South also possessed a masculine culture of honor that prized self-assertion and devalued shame in inverse proportion to the way evangelicals distrusted the self and pumped up a spiritual culture of shame for one's sinfulness. Women were the critical mediators of evangelicalism into southern life, particularly in the way they invited Methodist circuit-riding preachers into the households of their suspicious husbands and sons and brothers. Gradually, enough men (such as the wealthy planter in Liberty County, Georgia, Charles Colcock Jones) came to accept the message and to support the missionaries who evangelized among the slaves. Antebellum white evangelicals considered themselves faithful purveyors of the gospel message to a people bound down by heathenism and barbarism. Of course, the uses that slaves made of Christianity differed radically from the plans of the planters and missionaries.

In southern evangelicalism there was always a tension between involvement and non-involvement with the political system—the state. What is God's? What is Caesar's? White southern evangelicals historically preached a clear distinction between issues closely connected to personal morality, on which Christians were obligated to take a stand, and other issues of pubic policy and politics, which evangelicals were supposed to avoid as divisive and detrimental to the advancement of God's kingdom. For that reason, the suppression of alcohol became a matter for public activism among evangelicals (and remains so), while the tariff (in the nineteenth century) and the capital gains tax (in the twentieth) have largely been outside the realm of evangelical discussion of politics and public life. Not that this distinction prevented antebellum white southern evangelicals from vigorously supporting and defending slavery. Nor did it block a heavy involvement in public life during the Civil War through army service, chaplaincies, and fast-day sermons.

During the Civil War, evangelicals entered the public arena as never before, gradually coming to dominate their culture in a way that simply was impossible in the antebellum era. The Confederate cause increasingly was defined as a righteous and godly one, and the South's military heroes—Robert E. Lee, Stonewall Jackson, and others—became demigods to be praised as much for their piety as for their military prowess. Taking a lead in creating the religion of the "Lost Cause," evangelicals not only Christianized the Civil War but the white South as a whole. With a period of sharp post-war decline due to southern defeat and even moreso because of the mass withdrawal of African Americans from the major religious institutions of the region, it took a while for the white evangelical churches to get back on their feet. When they did, they still faced some of their old competitors and enemies, including the honor culture of the Old South that prized masculine assertiveness, to say nothing of the poverty and isolation that gripped so much of the region. But over time, white evangelicalism established its dominance over Southern culture. This included vigorous support for the new system of racial control—segregation—which white evangelicals defended all the way through the 1950s and 1960s.

Here it is important to make clear that the term "evangelical" has been coded "white," despite the fact that black believers have overwhelmingly worshipped in evangelical denominations—for the most part Baptist and Methodist. For as Michael Emerson and Christian Smith have pointed out in *Divided by Faith*, white and black evangelicals remain deeply divided in their approach to social engagement, as well as on important social issues. Specifically, evangelicalism among whites has reinforced individualism, thus making it difficult to comprehend issues like race and poverty that are relatively immune to individual remedies. Black evangelicals, in contrast, have used their religious institutions—churches for the most part—for collective sustenance and empowerment (a point developed further in William Montgomery's chapter in this book).

This is not to suggest that the distinction between the moral and the political (paralleling the private and the public) was ever so clear as white evangelical leaders claimed. And the fact that the distinction has collapsed almost entirely in the present day owes something to the example of black churches. (In recent years, white and black evangelicals have sometimes found common cause.) Nonetheless, the public life that emanates from the two groups generally leads in such opposite directions that it is necessary to consider them separately. What we are here calling the "Evangelical Belt" refers largely to the *white* evangelical South. It is a South that lines up overwhelmingly on the same side of moral and social questions, and is also closely aligned on issues that at first glance do not appear to have any particular moral coding. The white South may have changed political parties over the last generation, but it is still solid.

Social Activism in the Evangelical Belt

Social activism rarely comes to mind when thinking of this religious tradition. Historically, most southern evangelicals emphasized obedience to the powers that be, political conservatism, an overriding emphasis on personal (as opposed to social) morality, and a suspicion of social activism as a distraction from the real business of saving souls for eternal life. Presbyterian theologians historically defended the venerable doctrine of the "spirituality of the church," and most southern churches advised political quietism. Social activists, moreover, often came tainted with that ugliest of southern epithets: "outside agitator." But the South harbored many inside agitators as well, and most of them came from church traditions.

Progressive and radical social activism in the South quite often came from people imbued by the same evangelical upbringings as those who adamantly defended the social order. Overcoming some of their suspicion of state power and governmental authority, white evangelicals seized on progressive initiatives to improve public life through education, sanitation, and the prohibition of alcohol. Indeed, despite their reputation for stalwart conservatism, they led the progressive movement in the early twentieth century. Good roads, better schools, improved sanitation, elimination of alcohol, and the proper ordering of the races through such "modern" mechanisms as urban segregation, they realized, could only aid their cause.

Religion in the post-Civil War American South has been prophetic as well as priestly, not only ungirding the social order but from time to time challenging it. If white southern theology generally sanctified southern hierarchies, evangelical belief and practice also at times subtly undermined them. Churches as institutions were conservative, but progressive Christians drew different lessons from southern spirituality than regional religious leaders intended. The actions of individual churchmen and women outstripped the cautious defensiveness that often marked the public stance of the religious institutions.

While religious institutions were resistant to change, many religious folk devoted themselves to social change precisely because they perceived God as the author of it. Writing about the rise of southern liberalism, the historian John Egerton explains that churches and universities were wellsprings "for the intellectual and philosophical stimulation out of which some reform movements came—but when the institutions themselves shrank from joining the fray, it was often their sons and daughters, acting in new alliances or as individuals, who moved the dialogue and the action to a higher plane."[3] Petty daily harassment, economic coercion, beatings, death threats, and even assassination have hounded religious prophets for social change in a region historically hostile to radical seers—most especially those committed to racial justice. But the very pervasiveness of evangelicalism in the region also provided the religious language from which these social prophets drew their inspiration. They knew that, as a severe and righteous judge, God would condemn the historic patterns of brutality and injustice endemic to an impoverished and racially segregated region.

Scholars have rightly seen evangelicalism as a legitimator of the southern status quo, of giving divine sanction to the peculiar social mores of the region. But religious belief was also a prophetic voice warning against God's judgment on a people willing to tolerate unrighteousness. In the 1960s, some of the most self-consciously religious social activists served in the Student Non-Violent Coordinating Committee (SNCC). SNCC's "distinctively idealistic belief that fortitude, determined action, and fearlessness would result in momentous social change," Southern Methodist daughter and civil rights activist Mary King has explained, "stemmed to a great degree from the Protestant upbringings of most of its workers." She connected her vision specifically to Wesleyan theology, that "through grace and redemption each person can be saved," a view that "reinforced" SNCC's belief that the "good in every human being could be appealed to, fundamental change could correct the immorality of racial segregation, and new political structures could be created."[4]

The South was transformed in the 1950s and 1960s, and the magnitude of that accomplishment should never be underestimated. The South's *de jure* segregation eventually crumbled, its last supports ultimately swept away by the historic civil rights legislation of the mid-1960s. Black and white evangelicals played important roles in that transformation. The Civil Rights Movement in many ways represented the culmination of a religious vision, the creation of the beloved community in spirit if not in actuality. Even if this utopian language ultimately was bound to disappoint, such a vision was critically necessary for energizing ordinary black southerners stifled by a repressive social system.

After World War II, the American creed of democracy and equality effectively required white southern theologians to mouth the words that all men were created equal. To justify inequality, they resorted to constitutional arguments ("interposition"), appeals to tradition, outright demagoguery, and obscurantist renderings of Old Testament passages (such as mythologies derived from the story of Noah and his sons). Speaking before the South Carolina legislature, W. A. Criswell, pastor of the largest Protestant congregation of his era (The First Baptist Church of Dallas, Texas), condemned *Brown v. Board of Education* with these words: "Let them integrate. Let them sit up there in their dirty shirts and make all their fine speeches. But they are all a bunch of infidels, dying from the neck up."[5] Yet *Brown* exposed the nakedness of the raw exercise of power that white supremacy entailed, depriving it of any compelling theological justification. Most segregationist theologians eventually capitulated—even Criswell. By 1970 he had changed his mind and confessed that he had "come to the profound conclusion that to separate by coercion the body of Christ on the basis of skin pigmentation was unthinkable, unchristian and unacceptable to God."[6]

Though not renouncing their views, segregationists by the late 1960s and early 1970s knew better than to air them publicly. What had been mainstream thought was now extreme. But a new battle for the soul of the white Christian South was ongoing. It would result in a very different conclusion from the drama of the civil rights years.

Whether in upholding the status quo (as in the case of those white believers who defended segregation to its dying breath, often by the very act of claiming that the South's reigning social system was God's plan for maintaining racial "integrity"), or in attacking that status quo (as in the case of Christian activists in the Civil Rights Movement), southern evangelicalism has never been as removed from engagement in this world's affairs as its adherents—and many historians since—typically have claimed. Such is certainly the case today, when the activist impulse has migrated rightward and lodged itself firmly in the hands of a (mostly) white evangelical leadership.

After the 1960s, social activism in southern religion largely passed from the civil rights coalition, whose primary focus was racial justice in the South, to the Religious Right, seen in the rise of figures such as Jerry Falwell, Pat Robertson, and Ralph Reed. Learning from the techniques of the Civil Rights Movement—indeed, from the *black* evangelical churches—the contemporary religious-political right has deployed the language of social righteousness. In this case, though, social activism has been used not so much to pull a backward region forward as to reclaim a lost heritage of a once supposedly "Christian America."

By the 1970s, many white southern believers were accommodating themselves with remarkable ease to the demise of the idea that white supremacy was fundamentally constitutive of their society. Thus, in the recent controversies within southern church organizations, and involving the political activities of white evangelicalism, race has been one of the very few items on the agenda *not* in dispute. Today's conservatives have for the most part repudiated the white supremacist views of their predecessors; note the 1995 resolution of the Southern Baptist Convention (SBC) officially apologizing for the role historically played by white southerners in defending slavery and segregation.

Today, the standard biblical arguments against racial equality are relics, embarrassments from a bygone age. But their philosophical premises have not shriveled up and died. Instead, they have migrated into the contemporary religious-conservative stance on gender. For religious conservatives generally, patriarchy has supplanted race as the defining first principle of God-ordained inequality. Nowhere is this more evident than in the recent history of the SBC, the country's largest Protestant denomination.

In 1979, a group of conservative Southern Baptist men led by Paige Patterson and Paul Pressler, one a theologian and the other a lawyer and conservative district judge, set out to win control of the SBC. Prior attempts by less well-connected fundamentalists in the early 1970s had failed. But this effort did succeed in formulating a strategy for ultimate victory: Place the right men in the convention's presidency, and then use the appointive power of the executive office to slot political and ideological allies in key positions. Patterson and Pressler, the theologian and strategist of the movement, put into action their plan to purge the SBC of liberalism. They estimated (with remarkable prescience) that in 10 years conservatives would own a controlling majority on seminary trustee boards and denominational agencies. A politically charged battle through the 1980s for control of the SBC ensued. By 1991, the conservatives had won a complete victory in what they referred to as a "conservative resurgence" and the defeated moderates called a "fundamentalist takeover."

Theological modernism and political liberalism, the conservatives argued, were weaning Southern Baptists away from their historic defense of Reformation Christianity. The moderates responded that the fundamentalists were conducting a political purge. The conservatives meant what they said: Put the SBC back in the hands of biblical inerrantists. The word "inerrancy," referring to a complete trust in the literal verity of the Bible, served primarily as a political slogan designed to smoke out skeptics who expressed the wrong kinds of deviance from the new theological orthodoxy. The moderates also meant what they said: Permit some limited theological diversity among local churches that would cooperate for the cause of missions.

The moderates, however, lacked any clear political leadership. One might say that, as moderates, they lacked the capacity to fight with a single-minded will. By contrast, conservative leaders pronounced they were "going for the jugular." In the end, Southern Baptist moderates and progressives, who were often accused of being too preoccupied with things of the world, turned out to be too spiritually and irenically inclined to organize themselves as a "movement culture" or to engage in effective power politicking in the convention. The conservatives, who proclaimed themselves defenders of the spirituality of the church, in fact were the savvy political operators.

In 1998, SBC delegates, meeting in Salt Lake City, approved a change to the Baptist Faith and Message that endorsed "wifely submission" to husbands. Although it was reported as a reactionary public announcement, the new language actually reiterated a time-honored position in southern religious life. But its adoption was portentous nonetheless.

It was in 1925 that messengers to the SBC adopted the first Baptist Faith and Message statement. Over time it became the closest thing to a creed this avowedly creedless denomination had. So it was no small matter to change the Message to address social themes. The Depression, World War II, the Civil Rights Movement, and the war in Vietnam spurred no such action. But the family values debate did. In the process, the convention soundly defeated a competing amendment calling for "mutual submission" between husbands and wives—a formulation that many biblical commentators regard as truer to the Bible.

Denominational leaders and representatives thereby arrogated to themselves the privilege to make church law not only in theology and social policy but also, for the first time, in private life. About the same time conservatives consolidated their power at the SBC's flagship school, the Southern Baptist Theological

Seminary in Nashville. This brought about the near-total turnover of the faculty, including one particularly well-known case, the forced resignation of the theologian Molly Marshall in 1994. Had she not resigned, Marshall, the first woman to receive tenure at Southern and a supporter of women's ordination, would have been charged with "failure to relate constructively" to the SBC and alleged deviation from seminary positions on issues ranging from atonement and salvation to God and the Bible.

Denying that gender had anything to do with the effort to dismiss her, the newly appointed president of Southern, R. Albert Mohler Jr., acknowledged that "feminist theology, as distinct from the issue of the service of women in the church, is and has been one of proper concern related to Southern Baptist theological education." The seminary, Mohler said, would "not be open to a revision of basic Christian doctrine or of the text and character of Christian scripture in order to meet the demands of what is now considered the mainstream of feminist theology." For her part, Marshall denied that she was a "mainstream feminist theologian," insisting rather that the SBC's leadership felt threatened by the views of a woman who happened to be a theologian.

Certainly, her ouster highlighted the gender politics of the new regime. So for that matter did the conflicts of convention leaders with the historic organization of Southern Baptist women, the Woman's Missionary Union, discussed in the chapter by Cynthia Lynn Lyerly.

Behind the battle for control of the SBC has been a deep divide between those for whom human equality and autonomy reign as fundamental principles, and those for whom communal norms and strictures and a divinely ordained hierarchy remain determinative of social life. In some ways, the struggle has taken the form of a classic division between philosophical liberalism and communalist conservatism. For adherents of the latter position, gendered patterns of hierarchy are fundamental to godly structures of religious, social, and political life. Of course, southern conservatism always intertwined race and gender hierarchies, particularly in its emphasis on social purity. The foundational conservative principles of order and hierarchy, and the literalist biblical exegesis undergirding the philosophy, underlay each. Just as was the case with the anti-slavery biblical argument, liberals have been compelled to rely on broader readings of the biblical texts, which by definition leave them suspect and intellectually vulnerable within an evangelical culture that prizes strict constructionist readings of sacred passages—whether of the Bible or of the U.S. Constitution.

It was no accident that religious conservatives came to national prominence following the demise of race as the central issue of southern life. Their political movements updated venerable philosophical defenses of social hierarchy as necessary for a properly ordered liberty. No longer defenders of a discredited racial hierarchy, the conservatives could advance their positions in favor of an unapologetic patriarchy. In the civil rights years, white southern evangelical identity began to shift away from old divisions based on denominational theology and polity to new ones based on social attitudes. Beginning with race and ending with gender, liberals, moderates, and conservatives came to form separate blocs across denominational lines, in the kind of ideological restructuring of American religion described by the sociologist Robert Wuthnow.[7]

As in religious, so in secular politics. Once upon a time—in the late 1930s—southern conservatives led by figures such as Josiah Bailey, a Southern Baptist newspaper editor and senator from North Carolina, formed a conservative coalition that effectively stymied FDR's social agenda. In particular, opposition to a federal anti-lynching law became an effective organizing tool for the proto-Dixiecrats. They argued that the Democratic Party had become something very different from the party of their fathers. It had become a vehicle for the schemes of the New Deal, not the stalwart defender of decentralized and limited government as was the southern Democratic conservative philosophy. Moreover, the southern conservatives looked on with dismay as their party became a multi-ethnic patchwork. They were especially uneasy as blacks deserted the party of Lincoln for the party of Roosevelt. A decade later their efforts would take shape in the Dixiecrat revolt of 1948. In later years many of the same figures led the attack on the civil rights revolution.

The heirs of this restructuring of southern politics and religion led the later conservative movements, this time with more success. For them, race was not the primary issue. If at times it lay just beneath the surface, there were also some tentative cross-racial conservative coalitions—organized particularly around the issues of abortion, public education, women's rights, and same-sex marriage. Thus far have contemporary southern religious conservatives distinguished themselves from their avowedly white supremacist predecessors. Yet even as the new groupings on the right parted from the dishonorable racist past of their predecessors, they maintained their well-honed theological defenses of hierarchy, submission, and order.

Politically, they have turned into solid Republicans, joining forces with conservative white evangelicals in Appalachia, whose Republicanism has been a mark of identity since the Civil War. Across the South, about 40 percent of the GOP vote now comes from white evangelicals who tell pollsters they go to church one or more times a week. The whites who vote Democratic in the region now do so as moderates and liberals—folks who go to church less frequently and share the same kind of ideological commitments as fellow Democrats in the rest of the country.

The peculiar religious demography of the Evangelical Belt significantly influences the character of its public life, and increasingly of its politics, as the Republican Party strengthens its hold on believers in the region. In exit-polling data from the 2000 election, 27 percent of voters surveyed in the South indicated an affiliation with evangelical Protestantism, the highest of any region. (The next closest was the Midwest, at 25 percent; both contrasted starkly with New England, where just 1.8 percent claimed evangelical affiliation and 5.8 percent mainline Protestant.)

In the 2000 and 2004 presidential elections, evangelicals voted for George W. Bush over his Democrat opponent by better than three-to-one margins—in the nation as a whole as well as in the South. But the impact of these voters was nowhere near the same. White evangelicals dominate in the South but not elsewhere; indeed, frequent-attending white evangelicals—the vital center of the Republican base—constitute 40 percent of the G.O.P. vote in the South but only 20 percent elsewhere. Thanks to them, the South has become almost as solidly Republican as it once was Democratic. Once upon a time, the only elected southern Republicans came from traditionally G.O.P. areas in the Appalachian counties of north Georgia and Alabama, Kentucky, upper east Tennessee, and West Virginia. Increasingly, now, elected Democrats (outside of Florida) come out of the formerly Republican but now solidly Democratic black communities in and around cities like Atlanta and Birmingham and in rural black areas like the Mississippi delta. The racial alignment of political partisanship in the South has, in short, become more monolithic.

In the past generation, the most important political development in the Evangelical Belt, portentous for the nation as a whole as well as the South, has been the rise of the Religious Right. Spurred by the social revolutions of the 1960s, by a new generation of evangelical leadership that actively pursued rather than shunned politics, and by the Supreme Court's 1973 abortion decision in *Roe v. Wade*, the conservative evangelical movement spread quickly through networks of direct mailing lists, caucuses, and church congregations. Indeed, its most sophisticated theoreticians and activists, such as Ralph Reed, understood that the models of earlier social movements with deep bases in religion (including abolitionism and the Civil Rights Movement) could be applied to organizing for conservative causes and against abortion rights, gay marriage, and other practices that seemed to threaten family values.

The Religious Right, of course, is hardly peculiar to the South. Midwestern states like Iowa and Kansas boast strong contingents of evangelical conservatives in politics. In many ways the current epicenter of such religious conservatism is in Colorado Springs, Colorado, where the mammoth evangelical organization Focus on the Family (headed by James Dobson, a native Louisianian and author of the classic child-rearing text *Dare to Discipline*) is one of the largest employers in a city that includes a large number of sizable military installations. And, in national polling data, midwestern states often score close to southern states in the high degree of conservative responses to questions on social issues.

Nevertheless, in many ways the contemporary Religious Right was conceived and first grew into a significant political force in southern states. In Virginia, the Baptist pastor Jerry Falwell and the Pentecostal broadcaster Pat Robertson engineered many of the techniques that would became staples of Religious Right politics, and Robertson became the movement's first candidate for president. Although it collapsed in the late 1980s, Falwell's Moral Majority was a formative grouping, a forum in which southern evangelicals who historically had been suspicious of politics felt their way into involvement in local and state issues such as pari-mutuel betting, as well as national controversies on abortion and gay rights. After his unsuccessful run for the G.O.P. presidential nomination in 1988, Robertson (with Georgian Ralph Reed as executive director) built the Christian Coalition into a formidable grass roots organization. Unencumbered by the Baptist legacy of attachment to strict church-state separation, the Christian Coalition served as the beacon for faith-based politicking across the region.

To be sure, the enthusiasm and passion generated by the Religious Right frequently was not matched by substantive victories. From the 1970s to the 1990s, the Religious Right in the Evangelical Belt was compelled to learn the art of political pragmatism and coalition-building. In Virginia, for example, when the Republican Party itself was the state's dominant political force, it attracted a more diverse constituency, meaning that moral conservatives had to make nice with a variety of other groups housed in the big tent (although they drew the line at consorting with the "Log Cabin Republicans," an organization of gay party members). The Religious Right experienced considerable successes in Virginia, then, but could not press its full agenda without alienating many other groups and jeopardizing the Republicans' chances for statewide success at the polls.

The story of remarkable but ultimately limited success in the world of southern politics also has held true for evangelicals in South Carolina. The ultraconservative Bob Jones University, located in Greenville, served as a launching pad for evangelical politicos in South Carolina from the 1960s to George W. Bush's controversial appearance there in 2000 (by which time the formerly obscure institution was nationally known and ridiculed for its ban on interracial dating). In the 1980s, Bob Jones Republicans joined with the state GOP establishment in repelling the advance of Pat Robertson's Christian Coalition (and Robertson's own insurgent political campaign against then-Vice-President George H. W. Bush) in internecine party warfare. Over the next decade intra-party skirmishing continued as the Christian Coalition sought unsuccessfully to take over the state party organization.

In the 1990s, the Christian Coalition was extremely active on the campaign trail, distributing its voter guides in white evangelical churches across the region, and gradually welding those churches into a political machine for turning out voters. Very often this proceeded in a stealthy way, as some candidates found it necessary to avoid too strong an association with the Religious Right, lest they alienate moderate voters at the polls. As in other states, a delicate balancing game had to be played between older-style mainstream business Republicans, economic and social libertarians, and Christian conservatives.

When Republicans are able to unite these diverse factions, then they are formidable indeed. But such unity is far from assured in an Evangelical Belt state divided between fundamentalists associated with Bob Jones University, the Pentecostal/ Charismatic base of Pat Robertson's support, and mainstream Southern Baptists who have conservative inclinations but are difficult to mobilize (in part because of their historic reluctance to be too closely identified with specific candidates or political debates). As with other political coalitions, the division between ideological purists and electoral pragmatists remained a constant challenge. How much of the basic agenda could be sacrificed in the name of success at the polls?

A third example may be seen in Alabama, where in May 2003 Gov. Bob Riley, a conservative Republican and standard bearer for the Religious Right, shocked supporters by announcing his plan for a significant restructuring of the state's onerously regressive tax system. "Jesus says one of our missions is to take care of the least among us," Riley told the *Birmingham News*. As the *New York Times* reporter Adam Cohen put it, "Church and state are not as separate in Alabama as they are in most places."

The plan was the brainchild of Susan Pace Hamill, a University of Alabama tax professor fresh from receiving a master's degree in theology at Samford University's Beeson Divinity School, a Baptist institution in Birmingham. On the campaign trail, Riley attributed his conversion to progressive taxation to Hamill's book, *The Least of These: Fair Taxes and the Moral Duty of Christians*. As interesting as Riley's embrace of this neo-Social Gospel was the split it provoked in the Religious Right. The Christian Coalition of Alabama would have none of it. "Alabama does not have a tax crisis. It has a spending crisis," the CCA thundered in an eight-page "voter education" pamphlet distributed at Christian schools and bookstores, and at football games. "The road to a better future isn't paved with a tax increase."

But the national Christian Coalition took the governor's side. As its president, Roberta Combs, put it in an *Anniston Star* op-ed August 10, "I think this is a good plan and I think people of faith need to know about the plan." Riley tried to get pastors to trumpet his plan from the pulpit but in the end he failed to persuade them that a more equitable tax system was what Jesus would have wanted. On September 9, Alabama voters turned down the plan by an overwhelming two-to-one margin.

But was this a victory or a defeat for the Religious Right? Across the South, evangelicals influence but cannot expect to control, public life. Politicians are obligated to speak to issues important to evangelicals, and moral issues are a part of electoral campaigns. But voters do not always support the evangelical party line (assuming there is one). This is especially true regarding gambling and the lottery, where practical considerations of economic development and funding for education often supersede moralistic pronouncements. Evangelicals have placed many of their own in seats of political power at local and state levels, but there they must forge coalitions and often move more to the center or else remain outvoted and exiled. This reality is particularly true in states like Georgia and, above all, Florida, where greater ethnic and religious diversity makes it difficult to run exclusively on a hard-core religious right platform.

Evangelical Belt Christians are about as united as any group in the country on moral and social issues. Southern politicians ignore them at their peril. They use the language of "family values" and "what would Jesus do." But they often fail to deliver, and sometimes it's because the evangelicals don't want them to. In the Evangelical Belt, then, believers are at ease in Zion and, at the same time, uneasy in Babylon.

Endnotes

1 *New York Times*, March 31, 1996.

2 Virginia Brereton, *From Sin to Salvation: Stories of Women's Conversions, 1800 to the Present* (Bloomington: Indiana University Press, 1991), 47.

3 John Egerton, *Speak Now Against the Day: The Generation Before the Civil Rights Movement in the South* (University of North Carolina Press, 1994), 425.

4 Mary King, *Freedom Song: A Personal Story of the 1960s Civil Rights Movement* (New York: Morrow, 1987), 273.

5 Andrew Manis, Southern Civil Religions in Conflict: Black and White Baptists and Civil Rights (University of Georgia Press, 1987), 65.

6 Carl Kell and L. Raymond Camp, *In the Name of the Father: The Rhetoric of the New Southern Baptist Convention* (Carbondale: University of Southern Illinois Press, 1999), 120-121.

7 Robert Wuthnow, *The Restructuring of American Religion* (Princeton: Princeton University Press, 1990).

CHAPTER THREE

SEMI-INVOLUNTARY: AFRICAN-AMERICAN RELIGION

William E. Montgomery

In March of 2004, the Georgia Supreme Court agreed to listen to representatives of Speedwell United Methodist and Macedonia Baptist churches argue to stop Wal-Mart from building a supercenter adjacent to their houses of worship in the crossroads town of Sandfly, 10 miles south of Savannah. Some of the locals trace their ancestry back hundreds of years to Africans forced to toil on nearby rice plantations. Not much remains today of the original eighteenth-century community; Savannah's suburbs have wiped most of it away, and now there's Wal-Mart. But a commitment to preserve what's left of their cultural heritage and their once-segregated but always communal world in the rural South has led members of these two churches to spearhead this community-action effort. Understandably, it's the older folks who are the most involved. Younger people seem less distressed; in fact, 62 percent of Sandfly's residents say they welcome Wal-Mart and its 24-hour offerings of food, clothes, sporting goods, CDs, and other products of modern life.[1]

The story of Sandfly's African-American churches offers insight into the position the church holds in the personal and public lives of black Southerners. Many churches are actively confronting the dynamic forces of urbanization and social integration that have reshaped the lives of African Americans since the days of strict racial segregation in the South. Apart from worship, prayer, and other religious activities, churches like those in Sandfly have channeled political activity, accorded status, provided important social services, and maintained a sense of community for African Americans, who in varying degrees are still marginalized in Southern society. Mainline African-American Baptist and Methodist churches have historically claimed the largest membership and continue to be the most socially and politically active components of the African-American religious establishment. The more fundamentalist organizations have focused on otherworldly spiritual salvation, but that may be changing. The new Wal-Mart store exemplifies the competition with which urban churches must contend for influence in the social marketplace, as well as the integrative forces that some say are weakening the bonds of African-American community. Indeed, some churches are literally battling to stay alive under modern pressures.

"The Black Church"

This chapter aims to describe African-American churches and the roles they play in the South today; to assess the significance of churches in the lives of African American southerners; and to identify the issues that African Americans in the South face and interpret their churches' responses to those issues. All this requires addressing some tricky problems. For starters, many scholarly, journalistic, and lay commentators use the concept of the "black church" or the "African-American church" to imply the existence of a unified African-American institution in which internal differentiation—denominational or other—is relatively unimportant. Does such a "black church" exist?

The historian David L. Chappell complains about the "mushy generalizations" about the influence of African-American religious tradition on Martin Luther King. "It is no more useful," he says, "to say that King was shaped by the black church than to say that he breathed air or was a Georgian."[2] But it did matter that Martin Luther King was a Georgian and not a Bostonian. And it did matter that he grew up in and imbibed the religious culture of an African-American church. African-American churches provided a framework for his life's work, and it is necessary to understand that framework in order to understand the churches today. Mushy as it can seem, the "black church"—thought of in terms of the broad historical development of African American religion—has been and remains, especially in the South, inseparable from the African-American people, to a degree unlike any other Christian religious group in the country. Themes of unity and freedom have run through the religious life of African-Americans from the eighteenth century through the civil rights movement to the present time. African-American ministers have persistently declared that God demanded freedom for African Americans because He made them in His image. And that freedom had to be collective, not individual. This lies at the core of the African-American Sacred Cosmos.

That said, should "the black church" refer only to historically independent African-American denominations? As Ted Ownby points out in chapter 1, the North American Religious Atlas (NARA) fails to provide a separate count of mainly African-American congregations that exist within predominantly white denominations, but in fact, perhaps as many as 13.5 percent of all African-American churchgoers nationwide belong to such congregations.[3] This significant omission is compensated for to some degree by the American Religious Identification Survey (ARIS), which indicates that the South's 6.7 million black Protestants make up 14.2 percent of the region's population. ARIS also shows that African Americans residing in the South comprise 41.1 percent of the nation's black Protestants, more than double the percentage for any other region. Unfortunately, however, ARIS does not classify African-American Protestants by denomination, as it does whites. ARIS does reveal that black Catholics represent 0.9 percent of the South's population; these 424,583 black Catholics constitute 29.7 percent of all the black Catholics in the country—almost double the percentage in the Southern Crossroads, with its famous Louisiana Catholic traditions, and exceeded only by the Middle Atlantic's 30.3 percent.

Most seriously, the failure of the traditionally African-American denominations to report membership data means that the NARA estimates of their county-by-county strength must be understood as highly conjectural. It would be useful to know, for example, if rural-urban differences manifest themselves in denominational affiliation. Is there a significant disposition for urban African Americans to affiliate with the multiracial United Methodist Church or for rural people to belong to the traditionally and still predominantly all-black African Methodist Episcopal (AME), African Methodist Episcopal Zion (AMEZ), or Christian Methodist Episcopal (CME) churches? The state of the data makes such a question impossible to answer.

Historical Considerations

History is an essential element in how African Americans regard their churches and their religious experience. Through the years, African-American churches have built strong traditions, some liberal (even revolutionary) and others conservative, and many enduring cultural patterns were laid down long before the civil rights era of the 1950s and 1960s.

African-American religion originated in a meld of African and Christian beliefs and practices. In the eighteenth century, hundreds of thousands of enslaved people from different regions of Africa poured into colonial South Carolina and Georgia to clear land, drain swamps, and cultivate rice, sugar, and cotton. Those who survived the harsh conditions developed a new way of life, borrowing culturally from each other and from Europeans. Protestant missionaries conducted revivals and established churches among them. African Americans responded to the missionaries, for the gospel of salvation touched vital chords among these enslaved people whose blighted existence filled them with hopelessness and despair. And although it was spiritual salvation rather than earthly liberation that the missionaries promised, African Americans did not make such distinctions.

Missionaries allowed them to preach, and they exhibited such remarkable enthusiasm in doing so that the missionaries were certain that the "Spirit of God" dwelled within them. The African way of experiencing the sacred world was holistic and communal, unlike the differentiated cosmos inhabited by European Christians.

During slavery, African-American churches imparted faith in a just God, a God who demanded liberation for all His people. Indulgent masters allowed enslaved people to worship together, but usually under white supervision, for plantation slave owners worried far more than the evangelists about unsupervised slave gatherings, and rightly so. Methodists fretted about church structure and orderliness, and although Methodist missionaries and regular ministers allowed blacks to preach, they only slowly sanctioned separate African-American churches. First in Philadelphia and later in New York, African Americans withdrew from predominantly white Methodist churches. In 1816, African-American Methodist churches, under the leadership of Richard Allen, united to form the AME denomination. Six years later, other African Americans organized the AMEZ.

African Methodism signified race consciousness and an African cultural identity, two levels of self-awareness that have not always been compatible. For example, in 1820, the AME minister Daniel Coker founded the first African-American settlement in Liberia. Richard Allen rebuked Coker and condemned colonization as a ploy to strengthen the institution of slavery. Allen's stance, and that of most AME and AMEZ churches, was overtly abolitionist and committed to racial justice. The association of African Methodism with antislavery made white Southerners suspicious of AME and AMEZ congregations. The revolutionary message inherent in the Christian gospel stirred the spirit of rebellion. In 1822, after disclosure of the terrifying Denmark Vesey slave revolt conspiracy, a white resident of Charleston voiced the complaint of many that Christian missionaries came into the South "with the Sacred Volume of God in one hand ... [and] scatter ... with the other the fire-brands of discord and destruction." As a solution, whites banned unsupervised African-American Christian worship. An 1845 Georgia statute typically ordered "Negroes not to assemble under pretense of divine worship."[4] Whites clearly recognized the alienness of African-American churches and African-American Christianity.

African-American churches comprised a distinctive religious milieu. Worship transported African Americans temporarily into another world through forms derived from Africa. As the foreign traveler Fredrika Bremer observed: "They sang ... with all their souls and with all their bodies in unison; ... their bodies wagged, their heads nodded, their feet stamped, their knees shook, their elbows and their hands beat time to the tune and the words which they sang with evident delight."[5] Slaves also filled sacred music with double entendre that made otherworldly lyrics expressive of their worldly yearning to be free.

> "Go down to Egypt—Tell Pharaoh
> Thus saith my servant, Moses
> Let my people go."[6]

And as Federal troops took their former masters away at the conclusion of the Civil War, they erupted in song.

> "De Northmen dey's got massa now,
> De Northmen dey's got massa now,
> De Northmen dey's got massa now,
> Glory Hallelujah."[7]

God had fulfilled his promise, and religious commitment burrowed itself even deeper into the marrow of African-American culture.

African Americans were now on their own, with God's blessing but little else. What they desired most were schools and churches. The federal government did provide schools through the Freedmen's Bureau, but when that agency became defunct, black religious organizations took over much of the task of educating the people. As for establishing churches, black missionaries from the North joined former slave preachers. AME and AMEZ missionaries incorporated former slave congregations into their denominations. Tension frequently developed between educated and relatively cosmopolitan missionary clergy and poor and mostly uneducated people of the rural South. AME bishop Daniel A. Payne complained of hand clapping, "heathenish" shouting, and "savage" dancing to string and percussion instruments.[8]

Some people chose to remain attached to white denominations. Methodist missionaries from the North appealed to former slaves by promising to treat them respectfully as free and equal Christians. "There will be no [segregated] galleries in Heaven," they declared.[9] Yet even as thousands of African Americans joined the Northern Methodist Episcopal Church, de facto segregation became the practice. When, in 1939, the Northern and Southern Methodist Episcopal churches merged into the United Methodist Church (UMC), the new denomination segregated all African-American congregations into a Central Jurisdiction under an African-American bishop. Not until 1966 did the UMC dissolve the Central Jurisdiction, and issues of racial reconciliation remain. This is why it is problematic to exclude African-American congregations within the UMC from "the black church."

Some African-American Baptist congregations existed during slavery, but most Baptists withdrew from white Baptist churches immediately after emancipation, and Southern whites made little attempt to stop them. The less bureaucratic Baptist polity made it easier for congregations to control the type of worship, which partly explains the Baptist appeal to those who wished to express religious sentiments in physical, highly emotional ways. African-American Baptists also organized regional associations and state conventions, and by the 1880s had begun to organize nationally. In 1895, African-American Baptists formed the National Baptist Convention, USA. Five years later, Baptist women founded the Women's Convention. Within 20 years, the denomination claimed 3 million members, was the largest organization in the world controlled entirely by Africans, and was firmly anchored in the South. In addition to missionary activity, both in the United States and abroad, the National Baptist Convention operated a publishing house that supplied African-American Baptist churches with Sunday school materials and hymnals written by African Americans. These were all sources of pride and satisfaction.

By the early years of the twentieth century, African Americans had taken great strides in education and income, creating a "black bourgeoisie." Many rural people also crowded into cities like Jacksonville, Atlanta, Birmingham, Nashville, Memphis, and Jackson. But African Americans remained segregated and excluded from the general life of the city. Urban churches became the most important social and spiritual institutions inside those segregated worlds. Churches erected large buildings, assembled marvelous choirs that performed standard denominational hymns, and employed college-educated and often seminary-trained ministers as well as lay staff. Bourgeois values and norms, a Social Gospel theology, and bureaucratic organization characterized mainline Baptist and Methodist churches. But many poor, uneducated people felt alienated and dissatisfied with unsanctified churches and ministers who preached from the head and not from the "spirit." Sacred music was not sanctified either; it came right out of a hymnbook. Furthermore, high-toned "secular" churches frowned on dancing, shouting, and "praising"—a staple of traditional African-American worship. Such dissatisfaction fueled the holy fires of sanctification, or holiness, which in turn gave rise to Pentecostalism.

An African American, William J. Seymour, was an early leader of the Pentecostal movement. During the summer of 1905, after leaving the Methodist Episcopal Church, Seymour learned of a Bible school where participants spoke in tongues, which they regarded as a sign of the Holy Spirit. Seymour became a disciple, and moved to Los Angeles where, in 1906, he conducted a successful revival on Azusa Street among racially diverse worshippers. As he wrote in the newspaper *The Apostolic Faith*, "God makes no difference in nationality. Ethiopians, Chinese, Indians, Mexicans, and other nationalities worship together."[10] Those were intoxicating sentiments in African-American culture at a time when Jim Crow had all but extinguished the hope of racial justice.

One African-American participant in the Azusa Street revival, Charles H. Mason, recalled the powerful impact that Pentecostalism had on him. "The Spirit came upon me, and all of my being was filled with the glory of the Lord .... When I opened my mouth ... a flame touched my tongue which ran down to me. My language changed and no word could I speak in my own tongue."[11] In 1907 in Memphis, Mason organized several sanctified congregations into the Church of God in Christ. Pentecostalism fulfilled the African-American desire to experience religion in a more traditional way. Indeed, in many respects it came closest of all African-American religious milieus to typifying the syncretistic nature of African-American religious culture. Early in the twentieth century Pentecostalism grew faster among African Americans in the urban North than among black southerners. But a recent reversal of that migration has brought northern urban Pentecostalism to the urban South. This religious tradition has also shaped popular culture, white as well as black, especially through music.

Culture

The impact of religion on the cultural lives of African Americans extends to folklore and music. The otherworldly religion of black folks, their belief in ghosts ("hants"), and the moral shortcomings of the "jackleg" rural preacher whose love of Sunday fried chicken and the sexual favors of church sisters surpasses his love of God—all had become staples of black Southern folk tales by the early twentieth century. The notion that the allure of the charismatic preacher man accounts for the predominance of female church members is implicit in African-American folklore. In addition, many folktales suggest a turbulent, conflicted relationship between God and black men.

In *Tales of the Congaree*, compiled in the 1920s by Edward C. L. Adams, Deacon Jones asks God to guide him safely through the dangerous woods. After a terrifying encounter with a bear that ripped his clothes to shreds, Deacon Jones attends an "experience meetin'" at church, where members of the congregation relate their experiences with God. Deacon Jones tells those gathered: "My brothers an' sisters, all I can say is: God is good ... I loves God. I sho' loves Him, an' I puts my faith in Him ... [B]ut, my brothers an' sisters ... He ain' worth a damn in a bear fight."

By contrast, the sisters of the church find peace and happiness in God's heavenly embrace. As a fragment of one funeral sermon goes:

On Jordan's chilly flares,
In tempest and storm,
Her boat sailed safely
In de harbors of heaven;
An' she rests in de arms

Of her Maker,
In de love of her God;
Her sins are forgiven,
Paid in repentance full.

Her soul is a heavenly mansion,
Her guard an angel of rest,
For she sleeps on a hillside
Wey de peach blossoms bloom,
An' de wild birds sing,
Sing to de soul dat is flown.[12]

In light of the strong African-American oral tradition, it is not surprising that religiosity would find full expression in popular music. Religious themes, instrumentation, and performance styles are in evidence from early twentieth-century blues to '50's doo-wop and rock 'n' roll, to the soul and funk sounds of more recent years. Besides importing elements of religion into the American musical mainstream, African-American musicians also took it upon themselves to comment on their religious culture—especially during the 1920s and 1930s, when black Southern churches retreated from political and social activism into otherworldliness. In "Broke Down Engine," Blind Willie McTell sang of preferring romantic love to religion.

Feel like a broke down engine; mama ain't got no driving-wheel
You ever been down and lonesome; you know just how Willie McTell feels
I been shooting craps and gambling; good gal I done got broke
I done pawned my thirty-two special; good gal and my clothes is soak
I even went to my praying ground; dropped down on bended knees
I ain't cryin' for no religion; Lordy give me back my good gal please.[13]

Hi Henry Brown's 1932 recording of "Preacher Blues" trashes the lascivious ministers.

Preacher in the pulpit; Bible in his hand
Sister in the corner; crying there's my man
Preacher comes to your house; you ask him to rest his hat
Next thing he want to know; sister where your husband at
Come in here Elder; and shut my door
Want you to preach for me the same text you did night before.[14]

Because of Southern blues' bitter satire and the fact that its venues included juke joints and other ungodly places, religious people regarded it as the "Devil's Music." Blues great Robert Johnson's death by poisoning, many religious people believed, was the Devil's payback for singing the blues. But some blues performers, including Blind Lemon Jefferson, Memphis Minnie, and Johnson himself, sang sacred as well as profane songs.

During the civil rights years of the 1950's and 1960's, the African-American church regained some of its prestige through its involvement in the freedom struggle. Religion became less vulnerable to parody. Moreover, as the South moved toward integration, black musicians crossed over into the lucrative white musical market. The Devil's Music became known as "Rhythm and Blues," and many singers reared in Pentecostal churches moved over—Tina Turner and James Brown for instance—into popular music. But their religious roots clearly showed. Brown, who joined the Gospel Starlighters after a four-year jail term for robbery, exemplifies the soulful, animated, "spirit possessed" preacher of the sanctified church.

Souls of Black Folk

If the concept of the "the black church" signals anything in American culture, it is the high degree of religiosity of African Americans. At least by their own reckoning, they have followed the Christian precepts of love and tolerance more closely than white people have. In his autobiography *Born to Rebel*, the theologian and social scientist Benjamin E. Mays called the white church "society's most conservative and hypocritical institution." Apart from that, white Christian folks, at least as far as many African Americans believe, have lacked religious enthusiasm. A young Zora Neale Hurston noticed how lifeless white church singing was where she grew up in Florida. "If white people liked trashy singing like that," she wrote in *Dust Tracks on a Road*, "there must be something funny about them." Of course, whites have also expressed religious zeal; and besides, overt excitability is not necessarily a measure of genuine religious conviction.

Besides such impressionistic evidence of greater African-American religiosity, several data sets—the most useful being the University of Chicago's General Social Survey—indicate that African Americans are, by various measures, more religious than whites. They are significantly more likely to belong to churches, to attend worship services, to identify strongly with their churches, and to read the Bible and pray regularly. However, when confined to rural areas, the data indicate no measurable difference between whites and African Americans. Thus, it's in the urban South where African Americans are more religious than whites (though somewhat less religious than their rural counterparts).

How to explain these higher levels of religious involvement? For decades, both before and after emancipation, African Americans possessed few other organizations and facilities they could call their own, that brought them together for pleasure and comfort. Whites, on the other hand, have always had secular clubs, concerts, teams, public and private schools, and countless other groups and organizations with which to associate and derive benefit. This has led scholars to develop a model called the "semi-involuntary institution" to characterize African-American churches in the segregated South.[15] The basic idea is that many African Americans join churches or say they belong to churches for the secular purposes of recreation, personal support, and status, even if they aren't religious believers and wouldn't do so voluntarily. They are rewarded if they do and punished through deprivation and disapproval if they don't. African Americans' participation in religion is so high, in short, because it is not altogether voluntary.

Denominationalism remains strong among African-American churchgoers. A recent survey taken by Atlanta's Interdenominational Theological Center shows that 56 percent of African-American congregations give strong voice to the heritage of their denominations.[16] Most churchgoing African Americans in the South, as in the rest of the country, are Baptists; today, the three largest denominations of African-American Baptists are the National Baptist Convention, U.S.A (incorporated); the National Baptist Convention of America (unincorporated); and the Progressive National Baptist Convention. A somewhat smaller number of black Southerners are Methodists, belonging to the historically African-American Methodist denominations (AME, AMEZ, and CME), as well as to the predominantly white United Methodist Church. Both Baptists and Methodists—the African-American mainline—share an attachment to the Social Gospel, which emphasizes the importance of improving social and economic conditions in this world rather than putting everything off for the world to come.

Black Protestantism is growing fastest in the holiness/Pentecostal/non-denominational world typified by the Church of God in Christ. Historically the theologies of these churches have been otherworldly, their worship patterns emotional, and their moral tenets conservative, modest, and ascetic. Yet they are beginning to follow in the footsteps of the Baptist and Methodist churches, which became more buttoned-down and bureaucratic following Emancipation, when Northern missionaries with middle-class values took control and organized them into denominations. Church of God in Christ members have begun to involve themselves in politics, while Church of God in Christ ministers are more likely than once upon a time to stress thisworldly goals. Meanwhile, race pride and self-confidence have reduced the level of disapproval that folk religion once created in aspiring African Americans, so that it is sometimes hard to tell the difference between mainline and more evangelical churches when it comes to worship practices.

But African-American church life is not coalescing in all respects. For one thing, class matters. As in the past, poorer African Americans continue to look to their churches for compensation for the hardships of a harsh world. They draw psychological comfort from their religion—temporary escape and the promise of ultimate redemption. Their worship involves shouting, uninhibited singing, and trance-like or possession-like behavior indicating the powerful presence of the Holy Spirit and African traditions. Because of their more limited resources, lower-class congregations often find it hard to build and maintain churches, pay decent salaries, and finance support services.

Conversely, the well-to-do have their own spiritual and social needs. Financially independent, they need less from their churches by way of material support, recreation, or social interaction. They are especially susceptible to social pressure to behave respectably, and thus often go to church regularly whether they are religious or not, and recognize that they stand to benefit from church connections with banks, insurance companies, mortuary businesses, and real estate enterprises. They prefer a style of worship that tends toward the formal, and look to take advantage of church-sponsored educational and training programs. They expect their well-to-do congregations to build and maintain large facilities, pay high clergy salaries, and support extensive community-outreach activities.

Generational differences matter too. Researchers have documented a degree of disaffection from Christian churches on the part of young African Americans. Some are turning to Islam; more are choosing no religious affiliation at all. In part, this may signal a rejection of the African-American church's conservative morality. The church, for example, teaches avoiding premarital sex, but between 1998 and 2000 in Alabama's Black Belt, three-quarters of African-American babies were born to unwed mothers, and a third of those mothers were teenagers. At minimum, it's clear that the churches have had limited effect on the sexual behavior of young people there. Significantly, documented declines in young people's participation in churches are largely confined to Baptist and Methodist churches. The more conservative Protestant sects seem to hold greater appeal for young people. Moreover, the younger members of conservative sects show higher income and education levels than their peers in Baptist and Methodist churches.

Although women have been extremely active and important to the success of church outreach and in the calling of church pastors, church authorities have generally barred women from pulpit. The tradition of female submissiveness, as enunciated by the apostle Paul, combined with old-fashioned Southern patriarchy with its ancillary "cult of womanhood," has prevailed over the African tradition of female religious leadership. In places like the Sea Islands and New Orleans, African women have long functioned traditionally as healers, fortune-tellers, and mediums between the spirit and living worlds. African and African-American oral traditions nurtured women's aspiration to preach, and despite determined efforts by men to maintain the ordained ministry as an exclusive male domain, women did preach as exhorters and evangelists.

In the Methodist denominations, a few have achieved ordination. In 1888, Bishop Henry M. Turner ordained a woman, but the General Conference immediately overruled him. In 1891, the AME Zion bishop James W. Hood declared that women held the same rights within the church as men; however, the church was slow to ordain them. The AME and CME churches were even more reluctant. All three Methodist denominations permitted licensed female preaching, and in 1900 the AME church created the position of "deaconess," but without ordination. The CME church was the last Methodist denomination to allow the ordination of women (1954). Baptist polity and African traditions once made it relatively easy for women to assume spiritual leadership; however, after the formation of the National Baptist Convention and more centralized control, women scarcely ever achieved ordination, and that unfavorable climate persists. The Church of God in Christ holds firmly to a policy against ordaining women ministers. In the late 1980s, an estimated 5 percent of the African-American clergy in the country were women. A 1997 *Ebony* list of 35 prominent women ministers contained only nine from Southern churches. And the 2001 survey performed by Atlanta's Interdenominational Theological Center found that only 4 percent of the pastors of African-American churches were women.

Some women have organized non-denominational churches. One of the most successful, Barbara King, began her ministry in 1971 in her Atlanta home. By 1996, King's Hillside International Truth Center and Chapel occupied a major-league facility and claimed 4,000 members. The politics of gender make it likely that black women will gain more acceptance as ministers of the gospel. But it should come as no surprise that African-American churches have been less inclined to address sexism than racism.

Rural and Urban

Recalling his boyhood in Greenwood County, South Carolina, Benjamin E. Mays remembered that Old Mount Zion Baptist Church was the focal point of community life. Adults found solace, escape, and compensation for worldly deprivation in church and during church-sponsored picnics, excursions, barbecues, and ballgames. Kids went to church because their parents made them. Besides, on most Sundays in Greenwood County "there was no other place to go." In addition, respectable people regularly went to church (although regularly did not necessarily mean every Sunday).

Old Mount Zion offered preaching only on the second Sunday of the month, for the pastor and community patriarch, Rev. James F. Marshall, had other congregations to look after. Although Marshall had no more than a fifth-grade education, the title "reverend" conveyed high status. His sermons were not so much theological as didactic, and he was not overtly political. That he did not directly confront Jim Crow suited the members of Old Mount Zion just fine. They believed the admonition in the old spiritual: "Take All the World and Give Me Jesus." As Mays put it, "Beaten down at every turn by the white man, Negroes could perhaps not have survived without this kind of religion."[17]

The early-twentieth-century economic situation described by Mays has not changed that much for African Americans in the Black Belt. Integration has brought change but not racial equality. Thus, during the 1990s family incomes in Alabama increased overall, but with a vast and widening disparity between whites and blacks; the 2000 Census found that while the statewide median family income stood at $41,657, fully 37 percent of the households in Alabama's Black Belt counties earned less than $15,000 per year. Is it any surprise that African Americans' opportunities for a decent standard of living, for recreation, and for social status are severely limited in the rural South? In Gee's Bend, an isolated Black Belt town, the community gathers for Sunday worship at the Ye Shall Know the Truth Baptist Church. The alternatives to church activities are illicit sex, drugs, alcohol, and violence. So the church is attempting to build a community activity center equipped with exercise gear, a skating rink, and anything else that the minister and congregation can think of and pay for to lure young people into the church.[18] In the country, if the churches don't do it, no one will.

In one recent study, researchers found that when asked if they attended church at least once a week, 35.6 percent of the respondents from the rural South and an almost equal 34.6 percent from urban areas answered "Yes." But when queried about their participation in non-religious activities sponsored by churches, 31 percent of the rural residents said they participated at least a few times a month compared to just 18.7 percent of those who resided in metropolitan areas. Significant too is that almost half (47.6 percent) of urban respondents said they never participate in non-religious activities associated with churches while only one-third (32.7 percent) of rural respondents reported no participation. This rural-urban split holds up even when the analysis controls for such variables as age, gender, and socio-economic status.[19] What it suggests is that, not surprisingly, the black church is less voluntary in the countryside than in the cities.

Sharp differences exist between rural and urban churches, even within the same denomination. In general, urban areas have more large churches, are richer in resources, are more inclined to have educated ministers and congregants, and offer more social support and political action than their rural counterparts. And discrepancies in levels of participation between conservative Protestant sects and mainstream Baptist and Methodist churches are more pronounced in cities than in the countryside. More rural African Americans attend church than do urban residents. Most surveys reveal that the number one reason rural people belong to churches is the preaching, since rural churches have a harder time financing social activities. A much larger percentage of rural churches than urban churches conduct revivals. Rural churches have a higher proportion of part-time, absentee pastors than urban churches, and as a consequence, lay members of rural churches exercise greater control over church programs and have acquired a greater sense of church ownership than has been true in larger urban churches, which generally maintain one or more permanent pastors.

Urban churches, both mainline Protestant and conservative Protestant, have in some cases grown to mammoth size. These megachurches are imposing on the outside and plush on the inside, with sophisticated sound systems and comfortable pews that seat thousands. New Birth Baptist Church, which claims 25,000 members, is the largest church in Atlanta, and World Changers, a non-denominational holiness congregation with over 20,000 members, ranks second. What those members hear in such places is very often quite different from the "pie in the sky when you die" message of yesteryear. At World Changers, for example, Rev. Creflo Dollar preaches an African-American version of what's known as the prosperity gospel. "We settle for being broke, for being poor, for being in debt," he tells his followers. "I've heard people in church say, 'I may not have this, I may not have that, but praise the Lord when I get to heaven on the other side.' Well, honey, God wants you to get it on this side." Dollar's message reaches not only the 20,000 members of his own congregation but also countless others who tune into his televangelism.[20]

Even as the post-civil-rights era has improved the lot of African-American southerners, particularly in the cities, it has brought new stresses. Over the last 35 years, integration has transformed African Americans, their communities, and their cultures. Neighborhood demographics have changed as upwardly mobile African Americans have moved into previously white suburban neighborhoods. Hispanics, Asians, and Caribbean islanders have settled into historically African-American neighborhoods. Consequently, some historically and predominantly black churches now function in multi-ethnic/multi-racial worlds. A number of communities in the Atlanta suburb of Gwinnett County, for instance, have almost equal numbers of whites, blacks, and Hispanics, and churches like the predominantly African-American Hopewell Missionary Baptist Church are trying to adjust to this environment. Integration has challenged the African-American church and led to awkward moments. On New Year's Eve of 2000 in Ft. Lauderdale, one African-American church, one white church, and one Brazilian church held a joint worship service under the leadership of Ben Williams, pastor of the African-American Ebenezer Baptist Church. Williams integrated the traditional black "Watch Night" service, an observance foreign to the other groups but derived from the experience of slaves awaiting the issuance of the Emancipation Proclamation on January 1, 1863, into the service.[21] The innovation caused a little tension within the mixed congregation. Yet despite integration, on Sunday morning most urban African-American churchgoers head to a black church rather than a multi-racial church.

Political Action

In the eighteenth century, Richard Allen and other founders of African Methodism set a pattern of religious activism by standing up (or rather, kneeling down) to protest racial bias in church. During the Jim Crow era, there were ministers who used Christian principles to demand political and economic freedom, and employed religious media and denominational networks to attack racism. Yet this activist tradition should not obscure the African-American churches' longstanding history of passivity when it came to social issues, or at least their preference for urging restraint and "moral suasion" rather than direct confrontation of racial oppression. Over the years, people in and out of African-American communities have criticized conservative church leaders as cop-outs who substitute promises in the millennial future—the "opiate of the masses"—for freedom and justice here and now. During the civil rights era, young radical activists ridiculed preachers in a song sung to the tune of the spiritual "Down By the Riverside": "Goin' to leave my shufflin' shoes, down by the parson's door." At the time, the Student Non-Violent Coordinating Committee's (SNCC) radicalism probably convinced leading white Southerners that resistance to integration was bad business before church ministers persuaded them that segregation was morally wrong.

In fact, the National Baptist Convention, Martin Luther King, Jr.'s own denominational body and the country's largest African-American religious organization, refused to endorse his strategy of civil disobedience. King grew up in Atlanta's mainline Ebenezer Baptist Church, where his father served as pastor. Ebenezer was a conservative church with a conservative, middle-class congregation that did not want to rock the boat, though it took responsibility for providing for the social welfare of Atlanta's African-American community. The younger King considered King Sr. a model for his own ministry before developing his own activist one. Taking his Christian identity for granted, King once wrote, "Conversion for me was never an abrupt something. I have never experienced the so called 'crisis moment'" that leads to conversion.[22] Graduate theological training exposed him to various liberal theological views, causing him to question his own conservative roots. He emerged with faith in divine love, but it was the revolutionary theology of Reinhold Niebuhr that led him to launch a confrontational social and political movement that redeemed the clergy from the "old black preacher" stereotype personified by Old Mount Zion's James Marshall. But even as King and others like the seminary-trained John Lewis, an early SNCC leader and a current U.S. Representative from Georgia, demonstrated the effectiveness of greater militancy, leaders of the National Baptist Convention continued to argue that churches should not involve themselves in political activism regardless of how righteous the cause.

Nevertheless, the black church as a whole deserves a large share of the credit of the civil rights movement's achievements by appealing to the conscience of whites while demonstrating the strength of Christian faith in the face of snarling dogs, police batons, and terrorist bombs. During the struggle, Christian precepts reinforced the principle of non-violent disobedience; ministers inspired direct action; and congregations supplied the masses of demonstrators, who marched to the civil rights anthem taken from a spiritual, "We Shall Overcome." Since that time, ministers and congregations have worked for racial justice, while African Americans have come to expect political leadership from the church. Surveys from the mid-1960s through the 1980s showed that, overwhelmingly, African Americans wanted their churches to become actively involved in civil rights. In due course, more than half of the South's African-American churches established some sort of relationship with civil rights organizations and began participating in civil rights activities. Under the circumstances, it's no accident that the National Baptist Convention has changed the denomination's image. At its 2001 national convention in Charlotte, for example, speakers rallied support for greater social action. "You've got to hit the streets and raise hell," one pastor insisted. "History has shown that nothing happens in this country unless the church takes aggressive leadership."[23] Although a longstanding concern to prepare followers for Christ's second coming continues to restrain conservative groups like the Church of God in Christ from working for social change, these churches too are responding to charges that their religious zeal is irrelevant by becoming more politically active.

Indeed, since the civil rights revolution African-American churches in the South have become powerful instruments of political mobilization. Serving as the primary means for politicians to reach into African-American communities, mainline Baptist and Methodist churches in particular offer forums for candidates and vital election networks. In 1973, for example, black ministers in Atlanta played a key role in the election of Maynard Jackson as that city's first black mayor. Their strategy relied heavily on using their churches to turn out the vote. White candidates also now plug themselves into the African-American church network. Former Virginia governor Douglas Wilder, an African American, claims that it was because he introduced white Democratic senator Chuck Robb around at black churches that Robb managed to eke out reelection in the decidedly Republican year of 1994.[24] In December 2003, six weeks before South Carolina's Democratic presidential primary, Rev. James Darby counted the candidates who had already appeared at his Morris Brown African Methodist Episcopal Church in Charleston: Joseph Lieberman, John Kerry's sister, John Edwards twice, Howard Dean twice, Wesley Clark, and Al Sharpton. "We are being treated like the belles of the ball," Darby exclaimed.[25]

To be sure, as African Americans join the mainstream, the kind of political monopoly enjoyed by the church has suffered some erosion. In 2002, for instance, Artur Davis—a graduate of Harvard's college and law school—was elected as Alabama's first African-American congressman since Reconstruction thanks not only to the black churches but also to extensive use of secular opinion shapers, Web sites, and e-mail. No one should, however, underestimate the importance of the churches when it comes to electoral politics—and to the capacity of the black clergy to influence black elected officials in the South. In the spring of 2004, as Georgia's African-American legislators considered a state gay marriage ban, Rep. Randall Mangham felt extreme pressure from Bishop Eddie Long, pastor of the 25,000-member New Birth Missionary Baptist Church—even though Long did not confront Mangham directly. "But he's my pastor," Mangham explained. "I go to church there. He doesn't have to call me. He speaks from the pulpit." The legislature first voted against the ban by a four-vote margin, then approved the measure when four members of the House Legislative Black Caucus who had initially abstained felt the clerical heat and voted in favor.[26]

The issue of gay marriage, which rose to national prominence in 2004, clearly pointed out the limits of African-American Christian liberalism. In several Southern states that considered measures to ban gay marriage, African Americans became the objects of intense lobbying by groups on both sides of the question. Opponents of the ban hoped to win African-American support by linking gay rights to civil rights, but the linkage proved more offensive than effective, especially in light of the African-American church's assertion that homosexual marriage is ungodly. Sounding like any white evangelical, John Timmons, pastor of Calvary Missionary Baptist Church near Savannah, declared, "Marriage is just between a man and a woman. That's the way God ordained it, and that's the way it should be." As for the civil rights analogy, Timmons added: "Gay marriage has nothing to do with civil rights. The civil rights movement was about racial discrimination. How can you discriminate against something that God said no to?"[27]

Nor is gay marriage the only issue on which the African-American church's responses to public issues reflect longstanding and often conflicting liberal and conservative ideological traditions. The church firmly supports the cause of civil rights when it comes to political and economic freedom but is conflicted on matters where the principle of freedom clashes with conservative Christian moral values. Combining the National Surveys of Religion and Politics from 1992, 1996, and 2000, John Green and his colleagues at the University of Akron found that 66.7 percent of Southern African-American Protestants favored more public spending for welfare (compared to 65.6 percent nationally). On school vouchers, Southern black Protestants were divided (43.8 percent in favor, 45.7 percent opposed, and 10.5 ambivalent), as were African-Americans nationally (50.6 percent in favor and 49.4 percent opposed or ambivalent). On abortion, though, Southern African-American Protestants were pro-life (48.3) more than pro-choice (37.6), very close to the national figures for African-American Protestants (46.4 pro-life and 38.9 pro-choice). In line with such conservatism on moral issues, African-American churches have also opposed state lotteries.

Social Welfare

Even before they could, or would, engage in political activism, black churches involved themselves heavily in promoting the social welfare of African Americans. In the past, much of the burden has rested directly on the shoulders of the clergy. Besides preaching against sinful behavior, preachers have traditionally given personal comfort to the distressed and advice to the wayward. Admonitions to quit "cussin', lyin', stealin', crap shootin', whiskey drinkin', and backbitin'" have been common in sermons in lower-class churches for generations. But when it came to social outreach programs, women played a role equal to if not greater than men.

During the Progressive Era of the late nineteenth and early twentieth centuries, young, professional African-American women participated in social reform through Christian-based settlements, where needy citizens received instruction in skills that would help them get ahead and maintain a healthy, wholesome home life. The settlements also taught the virtues of bourgeois Protestant Christianity. In 1897, Margaret Murray Washington, the wife of Tuskegee Institute's president Booker T. Washington, organized a settlement in Tuskegee that conducted a day school with classes in cooking, sewing, and gardening, along with a Sunday school. The purpose was "to better family conditions of the colored people ... in the matter of cleanliness, education, [and] uprightness—to teach them how to live."[28] At the same time, women in the churches formed alliances with African-American women's clubs to lobby for women's suffrage and anti-lynching laws. Other African-American churchwomen duplicated these activities throughout the South.

Before the civil rights era, black Baptist and Methodist churches also operated day schools to help provide religiously based education for black children. At a time when higher education was otherwise hardly available to African Americans, Baptists and Methodists also operated numerous colleges, most of which offered high school as well as college-level education. For example, until the opening of Booker T. Washington High School in 1924, the only secondary education available to African Americans in Atlanta was through colleges like the AME's Morris Brown. A recent survey of 150 Atlanta-area churches showed that 94 percent offered some form of Christian education.[29] Operating full-time schools, however, is much harder for the African-American church today because of cost, but school voucher programs could open up new possibilities for Christian education.

Today, the African-American religious mainstream remains committed to improving the worldly situation of its adherents. Many churches sponsor faith-based programs of education and welfare, and by employing clergy and lay people provide them with valuable business, managerial, and political experience. In general, black-church community outreach has taken two forms: (1) programs funded and administered directly by the churches and (2) those operated by various non-church groups, including the government, in which the churches participate. This tradition began before the Civil War and continued during and after Reconstruction on a much-expanded scale, even with paltry resources. One survey of 79 churches conducted in 1897 found that 65 contributed to some form of charity. By the beginning of the twentieth century, almost 20 percent of black Southerners lived in cities. Removed from rural family networks, urban African-American needs were particularly great. They suffered higher rates of poverty, vice, crime, disease, and mortality than other urban groups. A large proportion of black urban residents were young and unmarried. With increasing violence and intimidation, more and more churches turned away from direct political action toward social betterment behind the walls of racial segregation. And with the onset of the Great Depression, welfare needs multiplied.

Today, poverty, malnutrition, alcoholism, drug abuse, and teenage pregnancy plague African-American communities, and in rural areas particularly neither public nor private agencies have the resources to deal with them. With more material resources, urban churches do more than their rural counterparts. The survey of 150 Atlanta-area churches found that 91 percent offered personal counseling services; 85 percent, youth activities; 74 percent, character building and leadership training; and 67 percent, "family enhancement." These, however, cost relatively little. Only 20 percent offered before- and after-school child care; 11 percent, day care; 9.3 percent, health care; and 5 percent, Head Start.

With its background of community outreach, the African-American church continues to function as a multi-purpose institution—but perhaps with a more conservative set of ideas than in the recent past. Black consciousness has long been a prominent feature of African-American religion; however, in contrast to 30 years ago, when roughly two-thirds of the black clergy indicated a positive response to the radical liberationist theologies of writers like Gayraud Wilmore, James Cone, and Pauli Murray, only a third now claim to be so influenced. Age, education, and denomination are important variables. Thus, 66 percent of younger ministers in the Methodist denominations, who generally have considerable formal education, report being positively influenced by radical "black" theological scholarship. By contrast, Pentecostal ministers, on average less educated than the Methodists, are the least positive (18 percent).[30]

On a practical level, race consciousness shows up strikingly among African-American churches through a wide variety of community-outreach programs that deal in particular ways with problems confronting African Americans. This list includes joblessness, poverty, disease, drug abuse, HIV/AIDS, and violent juvenile crime. The African-American churches, to the best of their abilities, operate remedial programs and cooperate with public and private social service agencies. HIV/AIDS is difficult to deal with because of many churches' reluctance to address issues that involve sexual practices. As one Baptist pastor put it, "When we go to church, we don't like to talk about sex. But we have to talk about it. Our silence is costing too many lives." The Interdenominational Theological Center's recent survey found that pastors often shift the focus of attention to spiritual matters. However, that same survey reported that two-thirds of ministers who participated "strongly approve" of churches addressing social issues.[31]

Financial resources are critical to the African-American church's ability to provide important welfare services. In general, African-American churches remain strapped for the necessary funds—which helps explain their positive response to the Bush administration's "faith-based initiative." Well before the president made this a central feature of his administration's domestic policy in the first weeks after taking office, church leaders voiced their support for this approach to social welfare. In a 1998 survey of 1,200 religious congregations conducted by Mark Chaves of the University of Arizona, 64 percent of black congregations—as opposed to only 28 percent of white ones—indicated a willingness to apply for federal funds. While white church leaders expressed concern about government interference in religious affairs, black church leaders welcomed government assistance for their social programs. At a meeting of black and white Southern church leaders in Augusta, Georgia, in March 2001, the same reactions divided the two groups in response to a Bush administration official's presentation of the faith-based initiative.[32]

Atlanta's Wheat Street Baptist Church exemplifies the multi-purpose role of the modern church in the lives of African Americans. The church emphasizes economic stimulation in the community. It has itself become a powerful economic institution. Through a nonprofit corporation, the Wheat Street Charitable Foundation, the church has acquired and manages two housing developments as well as various smaller houses, an office building, and two shopping centers, real estate holdings totaling $33 million. To spur economic growth, the church operates a credit union. One of its former pastors, William Holmes Borders, explained the fusion of business and religion this way: "In my judgment, education, economic opportunity, and the vote are of equal importance. These gains must be harmonized with religion, with the love of man for his fellows, and his obedience to God."[33]

In the Interdenominational Theological Center's 2000 survey of 2,000 African-American churches, two-thirds of the leaders characterized their congregations as "spiritually vital and alive" and described their churches' financial condition as "good." And yet they listed "money and finance" as their primary concerns.[34] This was a national survey but undoubtedly reflects attitudes within the African-American church in the South. Race still matters in the South, but not the way it used to. Even as the black middle class grows, the prevailing conservative political winds suggest that public sources of welfare will continue to shrink. In all likelihood, it will be up to African-American religion and African-American churches to pick up the slack—whether they like it or not.

Endnotes

1 *The New York Times*, March 6, 2004. Most of the significant nuances of the Sandfly story are not apparent in the article.

2 David L. Chappell, *A Stone of Hope: Prophetic Religion and the Death of Jim Crow* (Chapel Hill: University of North Carolina Press, 2004), 54.

3 C. Eric Lincoln and Lawrence H. Mamiya, *The Black Church in the African American Experience* (Durham: Duke University Press, 1990), 407.

4 Dena J. Epstein, *Sinful Tunes and Spirituals: Black Folk Music to the Civil War* (Urbana: University of Illinois Press, 1977), 195, 197.

5 Fredrika Bremer, *The Homes of the New World: Impressions of America*, trans. Mary Howitt (New York: Harper & Brothers, 1853), I, 393-94.

6 *National Anti-Slavery Standard*, 22 (October 12, 1861), 3.

7 *Ibid.*, (December 21), 1.

8 Daniel A. Payne, *Recollections of Seventy Years* (Nashville: Publishing House of the A. M. E. Sunday School Union, 1888), 262-74.

9 Ralph E. Morrow, *Northern Methodism and Reconstruction* (East Lansing: Michigan State University Press, 1956), 130.

10 Ian MacRobert, "The Black Roots of Pentecostalism," in Timothy E. Fulop and Albert J. Raboteau, eds., *African American Religion: Interpretive Essays in History and Culture* (New York and London: Routlege, 1997), 304.

11 Lincoln and Mamiya, *The Black Church in the African American Experience*, 81.

12 Edward C. L. Adams, *Tales of the Congaree*, Robert G. O'Meally, ed. (Chapel Hill: University of North Carolina Press, 1987), 274, 299.

13 Teresa L. Reed, *The Holy Profane: Religion in Black Popular Music* (Lexington: University Press of Kentucky, 2003), 41.

14 *Ibid.*, 51-52.

15 See for example Hart M. Nelson and Anne K. Nelson, *Black Church in the Sixties* (Lexington: University Press of Kentucky, 1975) and Christopher G. Ellison and Darren E. Sherkat, "The 'Semi-Involuntary Institution' Revisited: Regional Variations in Church Participation among Black Americans," *Social Forces*, 73 (June 1995), 1415-1437.

16 *The Atlanta Journal Constitution*, March 17, 2001.

17 Benjamin E. Mays, *Born to Rebel: An Autobiography* (Athens: University of Georgia Press, 1971, 2003), 13-17.

18 *The Birmingham News*, May 24, 28, 2002.

19 Matthew O. Hunt and Larry L. Hunt, "Regional Religions?: Extending the 'Semi-Involuntary' Thesis of African-American Religious Participation," *Sociological Forum*, no. 4 (2000), 569-594; and Ellison and Sherkat, "The 'Semi-involuntary Institution' Revisited," 1423.

20 The *Atlanta Journal Constitution*, March 5, 2000.

21 *The Atlanta Journal-Constitution*, August 21, 2003; Ft. Lauderdale *Sun-Sentinel*, December 30, 2000.

22 Clayborne Carson, "Martin Luther King, Jr., and the African-American Social Gospel," in Fulop and Raboteau, eds., *African-American Religion*, 349.

23 The Charlotte *Observer*, June 20, 2001.

24 Andrew W. Billingsley, *Mighty Like a River: The Black Church and Social Reform* (New York: Oxford University Press, 1999), 81.

25 *The New York Times*, December 21, 2003.

26 *The Atlanta Journal Constitution*, July 14, 2001 and March 1, 2004.

27 *The Atlanta Journal Constitution*, March 1, April 1, 2004 and *The New York Times*, March 1, April 1 2004.

28 Leon F. Litwack, *Trouble in Mind: Black Southerners in the Age of Jim Crow* (New York: Alfred A. Knopf, 1999), 166.

29 Billingsley, *Mighty Like a River*, 221.

30 Lincoln and Mamiya, *The Black Church in the African American Experience*, 176-82

31 *The Atlanta Constitution Journal*, October 24, 1999, March 17, 2001 and the Charlotte *Observer*, June 20, 2001.

32 *The New York Times*, March 24, 2001.

33 Billingsley, *Mighty Like a River*, 162-63.

34 *The Atlanta Constitution Journal*, March 17, 2001.

Chapter Four

In Service, Silence, and Strength: Women in Southern Churches

Cynthia Lynn Lyerly

Since the earliest decades of European settlement, churches have been the single arena in southern public life in which women have visibility, standing, and power. From sermons and books published to honor pious colonial women, to women exhorters and prayer leaders in antebellum revivals, to women's benevolent organizations and church fundraising, to black "church mothers'" pivotal roles in the Civil Rights Movement, women have been important in southern public life. Although women's inclusion in and exclusion from church leadership roles continues to attract the most media attention, southern women have long been leaders of sex-segregated church groups.

Historically, these organizations evolved out of women's exclusion from churches' governing bodies, their unique social and religious interests, and their sense of religious mission. Scholars call the separate women's groups that exist alongside the denominational governing bodies at the congregational, state, regional, and national levels "the parallel church," because these groups mirror the general organizational ladder of historically male-dominated governing bodies, yet are usually separate in finances, government, and ministry.

Even these separate women's organizations have had to struggle for autonomy and acceptance. In antebellum Petersburg, Virginia, notes the historian Suzanne Lebsock, "voluntary, organized charity was the exclusive province of women."[1] Until 1858, that is. In that year, Petersburg's leading men took control over an orphanage that women had operated for a decade.

The Woman's Missionary Union (WMU) of the Southern Baptist Convention (SBC) is another case in point. The WMU was organized in 1888, but not before years of opposition from SBC male leaders, who feared that approving a separate

101

women's organization would lead to women speaking in public and would be an entering wedge for discussions of the burgeoning women's rights movement. The WMU organized as an auxiliary to the SBC; though the WMU was self-governing and self-supporting, the status as auxiliary signaled the founders' intentions not to usurp male authority. The WMU grew wildly and supported both foreign and home missions, causes extremely popular with nineteenth-century Protestant women.

Before 1927, the WMU's annual report was read by a man at the SBC convention. Beginning in 1928, when the practice changed and the WMU president read the report, the SBC meeting adjourned from the church in which it was assembled to the Sunday school rooms to hear the presentation—all to avoid the problem of a woman in the pulpit.[2] Women's success in fundraising and institution-building was not always received with hostility by male church leaders, but these examples illustrate a common pattern.

In no region of the country are religious debates over proper gender roles as publicly polarized as they are in the South, where the roots of these tensions run deepest. Southern religious history is replete with stories of women striving for a greater role in church work or more control over their churches' public ministries and charities, while men renegotiated, accommodated, or resisted women's efforts. These disagreements, frequently acrimonious and sanctimonious, were often aired in public. During the First Great Awakening, South Carolina ministers argued in print over whether George Whitefield's sermons had a salutary or a baleful influence on the colony's women. Southerners opposed to and in favor of the Equal Rights Amendment (ERA), to take a far more recent case, could be seen debating on television as well as in print. Even when women's participation was off-stage or behind the scenes, their actions could occasion public controversy.

Today, when Southern women have numerous routes to participation in public life, they still choose to direct much of their energy into church work. And today, when women religious leaders are not rare, public debates over gender roles in churches and families are still ubiquitous in the South. There are many places one could begin to explore the modern-day legacy of these tangled historical roots, but the story of the Gardners, a couple who did not seek to be newsworthy or to create controversy, is, for many reasons, a perfect place to start.

On September 10, 2002, Don and Esther Gardner received the bad news: Their application to be missionaries in Africa had been rejected, even though the two had experience volunteering in African missions and the head of missions work in Africa had urged them to return. The reason? The Gardners support women in ministry and belong to a congregation, Baptist Church of the Covenant in Birmingham, Alabama, that has a woman pastor.

In 2001, the SBC changed the denomination's doctrinal standards, called the Baptist Faith and Message, to assert that women pastors were not sanctioned by the Bible. The SBC's International Mission Board (IMB) then required all missionaries to endorse the revised standards. In response, the Gardners appended lengthy explanations of the points of doctrine with which they disagreed. The president of the IMB, Jerry Rankin, told reporters that the Gardners had "made it very clear that they supported women pastors. It was discussed with them, and they did endorse their pastor." Esther Gardner was saddened at the news. "We've been Southern Baptist all of our lives," she said in an interview. "It just hurt down deep in our gut."[3]

The South remains the region most hostile to women pastors,[4] and the SBC's 2001 revisions to its doctrine sought to buttress male authority in the church. Yet the Gardners' story also reveals the complexity of women's roles in southern religion. First, the Gardners supported Reverend Sarah Jackson Shelton, who on August 11, 2002, was called to the pastorate in the heart of the deep South by a congregational vote of 131 to 2.[5]

Shelton is unusual but not unique. In Greensboro, North Carolina, St. Andrews Episcopal Church is led by the Reverend Wendy Billingslea. Trinity Lutheran Church of Greenville, South Carolina, is co-pastored by reverends Susan Crowell and Shannon Mullen. Lisa Stone is pastor at Sinking Springs United Methodist Church in Clinton, Tennessee. The all-black membership of Bethany Congregational Church in Thomasville, Georgia, called their first woman and first white person to the ministry in May of 2002. In hamlets and cities across the South, women pastors are becoming more prominent.

The Gardners' story also suggests the variety of ways women have served their churches even when being excluded from the pulpit. Some of the most well-known women in southern churches have been missionaries, like Lottie Moon, a pioneering southern woman who was a missionary to China from 1873 to 1885. Women's support for foreign and home missions, moreover, has been crucial to southern religious outreach and organizational life. Today the WMU has a membership nearing 1 million and claims to be the largest organization for Protestant women in the world. Finally, the Gardners' rejection helps illuminate the fault lines in many southern faiths around gender roles and expectations. The SBC Mission Board rejected the Gardners, who were clearly able and willing to serve, because their beliefs about women do not accord with the SBC's literalist interpretation of the Bible.

Fault Lines of Gender in the South

Southerners are far more likely than Americans in other regions to believe that "[e]verything in the Bible should be taken literally, word for word."[6] Data from 2001 and 2002 studies by the Barna Research Institute also show that Southerners are more likely to consider themselves "born again" and that half of all self-described evangelicals live in the South. These conservative Protestants are active in their churches, communities, and state and national politics. The political scientist John C. Green argues that the "church-based mobilization of white evangelical Protestants in the South" was key to Republican victories in the 2002 elections.[7] Among these same conservative Protestants were the delegates to the SBC 2001 convention.

The Religious Right was born out of discontent with liberalism and social protest in the 1960s and 1970s. Virginia's Jerry Falwell, founder of the Moral Majority, credits his initial alienation to the Supreme Court's decision to ban prayer in the nation's public schools. But by the time he wrote the Religious Right's manifesto, *Listen, America!*, in 1980, his list of America's national sins was heavily influenced by the women's movement and the cultural revolution of the 1960s.

Falwell's top five sins, in 1980, were abortion, homosexuality, pornography, humanism, and the "fractured family," a category in which he included divorced couples, unmarried couples living together, homosexual couples, and those living communally. The Supreme Court's striking down of anti-sodomy statutes in 2003 and the Massachusetts Supreme Judicial Court's legalization of gay marriage have again mobilized the Religious Right, which is organizing on behalf of a proposed Federal Marriage Amendment, which would define marriage in the nation and its states as the union of one man and one woman.

A perceived threat to traditional gender roles has long been at the heart of much of the Religious Right's concerns. Feminists, conservative Christians argue, are trying to destroy the family as God intended it. Feminists are only concerned with self-fulfillment. Feminists denigrate women's traditional roles as homemakers and mothers. Feminists sanction a selfish agenda that includes the right to kill unborn children when women should be embracing pregnancy and child-bearing. Feminists who have children neglect them by going to work instead of staying at home and caring for them. Feminists promote "secular humanism"—a philosophy that emphasizes, as Falwell put it, "that within each individual there is a glorious talented personality...an inner divinity that he alone can bring out in himself," and which leads directly to moral relativism. And feminists refuse to be submissive to men in both church and family, which the Religious Right views as anti-scriptural. Feminists, per Falwell, "have never accepted their God-given roles."[8]

Conservative women share many of these opinions, and they mobilized in the 1970s and 1980s in opposition to the ERA, which read: "Equality of rights under the law shall not be denied or abridged by the United States or by any state on account of sex." Opponents of the amendment feared a host of evils would result from its passage. One main fear was that women would be subject to the draft and would have to serve in combat. Another was that the amendment would abolish special protections women had under existing laws, such as safety legislation designed for women in their childbearing years. Opponents argued that the ERA would invalidate laws against rape, abrogate states' rights, make single-sex schools illegal, legalize homosexual marriages, and abolish alimony. But behind all of these arguments lay two core beliefs: that the ERA and its proponents were seeking to erase gender differences and that the ERA and its supporters were seeking to undermine the traditional family.

Currently, there is an effort to revive the ERA in a number of states, including Florida. Opponents are drawing on some of the same themes used two decades ago, but in particular they stress two familiar issues with new piquancy. A Stop ERA flyer for Florida boldly declares that: "ERA would require taxpayer funding of abortions." The National Right to Life Committee agrees. Once more, abortion is at the center of conservative opposition to a women's issue. Yet just as urgent, in the minds of new ERA opponents, is the impact an ERA would have on marriage regulations in the country. Now, as earlier, opponents of ERA claim that the language of "sex" in the amendment could be construed to grant rights to homosexuals. As the Florida Stop ERA flyer asserts: "ERA would legalize same-sex marriages." The battle against the ERA and the battle for the Federal Marriage Amendment have been merged.

Conservative Christians, especially fundamentalists, seek to counter feminism and the evils associated with it. Dorothy Patterson, a leader in the fundamentalist movement and a professor of women's studies at Southeastern Baptist Theological Seminary, does not let men take her classes, as it would be unbiblical for a woman to teach men. Patterson portrays feminists in the worst possible light. "Radical feminists," Patterson warns, "accuse the family of oppressing all people and especially women. They would portray dutiful wives as 'dishonest prostitutes,' nurturing mothers as pitiful prisoners descending into terminal social decay, and traditional homes as the origin of the most evil against women." Feminists have spent two decades "aggressively denying" that there are "gender differences in a bid for equality (by which feminists or egalitarians mean sameness or unisex)," she reports. Patterson blames the skyrocketing rates of divorce on feminists who put self first. These same women have made the home "a way station for people passing through" in which "food preparation may become a thing of the past." The Conservative Theological Society is more blunt:

"Feminism has an evil agenda; the destruction of the home and the husband's spiritual leadership in that home."[9]

Efforts to undermine the traditional family or traditional gender roles, the Religious Right says, will imperil the nation. Shortly after the September 11, 2001, attacks on the World Trade Center, Jerry Falwell opined that "the pagans, and the abortionists, and the feminists, and the gays and lesbians who are actively trying to make that an alternative lifestyle" had "created an environment which possibly has caused God to lift the veil of protection" from America. Falwell's ready mingling of various groups should not obscure the prominence of gender to his analysis. Two years later, he was still bemoaning "the willful blurring of sexual roles" seen when Madonna, at the 2003 MTV Video Music Awards, "kissed on the mouth" two younger female pop stars. It was a short step from this "willful blurring" to a violation of "the biblical mandate for man-woman marriage relationships," and from thence to abortion and homosexuality.

Conservative Christians in the South exert much energy to counter feminist views and offer support and advice for those attempting to live "scripturally based" gender roles. These efforts range from books and audiotapes like *The Power of a Praying Wife* and *There's No Place Like Home: Steps to Becoming a Stay-at-Home Mom* to special research centers and publications established to further a conservative Christian agenda.[10]

Phillip Lancaster, a member of the fundamentalist Presbyterian Church in America, publishes *Patriarch* magazine out of Willis, Virginia, and operates the Patriarch.com Web site as well. The mission of these forums is to promote a "Christ-like manhood" that is "neither wimpy nor tyrannical" and to encourage a "home-centered lifestyle." Lancaster and his colleagues advocate a new type of Christian manhood that eschews the "feminized emotionalism and sloppy doctrine of recent movements" in favor of "a manly pursuit of truth and a gutsy appeal to duty." *Patriarch* acknowledges that it presents "a direct challenge to feminism," which it blames for a host of social evils. Feminism has led to "women working outside the home," "unmarried daughters [leaving] home for college or career," "hyphenated last names," the advocacy of gender-inclusive language in churches, and the equality of the sexes in home and church. The sponsors of *Patriarch* support home-schooling, urge fathers to be thoroughly involved in every aspect of their families' lives, and believe that single daughters should remain in the father's household and under the father's control until they marry. Though these notions are not supported by all fundamentalists, *Patriarch*, in many ways, carries fundamentalist views to their logical, if extreme, conclusion.

An organization with many similar goals but with far more influence is the Council on Biblical Manhood and Womanhood, based in Louisville, Kentucky. The council grew out of a meeting of evangelical leaders concerned about modern sex roles. Its "Rationale" included 10 contemporary developments the leaders viewed with alarm, including the "confusion" over "the complementary differences between masculinity and femininity," the resultant "unraveling [of] the fabric of marriage," the increase in pornography, the claims for legitimacy of relationships not sanctioned by the Bible (homosexuality), modernist readings of the Bible "devised to reinterpret apparently plain meanings," women's entrance into church-leadership roles not sanctioned by the Bible, and the devaluation of motherhood and "vocational homemaking."[11]

The council issues the biannual *Journal for Biblical Manhood and Womanhood*, hosts a Web site with downloadable articles and audiotapes, and compiled, in 1991, the massive tome, *Recovering Biblical Manhood and Womanhood: A Response to Evangelical Feminism*. This collection of essays from conservative Protestants, setting forth the case for male leadership in the home and the church, could be a latter-day version of *The Fundamentals*, which helped launch the Fundamentalist movement in the early twentieth century. Each essay considers the counterarguments—from exegetical to historicist—in great depth before propounding a differing view supported by a host of scriptural references.

The authors promote a view of gender roles that they describe as "complementarian," which they counterpoise to "hierarchical" and "egalitarian." One essay defines the essence of scriptural gender identities in terms of men's "benevolent responsibility to lead, provide for, and protect women" and women's "freeing disposition to affirm, receive, and nurture strength and leadership from worthy men." The essay's author meticulously describes how husband and wife should carry out these roles in everyday life. While mothers can discipline children, for example, fathers are counseled to take "the initiative in disciplining the children when both parents are present." The volume's editors argue that God's plan is subverted when women executives have male secretaries. Wives can communicate sexual interest, but it is the husband's role to lead in "sexual relations by communicating an aura of strong and tender pursuit." Feminists' "minimization of sexual role differentiation," another author declares, "contributes to the confusion of sexual identity" and "gives rise to more homosexuality."

Women's roles in the churches are the second main theme of the collection, and the authors squarely assert that women "are not to teach Christian doctrine to men and they are not to exercise authority directly over men in the church." Women may teach other women or children. They may prophesy and pray in church. They may be missionaries and "tell the gospel story and win men and women to Christ."[12] They may vote in church. But they should not be elders, deacons, or pastors.

The impact of *Recovering Biblical Manhood and Womanhood* and the council's other work was most vividly demonstrated in the summer of 1998, when the SBC adopted a doctrinal article on the standards of family life. Two council members were on the committee that drafted this article and *Recovering Biblical Manhood and Womanhood* was, outside of the Bible, the "prominent" source the committee consulted. The article defined marriage as "the uniting of one man and one woman in covenant commitment for a lifetime." A husband's role is to "provide for, to protect, and to lead his family," while a wife's is to "submit herself graciously to the servant leadership of her husband." In their explanation of this creedal statement, the drafting committee stressed that male and female roles were "complementary," terminology adopted from the council.

The SBC, the largest Protestant body in the country, has forced many of its employees to endorse the revised Baptist Faith and Message or be fired. Southern Baptist Theological Seminary in Louisville, Kentucky, has played host to the most publicized purges. Fundamentalists took control of the Seminary's Board of Trustees in 1990 and appointed a young conservative president, Albert Mohler. Mohler required faculty to endorse a number of fundamentalist principles— including that abortion and homosexuality are sins and that women should not teach men or be pastors. A majority of the faculty resigned or were forced out, most notably two women who affirmed their support for women pastors.

The struggle of Molly Marshall, the first tenured woman at the Seminary, became the subject of a documentary film, *Battle for the Minds*, that aired on PBS and won numerous awards. Marshall was forced to resign in the fall of 2004 because of her support of women in ministry and what Mohler termed her "feminist theology." In March of 1995, Mohler forced the Dean of the Carver School of Social Work, Diana Garland, to resign because she wanted to fill a position with a candidate who believed that women's ordination was scripturally valid.

What is easy to overlook in the conservatives' focus on women's subordination is their equal emphasis on reforming men. The assumption that men need to be disciplined goes back to the foundational years of the Religious Right. Falwell, for example, cast equal blame for the decline of civilization on feminists and what he called "the cult of the playboy." As Falwell explained in 1980, "The playboy philosophy tells men that they do not have to be committed to their wife and to their children, but that they should be some kind of a 'cool, free swinger.'"

Opponents of ERA cited their fears that if the amendment passed, husbands would leave their wives for younger women, without having to pay child support or alimony. In a Father's Day sermon in 2003, Falwell identified America's most serious problems as "the absence of Godly fathers in our homes" and "fathers in our homes who don't keep their promises." This allusion to the Promise Keepers, the evangelical organization for men, is apropos of both the desire to reinforce men's authority in the home and to hold men to a high moral standard. Just as the Promise Keepers vow to lead in marriages and families, they also vow to practice "spiritual, moral, ethical, and sexual purity."

A sermon preached by the council's Chairman of the Board, Dr. Ligon Duncan, senior minister of the First Presbyterian Church in Jackson, Mississippi, and reprinted in the council's journal, nicely encapsulates the reasoning behind conservative views of male nature. Declaiming against the "bizarre spectacle of 'same sex marriages'" (his quotation marks indicate he finds this an oxymoron), Duncan warns his audience that "every assault on the ordinance of marriage…is an attack on the uniqueness of marriage." Duncan then conversationally adds, "Look, men especially are not instinctively committed to marriage. There have to be pressures at force in order to help men be connected and committed to that marriage." He further argues that the clothes made for Adam and Eve after the fall were needed because men "will look across the marriage bounds and outside the marriage bounds to experience some of the pleasures and blessings of the marital relationship." "That is why," Duncan concludes, "the beach is a very dangerous place for a man to be today, because there is not much covering going on out there."

These concerns can be seen at the congregational level, too. New Life Community Church, in Stafford, Virginia, is a case in point. This nondenominational fundamentalist church has an active multiracial membership of 100 families and offers a plethora of local and international missions, study, prayer, and other groups for members. New Life describes itself as a "family-based ministry." "We focus much of our energy upon discipling the priest of the family, i.e., the dad and husband" and "provide modeling and tools for the priest of the home to love and disciple the members of his own family." New Life's Web site is elaborate, with links to articles and sites on overcoming addiction, promoting a healthy sexual relationship in marriage, Christian matchmaking services, and "clean Christian humor." But a number of the site's links are geared to helping men become proper role models and leaders in their homes and churches.

One linked article, "The Man's Role in the Home," stresses not only men's responsibility to provide for, protect, and lead their families, but also their need to emotionally bond with their wives and children and be engaged in childrearing and strengthening their marriage. While a father is exhorted to "help your children know the joy of obedience," he is also urged to "patiently listen to his teenagers" and "wash the dishes and tend to the baby, so mother can have a break, even after his long day at work."

Another article linked on the site, "What Kind of a Husband Would Jesus Have Made?" blends scriptural references with pop psychology of the "men are from Mars, women are from Venus" type. This article lists 10 "freedoms" that Jesus provided women and includes the "freedom to ask questions." The author explains: "The typical woman speaks 25,000 words in a day; the typical man speaks 12,000...Women need to talk. Conversation is how they establish relationships and feel secure in relationships...A husband like Jesus would sacrifice his need in order to meet his wife's need to relate." Wives also need "freedom from accusation," from husbands' "criticism, put downs, and sarcasm....For her to grow, you need to give your wife ten compliments and encouragements, for every one criticism." The article laments that in "our radical feminist, unisex culture we try to ignore male/female differences" that are divinely ordained. Husbands, cognizant of these differences, need to give their wives the "freedom to be emotional."

Controversy over the Promise Keepers and the SBC's statements on women has obscured some of the main attractions conservative Christianity has for both men and women. The pastor of New Life Community Church, Dennis Rupert, in explaining why he does not allow women to be elders or pastors, makes a startling admission. "Men are more than willing to allow women to take the lead in spiritual matters," he confesses, just as Adam deferred to Eve in the Garden. Rupert emphasizes that this "is a weakness IN MEN, not women. God being well aware of this male tendency to [cop] out of spiritual matters reserves certain activities in the church for men only—forcing them to engage with the church and God." New Life intentionally places men "in front of the congregation leading, teaching, and directing" so that men "are very engaged in their relationship with the Lord and in the life of the church." Conservatives, by deliberately appealing to male leadership, hope to involve men in the churches and counter the long trend in America of women outnumbering men in church membership and attendance. An ABC News poll in 2002 concluded that the Americans who attend worship services the most are southern women aged 45 and older, 68 percent of whom attend church weekly.[13] By urging men to be gentle, loving, listening, and religious, conservative Protestants help ensure this female majority stays in the pews.

While women cannot be preachers in conservative Protestant churches, they are encouraged to be active in their churches, communities, and politics. Women are often in the front lines of demonstrations against abortion clinics and conservative southern women have been active in the Republican Party, Moral Majority, and other groups. Yet conservative women have other routes to public life through causes traditionally associated with women. Elizabeth Ridenour and Vicki Frost offer two examples of the political influence conservative Protestant women can exert. Ridenour, a resident of Greensboro, North Carolina, was called by the Holy Spirit, she maintains, to "get the Bible back into public schools." Ridenour began to study American education, and "discovered that since 1963, when the Bible was removed from public schools, the United States has become the world's leader in violent crime, divorce, illegal drug use and illiteracy."

Ridenour's research, aided by conservative legal foundations, showed that the Bible could be studied in schools as long as it was not used for religious indoctrination. Founded in 1993, The National Council on Bible Curriculum in Public Schools, with Ridenour as president, developed a curriculum for a Bible study course that could be used in public high schools.

The course purports to teach the Bible solely as literature and history and includes discussions of Passover, Chanukah, the Apocrypha, and the Dead Sea Scrolls to give it an ecumenical dimension. But Ridenour, when speaking to conservative Christians, is more open about her motives. "[T]eachers report that the Bible has a positive effect on the character of students," she told a reporter for *Believer's Voice of Victory*, a fundamentalist magazine, "even those who had previously been rebellious and those openly involved in the occult."

The National Council Web site provides links to a host of conservative Christian groups, including The Center for Reclaiming America, based in Florida. The Center offers useful tips on grassroots organizing, petitions to sign in favor of the Federal Marriage Amendment and in opposition to abortion, and a fact sheet on how to influence local school boards. The Council boasts that its curriculum has been adopted by 244 school districts and that 150,000 students have taken the course. Though the Council adds that their success is "not just in the Bible belt," 10 of the 33 states where the course has been offered are in the South, including every state covered by the essays in this volume.

Vicki Frost's saga in Church Hill, Tennessee, was given wide publicity in the press and in Stephen Bates's insightful account, *Battlegrounds*. In 1983, Frost discovered, in her daughter's sixth-grade reader, a reference to telepathy. Disturbed because of its association with the New Age movement and the Antichrist, she further examined her children's readers and found other values contrary to their faith: references to Hinduism, advocacy of the women's movement, positive depictions of Satanism, and anti-Christian messages.

Frost attempted to convince school-board members to replace the readers, but they refused. Next, she tried to persuade the school principals to allow her children to be released from English classes and use other readers under her supervision in the school libraries. When the school insisted her children use the approved readers, Frost pulled her daughter out of the classroom and was arrested for trespassing. Backed by other concerned fundamentalist parents, Frost filed suit against the local school board for violating the free-exercise clause of the Constitution, arguing that the readers promoted secular humanism and thus infringed on the students' beliefs.

This case became a cause celebre both for the Religious Right and for its opponents. Frost received legal aid from Concerned Women of America, a conservative women's group headquartered in California that has a strong base of support in the South. The local school board received assistance from the American Civil Liberties Union and People for the American Way, a national organization founded by Norman Lear to counter the Moral Majority. In the county court, the plaintiffs won a limited victory: the judge ruled that children could be allowed to opt out of a particular subject and be schooled at home in that subject if there were free-exercise infringements in the classroom. On appeal, Frost and her allies lost. As a result, most of the plaintiffs removed their children from the public schools and placed them in parochial schools.

Vicki Frost is but one example of a wider movement among southern fundamentalist women to keep abreast of, challenge, and influence what is taught in public schools. Fundamentalists expect women to be advocates for children and families, and therefore women's involvement in these issues does not contravene their beliefs about gender roles. Many fundamentalist women, moreover, do not work outside the home, because that violates biblical prescriptions for women, and thus have the time to closely monitor their children's public school education and the church networks to quickly gather interested people for meetings or to sign petitions.

A growing number of fundamentalist and conservative Christian parents are choosing to educate their children at home precisely because of their beliefs that public schools are hostile to Christianity while endorsing secular humanism, homosexuality, evolution, and feminism. The SBC's home missions board now promotes home schooling and the SBC publishing houses offer resources, textbooks, and curricula for parents choosing this option. The burden of home schooling, of course, largely falls on mothers, but by home schooling, conservative Christian women believe they are fulfilling their divine duty to their families and avoiding the sin of working outside the home.

The final fault line of gender that divides southern Protestants is over gender-neutral language in church liturgies and gender-neutral translations of the Bible. Mainline denominations like the United Methodist Church and the Evangelical Lutheran Church in America (ELCA) have attempted to change their liturgies and hymns to reflect modern usage, replacing words like "man" with "humankind." The United Methodists changed the hymn "Good Christian Men, Rejoice" to "Good Christian Friends, Rejoice" and even changed a line in Wesley's popular "Hark! the Herald Angels Sing" from "pleased as man with men to dwell" to "pleased with us in flesh to dwell." Two new translations of the Bible, the Today's New International Version and the New Revised Standard Version, also adopted gender-inclusive language. Conservative Christians are outraged at what they see as the latest attempt by feminists to impose "politically correct" standards at the expense of biblical truth. Women may feel excluded by masculine pronouns, conservative Protestants say, but that is no reason to alter God's word.

The fault lines of gender will likely continue to divide mainline from evangelical Christians in the South for years to come. Crucial to understanding the Religious Right's position is their literal interpretation of scripture. For conservative Christians, gender differences began with the creation of Adam and Eve and were essential to God's plan for humanity. Any effort to change the roles prescribed in the Bible for men and women or husbands and wives is tantamount to defying God's will. Feminism and the gay rights movement come from a secular mindset, say conservatives, and Christians must resist these threats to the family and gender roles or risk God's displeasure. But just as they tout women's submission, conservatives also promote a godly masculinity that sanctions marital fidelity, fiscal responsibility, and church involvement. For evangelicals who feel at sea in the swirl of modern life, the Christian Right offers eternal truths and fixed verities about men, women, sexuality, marriages, families, and relationships. And conservative Christians, as Elizabeth Ridenour and Vicki Frost show, are willing to advance their agenda in the public sphere.

Mainline and liberal Protestants in the South continue to ordain women and manline congregations are increasingly willing to call women as pastors or priests. One of the female bishop suffragans (assistant bishops) in the Episcopal Church is the Right Reverend Carol Gallagher of the Diocese of Southern Virginia. As of 1998, there were 368 women priests serving in Episcopal dioceses in the South. In some southern dioceses, the percentage of women priests is surprisingly high.

Sixty-three women (16.5 percent) serve as priests in the Diocese of Virginia. The North Carolina Diocese has 45 women priests, who comprise 20.7 percent of the total. Forty-one women priests, or 20 percent of the total, serve in the Diocese of Atlanta. In the deeper South, women comprise 11.4 percent of all priests in the Mississippi Diocese, 11 percent of all priests in the Alabama Diocese, and 5 percent of all priests in the Georgia Diocese.[14]

The statistics are similar in the ELCA. Of all ELCA pastors active in July 2003, 22.7 percent were women. ELCA's Virginia Synod had 30 women pastors, or 19.7 percent of the total. In the North Carolina Synod, 49 women served as pastors, comprising 17.8 percent of the total. South Carolina's Synod reported that 16 percent of its pastors were women, 31 in number.[15]

The Presbyterian Church, U.S.A. (PCUSA) also ordains women, and in 2002, 19.6 percent of all those ordained by the PCUSA were women.[16]

National statistics for the United Methodist Church (UMC) confirm the trend. Women comprised 18.5 percent of all United Methodist clergy in 2002, 75.3 percent of all ordained deacons, and 22 percent of all bishops. By October of 2001. the Western North Carolina Conference of the UMC (which is governed by a woman bishop) reported 219 clergywomen serving in its bounds while the North Georgia Conference had more than 150 clergywomen active.[17]

All of these denominations have shown significant, sometimes remarkable, increases in the number of women ordained and serving as pastors, even in southern churches.

A further sign that mainline denominations are growing more willing to ordain women and employ them as pastors is the fact that the number of women enrolled in American seminaries is on the rise. The Association of Theological Schools reported that in 2002 women comprised 36 percent of all students enrolled in degree programs. Thirty-one percent of those enrolled in Master of Divinity Programs, the degree that usually leads to ministry, were women. These figures are more significant when one takes history into account. The increase in women enrolled in Master of Divinity (MDiv) programs between 1977 and 2002 was a whopping 234 percent.

The Association of Theological Schools maintains that "[a]ll of the numeric gain in enrollment in the MDiv program across the past 25 years has been due to the increasing enrollment of women."[18] Considering that the largest Christian body in the United States, the Roman Catholic Church, and the largest Protestant denomination in the United States, the Southern Baptist Convention, do not ordain women, these numbers show that among mainline and other bodies, the number of women in ministry will continue to increase in the years to come. The divisions over proper roles for women in southern churches will likely be an issue for the foreseeable future.

The Parallel Church

Whether a southern church is mainline or storefront, conservative or liberal, it is sure to have organizations and groups just for women. Data on women nationally show that women are much more likely than men to be involved in a discipleship program in their churches, to participate in Sunday school, to hold a leadership position in their churches other than pastor, to participate in small-group activities in their churches, and to volunteer in their churches.[19] Regional studies show that southern women are more likely than men to attend church at least once a week, with 49.4 percent of women attending that often compared to 38.6 percent of southern men. And when asked whether their religious faith was extremely important, very important, somewhat important, or not important in their lives, 44 percent of southern women answered "extremely important" as opposed to 33.4 percent of southern men.[20] These figures help explain why even churches that ordain women, like the United Methodists and Evangelical Lutherans, have separate women's groups and organizations.

The parallel church is often in the local newspaper, hosting events, prayer meetings, conferences, or suppers. On October 6, 2001, for example, the *Chattanooga Times Free Press* announced upcoming women's activities at three area churches. The local Baptist Missionary and Educational District Association Women's Auxiliary was hosting its "annual state tea" to benefit various Baptist colleges it supports. The Highland Park Baptist Church was holding "The Joyful Woman Jubilee Retreat." The Mount Calvary Baptist Church women were sponsoring a women's seminar, "Women of Virtue." On September 7, 2002, the *Press Journal* of Vero Beach, Florida, announced a concert sponsored by United Methodist Women, a pancake breakfast by the Christian Women's Fellowship, classes on "Women of the Bible" for women at First Baptist Church, a luncheon and program by Episcopal Church Women, the first meeting of the Holy Cross Women's Guild at the Catholic church, and an interdenominational women's prayer meeting at the First Church of God.

From fundraising to social events to spiritual uplift, women's organizations at the local level constitute a vital part of southern religious life. These local groups are often bound together by state, regional, and denominational organizations for women. Perhaps the best way to appreciate the parallel church is to explore in depth two rich examples: the Southern Baptist's WMU and the Women's Department of the Church of God in Christ.

Church Mothers in the Church of God in Christ

The Church of God in Christ is a black Pentecostal denomination headquartered in Memphis, Tennessee, that believes in divine healing through prayer and in the gifts of the Holy Spirit, including speaking in tongues. While the Church of God in Christ does not ordain women, it does allow women in ministry, and bases this decision on its belief that the Holy Spirit can baptize all believers with exceptional gifts and on biblical references to prophesying women. To remain scriptural, however, the women in ministry operate under the putative guidance and leadership of male jurisdictional supervisors.

The Church of God in Christ has an elaborate parallel church, with a Department of Women and numerous women's ministries and auxiliaries. The women in positions of leadership have titles that indicate the deference due them. The General (denominational), Jurisdictional, and State Supervisors, as well as women leaders of congregations, are called Church Mothers, a title of respect historically used for pious women in black churches but here made formal. A pastor's wife is referred to as First Lady, and she is charged with keeping her husband informed of what the women's programs are doing.

Vivian Green, for example, is First Lady of St. John's Church of God in Christ in Newport News, Virginia. The St. John's Web site describes her as her husband's "co-pilot" who "demonstrates the virtues of submission and holiness."[21]

Local Church Mothers (who as a group are called the Mothers Board) lead the women of their churches and teach them proper Christian and womanly values. The Women's Department's literature maintains that although, in the past, pastors taught women from the pulpits, this teaching was "never proper" and "would only embarrass and drive out our present-day generation from the church." The Church Mothers thus hold monthly meetings with women and girls to "teach them things women should know."

The Church of God in Christ licenses Deaconess Missionaries to operate within local congregations. After two years service, these women may apply to become an Evangelist Missionary, who travels within her district (also called a jurisdiction) to conduct revivals. District Missionaries are women who preside over the Church Mothers, Missionaries, Auxiliaries and women's unit leaders within a jurisdiction and assist the Jurisdictional Supervisor, who is an ordained man. A woman can become a National Evangelist after she has conducted successful revivals in seven different states and is nominated by her Jurisdictional Supervisors.

In addition, the Church of God in Christ has a host of other groups for women, many of which have a local, state, district, and national leadership structure. The Prayer and Bible Band is one such auxiliary of the Women's Department. These bands combine women's Bible study with training sessions, for they aim to teach women "[h]ow to love their husbands and children" and "how to work in the church and retain their femininity at all times."

The Sewing Circle, which is a longstanding auxiliary, trains women to sew, knit, and crochet (and thus "has served to help women to become better homemakers"), and then raise funds for the church by selling their crafts. The church's Christian Women's Council is a group for women aged 40 and older. Another women's auxiliary with officers at the local, jurisdictional, and national level is the Business and Professional Women's Federation. This group embraces a mission of fostering young people's education, helping the poor, and visiting the shut-in. There are numerous other women's groups with a similar structure like the Usher's Board, the Hospitality Committee, and the Mission Board. Every year, church women assemble together at a National Convention to receive training, to worship together, and to help the church thrive.

As the Church of God in Christ's Women's Department and its auxiliaries show, the parallel church flourishes alongside of male-run denominational bodies. Church women operate independently of the male hierarchy even as they claim submission to it. With the numerous opportunities for women to engage in separate women's fellowship, service, and ministry, the parallel church is surely central to these women's experiences of religion. Although the Church of God in Christ does not ordain women (and only sanctions women Evangelists serving as church pastors when there is not a male available), women have numerous opportunities for leadership.

The Women's Missionary Union in the Southern Baptist Convention

The WMU also illustrates the strength of the parallel church and reveals how southern churchwomen still struggle for autonomy and acceptance. The two best-known women in Southern Baptist history were missionaries: Annie Armstrong, who pioneered in home missions, and Lottie Moon, who served with great success as a missionary to China. To this day, the two largest fund drives for missions in the SBC are the Lottie Moon Christmas Offering and the Annie Armstrong Easter Offering. In 2002, the SBC, largely because of efforts by the WMU, raised $115 million for the Lottie Moon Christmas Offering and $49 million for the Annie Armstrong Easter Offering.

The WMU sponsors missionaries in the United States and abroad; educates and involves "women, girls, and preschoolers" in "the cause of Christian missions"; raises funds through sales of books and products; and publicizes the need for missions and lay involvement. The WMU is highly organized, with separate missions groups for preschoolers (Mission Friends), primary-school-aged girls (Girls in Action), and teen-aged girls (Acteens), as well as numerous groups for adult women. The WMU is a publishing dynamo. In addition to books, cassettes, and videos, the organization publishes a wide variety of periodicals in support of missions: *Missions-Mosaic*, for women; *Dimensions*, for women leaders of missions; *The Mag*, for teen-aged girls; *Acteens Leader*, for teen-aged girls in leadership positions; *GA World*, for fifth- and sixth-grade girls; *Discovery*, for first- through fourth-grade girls; *Aware*, for girls in leadership positions; *Share*, for preschoolers; and *Start*, for teachers of Mission Friends preschoolers.

The October 2003 issues of *GA World* and *Discovery* are vivid examples of WMU efforts to educate girls about missions and inspire them to become missionaries. Both magazines focus on the McClendon family, SBC missionaries in Yemen. The magazines are filled with facts about Yemeni foodways, housing, customs, and women's lives. *Discovery* magazine tells young girls that a Yemeni woman loves dressing up but "would never show her beautiful clothes to a man who was not her husband." Paper dolls are provided so that girls learn about the sirwals (leggings worn under dresses when women leave their houses), baltos (coat-like garments that go over women's clothes), hejabs (scarves that covers women's hair), and burkas (veils that covers women's faces).

Older girls learn in GA World that Yemeni women "consider it shameful to show their hair, their arms, or their legs" in public and that "Mrs. McClendon" and her daughter dress according to local custom so that Yemenis will not conclude they are "dressing immodestly or shamefully." Both magazines ask girls to pray for the McClendons and for their efforts to Christianize Yemeni people, with *Discovery* doing so in a coloring page. Older girls learn that it is "against the law for Muslims to choose to follow Jesus" and are told of the three SBC missionaries who were killed in Yemen on December 30, 2002.

Both magazines publish stories sent in by girls in missions groups, where readers can see, to take one example, that the Girls in Action in Jacksonville, Florida, participate in the adopt-a-grandparent program, raise money for the Lottie Moon offering, and put together kits of needed supplies for 400 needy children at Christmas. Though the emphasis is clearly on converting Yemenis to Christianity, these publications expose Southern Baptist girls to a world very different from their own.

The WMU directly sponsors a wide range of missions both in the United States and abroad. Most of these involve women's work for women, a traditional emphasis of women's missionary organizations. The Christian Women's Job Corps, for example, is designed to help poor and uneducated American women acquire the skills to succeed in the labor force and in life. The Job Corps pairs a Southern Baptist woman with a woman in need, and the mentor conducts Bible studies with her client; assesses the client's needs; helps the client acquire skills for the job market; and assists her with health care, housing, childcare, or medical care, as needed.

The WMU also sponsors the Pure Water, Pure Love ministry, which provides missionaries overseas with a filter to purify water. The WMU puts the group that donates the money for the filter in touch with the missionary who receives it, and encourages the stateside group to become prayer partners with the missionary. The WMU also publicizes and supports smaller-scale missionary efforts, like the Haven of Rest Ministry in Kentucky. Eileen Mullins conceived of the idea after her long drives to visit her son in prison, where she saw poor families of incarcerated men making even longer drives with small children. Haven of Rest houses, feeds, and counsels families visiting men in prison. The WMU was careful to point out that Mullins developed her passion for missions from her mother, who was deeply involved in her congregation's WMU activities.[22]

Yet even this historically important and vibrant women's organization has been under threat from the Religious Right. To understand the struggle, we must return to the SBC's historic revisions of the Baptist Faith and Mission statement regarding wifely submission and an all-male ministry. In response to these revisions and the insistence that all SBC workers endorse them, several Baptist splinter groups, including the Cooperative Baptist Fellowship (CBF) and Mainstream Baptists, formed in opposition to the SBC fundamentalists.

On January 10, 1993, leaders of the WMU voted to support missionary work by all Southern Baptists, not just programs sponsored by the SBC. This independent tack was immediately met with hostility by the SBC's male leaders. A trustee of the SBC accused the WMU of acting like an adulterous woman. One member of the SBC's executive board implored the women to denounce mission efforts by breakaway groups and, as *The Christian Century* reported, "further suggested that if the women's group continues on its present course, the SBC leadership might consider starting its own women's group under the control of national church leaders."

When the WMU provided materials on missions to the moderate CBF, the SBC leadership demanded that the women's group affirm "faithful and solitary support" for SBC missions or risk its position in the denomination. One prominent fundamentalist and three-time president of the SBC, Adrian Rogers, called for a takeover of the WMU and "an end to what he termed the 'feminization' of missions." Rogers wanted the WMU "hard-wired" into the SBC, with delegates to the SBC electing WMU leaders rather than allowing the women of the WMU to choose their leaders. Echoing the fundamentalist concern about women's leadership, Rogers further argued that "mission promotion...should be led by pastors and the leaders of the Brotherhood, a men's mission group." A member of the SBC executive board suggested that the SBC consider "new approaches" for "promoting the Lottie Moon offering." In a secret move, the SBC's International Missions Board (IMB) tried to copyright the Christmas offering in Lottie Moon's name, but were stopped by the negative publicity when this effort leaked to the press. Under pressure, the WMU trademarked the name, then granted the IMB sole license to use it.

SBC leaders continued to undercut the WMU in subsequent years. In 1995, the SBC gave the Sunday School Board (now called Lifeway Christian Resources) rights to develop an educational program and to issue publications, which included missions educational material and devotional books for Baptist women—both had been the traditional purview of the WMU. These new efforts compete with the WMU and its publishing house, which is the Union's main source of fundraising.

The SBC's North American Missions Board started an "Alternatives for Life" ministry that not only set up Pregnancy Care Centers for women who would otherwise have had abortions but also actively campaigned to influence policy makers. The board also sponsors an evangelism kit to help Baptists persuade homosexuals to convert, and its Web site includes links to conservative articles, such as "How the Pro-Gay Agenda is Affecting Our Schools,...And How You

Can Make a Difference." Whether the women of the WMU approve of these initiatives is moot; when they raise funds to help the Southern Baptist mission board they have little control over how those monies are used or what agenda they are used to further.

In 1995, the fundamentalist president of Southern Baptist Theological Seminary, Al Mohler, closed its Carver School of Social Work, which effectively ended, as former WMU President Catherine Allen put it, "the only area of SBC theological studies in which women predominated." Mohler had concluded that "the tenets of social work are not compatible with biblical theology," the *Baptist Standard* reported on March 1, 2000. Ultimately, the WMU succeeded in having the Seminary return nearly $1 million in endowment funds earmarked for social work education.

A number of WMU leaders left the organization to found, in December of 2001, Global Women, a group that actively embraces women in ministry and women missionaries. Catherine Allen, the organization's treasurer, cited the SBC's "misogynist missiology" as a motivating factor for the defection of so many WMU women to the new group. Perhaps in response, and certainly in keeping with SBC's trajectory, the North American Missions Board announced in February of 2002 that it would stop employing women chaplains who were ordained. And of course, all missionaries under SBC sponsorship must now endorse the Baptist Life and Message, which includes the statements urging wifely submission and condemning women pastors.

Lives of Quiet Service

Fundamentalist attitudes towards women have not gone unchallenged in the South. In 1983, according to the ex-WMU President, Catherine Allen, "the WMU took the bold step...of helping to organize the Southern Baptist Women in Ministry." This group, now named Baptist Women in Ministry, celebrated its twentieth anniversary in June 2003. The group runs a placement service that collects resumes from ordained Baptist women, offers scholarships to women in seminaries, publishes booklets supportive of women in ministry and gender-inclusive language in church literature, and mentors women interested in the ministry. The group's Web site describes how the missionary Lottie Moon "endured censure by the Foreign Mission Board for 'preaching in the countryside,'" a fact in stark contrast to the sanitized version of Moon's life offered by the SBC.[23]

Individual churches have also challenged the SBC's stance on women. Glendale Baptist Church in Nashville, Tennessee, describes itself as a "caring community of equality and grace" and welcomes "all persons to worship with us, regardless of race, gender, or sexual orientation." Glendale boasts proudly of its history as "the first Southern Baptist church in Nashville to choose women as deacons." Five women have been ordained by the church and in 2002 the church, "in recognition and support of women's abilities and training in professional ministry," chose a woman pastor, April Barker.

Fellowship Baptist Church of Americus, Georgia, was founded in 1973 by men and women who were appalled by watching "white church leaders here in Americus actually [standing] guard at church doors to prohibit entrance to African Americans." Fellowship's founders decided on a policy of racial and gender inclusiveness, and from their beginning, opened the office of church deacon to both men and women. By 1989, the leaders of Fellowship began to be dismayed by the conservative turn of the SBC and in 1991 they stopped giving money to the SBC and donated it instead to the moderate Cooperative Baptist Fellowship. Membership fell, and by 1994 it was unclear if Fellowship would survive. Like an increasing number of rural congregations in such a crisis, and with its history as a church of inclusion, Fellowship decided on a woman pastor. In 1995, the church called as pastor Wendy Joyner, and became the first affiliated Baptist church in Georgia with a woman in that position. Joyner's salary was so low she initially had to take an additional job as a librarian. Fellowship continues to support women in ministry, inviting a female seminarian to preach on a special weekend each year.

Pastor Sarah Jackson Felton, whose members Don and Esther Gardner were turned down by the SBC missions board because they would not renounce their woman pastor, can best stand in for many southern church women. This Birmingham, Alabama, pastor delivered "A State of the Church Address" after having served the congregation for six months.

Baptist Church of the Covenant had much to be thankful for, Pastor Shelton said, pointing to 37 new members, an average increase in attendance at worship of 78, two new Sunday school classes, two new Bible study classes, and pledges for church gifts exceeding the projected budget by $27,000. Yet the year had not been without pain. Shelton reminded them of the Gardners' struggle, of how she herself had been "disinvited" from speaking engagements, and the threats by the Birmingham Baptist Association to "disfellowship" the church.

Although the Baptist State Convention was meeting in the city the day after this sermon, Pastor Shelton would not be in attendance. "I know that many of you long for me to make a stance," she admitted, "to raise a banner and wave it high…to preach words of such conviction that others will join up with us and begin a crusade." Yet Shelton did not feel called to that role; instead, she would spend the day planning for next Sunday's worship, "visiting with prospects, funeral preparation and visiting the sick."[24]

Southern women serve their churches in these ways whether they are pastors or not. Southern women are more active volunteering in their churches and in small-group church activities than men. And most of these women, like Pastor Shelton, are reluctant to "raise a banner and wave it high." Yet they sustain their local churches in numerous ways.

The *Salisbury Post* of North Carolina memorialized a few of these women in its obituary section of May 5, 2000:

• Lucille Clark, who had taught Sunday school and Bible School for West Albemarle Baptist Church

• Eunice Eller, who had been a church secretary, a past president of the Woman's Missionary Union, a Girls Auxiliary leader, church historian, church librarian, church pianist, 50 years a Sunday school teacher, and 40 years chair of the funeral food committee at Lakewood Baptist Church

• Alma Trexler, member of the Golden Age Sunday School Class and the Woman's Missionary Union, as well as a former Sunday school teacher at Dunns Mountain Baptist Church

• Vetra Brown, who taught Sunday school and was a member of the Women's Circle at Hardison United Methodist Church

• Grace Doyle, a former president of her local Women of the Evangelical Lutheran Church group, organizer of the Altar Guild, teacher in the church nursery, and honored for crafting the sanctuary banners at Christiana Lutheran Church.

Southern women like these will continue to lead lives of quiet service in their churches and for their faith.

Endnotes

1 Suzanne Lebsock, *The Free Women of Petersburg: Status and Culture in a Southern Town, 1784-1860* (New York: W.W. Norton, 1984), 215; William Wright Barnes, *The Southern Baptist Convention, 1845-1953* (Nashville: Broadman Press, 1954).

2 Harry Leon McBeth, "The Role of Women in Southern Baptist History," *Baptist History and Heritage* 12:1 (1977): 3-25.

3 Greg Garrison, "Baptists Reject Missionaries Over Woman Pastor Issue," *Birmingham News* 13 September 2002.

4 Mark Chaves, "Ordaining Women: The Diffusion of an Organizational Innovation," *The American Journal of Sociology* 101:4 (Jan. 1996): 840-873.

5 Bob Allen, "Couple says IMB Won't Appoint Missionaries With Woman Pastors," Associated Baptist Press News, 12 September 2002, Volume 02-83.

6 According to the data in the Economic Values Survey, 1992 (ARDA), 41.8 percent of southerners agree with this statement. The Barna Research Institute

poll of 2001 found that 52 percent of southerners believe "that the Bible is totally accurate in all of its teachings."

7 John C. Green, "The Undetected Tide," *Religion in the News* 6:1 (Spring 2003).

8 Jerry Falwell, *Listen, America!* (New York: Doubleday and Company, 1980), 150.

9 See *http://www.conservativeonline.org/questions/*.

10 Michael and Stormie Omartian, *The Power of a Praying Wife* (Eugene, OR: Harvest House Publishing, 1997) and Mary Larmoyeu and Ethan Pope, *There's No Place Like Home: Steps to Becoming a Stay-at-Home Mom* (Nashville: Broadman and Holman Publishers, 2001).

11 All of the CBMW material is posted on the Web, at *http://www.cbmw.org*.

12 John Piper and Wayne Grudem, eds., *Recovering Manhood and Womanhood* (Wheaton, Ill.: Crossing Books, 1991), 29, 33, 70, 75, 177.

13 ABCNEWS/Beliefnet poll, 19-20 February 2002.

14 1998 data compiled by Louie Crew of Rutgers University, available at *http://www.newark.rutgers.edu/~lcrew/womenpr.html*.

15 The ELCA's Commission for women gathered these statistics, which are available at *http://www.elca.org/cw/resources.html*.

16 This information can be found at *http://www.pcusa.org/cps/statistics.htm*.

17 The national statistics can be found at *http://infoserv.umc.org/faq/womenclergy.htm* and the data on the conferences at *http://umns.umc.org/backgrounders/clergywomen.html*.

18 The Association of Theological Schools in the United States and Canada, *Fact Book on Theological Education* (Pittsburgh: The Association of Theological Schools, 2003), 18.

19 Barna Research Group study and report, "Women Are the Backbone of the Christian Congregations in America," March 6, 2000, at *http://www.barna.org/*.

20 Southern Focus Poll, 1998, Institute for Research in Social Science of the University of North Carolina at Chapel Hill, available at the American Religion Data Archive, *http://www.arda.tm/*.

21 This information can be found at *http://www.stjohnscogic.com/*.

22 *Missions Mosaic* (April 2003); and "Haven of Rest Update," *http://www.WomenonMission.com*.

23 See *http://www.bwim.org*.

24 Shelton, "A State of the Church Address," *Covenant Word*, January 12, 2002, available on-line at *http://www.bcoc.net/*.

CHAPTER FIVE

TACTICS FOR SURVIVAL: RELIGIOUS MINORITIES

Charles H. Lippy

The popular perception of the South as the "Bible Belt" reflects the dominance of evangelical strands of Protestantism in regional public culture since the antebellum period. Some social and religious currents have challenged that dominance, but not ended it. The increasing urbanization and industrialization that started to produce the "New South" after the Civil War and the end of an economic system based on slavery made the region more attractive to immigrants and in-migrants, not all of whom were of an evangelical Protestant persuasion. But any significant transformation in the region's religious culture was to a large extent put on hold by world wars and economic depression in the twentieth century. Hence, an evangelical style shaped largely by white Baptists and Methodists has continued to exercise extraordinary influence in the region's public life. Only in the later decades of the twentieth century did a diversity that had always lurked beneath the surface begin to crack that hegemony, thanks in part to a new immigration that made some ethnic minority groups and their religious cultures more visible.

In one sense, though, Southern religious life was diverse even before the arrival of the first Europeans; the religious cultures of the Native American tribes were far from identical. Europeans brought a different kind of diversity; they too were not of a single mind in matters of religion. Spanish settlers, for example, planted a Catholic presence in Florida and Texas decades before the English came to Jamestown in 1607. French modes of Catholicism moved out from New Orleans to dominate the religious life of Louisiana and areas along the Gulf coast, such as Mobile, Alabama, long before U.S. political control came. When Irish Catholic immigrants arrived in the nineteenth century, they found a

Catholic culture already in place in parts of the South—a culture that in locales like New Orleans exercised an impact on public culture more powerful than that of evangelical Protestantism.

In such places as Charleston, South Carolina, and Savannah, Georgia, Jewish settlers were vital to English colonization efforts. If the numbers of Jews remained small, they nevertheless sustained viable religious communities that now in some cases stretch more than three centuries. In the days of slavery, there was also a Muslim presence, as some of those brought to the South as slaves came from areas of Africa where Islam prevailed. The conditions of slavery, though, made it impossible for Islam to flourish, and when Muslims became a more visible part of southern religious life in the later twentieth century, there were no direct lines back to these first Muslims in the South.

As evangelical styles of Protestantism came to dominate most of the region, the early Roman Catholic and Jewish communities adopted a variety of strategies to ensure their survival as minority cultures. These have proved useful to later religious and ethnic clusters that have extended the stratum of diversity beneath the surface. Some effective strategies, though, reflected the particular conditions that each minority group has confronted.

Roman Catholics, for example, benefitted from being part of an international religious institution. Even the smallest mission parish thus had ties to a larger tradition and could draw on its resources for support and strength. Although Roman Catholics comprised the largest single religious group in the nation by 1850, they were still dwarfed nationally by the total number of those inclined towards Protestantism. Hence some of the strategies that Catholics developed in the South were part of a larger effort to ensure that a culture dominated by Protestant thinking often hostile to Catholic ways could indeed provide the context for a minority group to prosper. For Catholics, the most well-known efforts of this sort came in the parochial or parish schools and the numerous colleges established to nurture a minority religious culture and sustain the commitment of the faithful.

In the northern states, parishes with their own schools were well on the way to becoming normative even before the Civil War; after 1884, the goal of having a school for every parish became a national goal for American Catholics. In northern cities, Catholic life was bolstered by the heavy concentration of immigrants from one cultural area in an urban neighborhood. That pattern of settlement meant that the parishes, along with their schools, often took on a particular ethnic cast and became centers not only to preserve a cultural heritage but also to aid an immigrant constituency make the transition from one cultural setting to another. The smaller number of Catholics in the South, however, made it more difficult for parishes to have the people and resources to support parish schools during the nineteenth century.

Louisiana was home to more than half the South's Catholic population for much of the nineteenth century, although Savannah, for example, gained a significant Irish immigrant community in the nineteenth century and Charleston a strong German immigrant community. Even so, outside such major centers, parishes were more like mission outposts than functioning congregations, with priests sometimes ministering to several, all of which were struggling to survive. In many parts of the South, a vital Catholic presence did not come until the later twentieth century, with the arrival of a growing Latino population and a rise in migration of Catholics from other regions into the South. Even so, the North American Religion Atlas (NARA) data shows that in 2000, just 8 percent of the South's residents identified themselves as Roman Catholic.

Yet Catholics and Jews alike recognized early that survival required building institutions. Institution-building in turn required having enough adherents in one area to support those institutions. Until well into the twentieth century the bulk of Catholics and Jews in the South were found in the region's cities. (Just 1.4 percent of Southerners belong to one or another branch of Judaism, according to NARA.) Even in instances where adherents of a minority religion are more dispersed, with small clusters of members in areas gathered around institutions, the pattern set by Roman Catholics and Jews served as a symbol of survival and even stability for other religious minorities.

This strategy has worked well for several Protestant groups that remain outside the Baptist-Methodist evangelical orbit. For example, when Seventh-day Adventists penetrated into central and southern Appalachia in the later nineteenth century, a training school in Graysville, Tennessee (now Southern Adventist University in Collegedale, outside Chattanooga), and then a health center near Nashville (now the Tennessee Christian Medical Center), became symbols that secured the identity of a minority tradition.

Institutions have also been vital in ensuring the survival of the Churches of Christ, a religious group that eschews the label of a denomination. Emerging in the frontier camp meetings among those who sought to restore New Testament forms in the then contemporary church, this group has looked especially to colleges in several locales in the South and Southern Crossroads regions (including Lipscomb University in Tennessee, Abilene Christian University in Texas, and Harding University in Arkansas), along with a publishing operation centered in Nashville, as links to connect members. Lectureships at the various schools and a host of periodicals sustain a vibrant minority identity, and as adherents have tended to locate near those schools and publishing agencies, in those communities the Churches of Christ are very much part of the public religious culture even if there is no central headquarters.

When Pentecostal stirrings moved through the South as the nineteenth century faded into the twentieth, those drawn to this more ecstatic expression of Protestantism coalesced into several denominations. In the case of two of these Pentecostal groups that are predominantly white, the city of Cleveland, Tennessee, has become a symbol of public presence. Both the Church of God (Cleveland, Tennessee) and the Church of God of Prophecy, which split off from the Church of God, have established headquarters there. For the Church of God Lee University, which began as a Bible training school, and the denomination's theological seminary adjacent to the university, have likewise served not only to signal the growth of Pentecostal expression in the South, but also to assure that Pentecostalism will maintain a public presence in the region. Using institutions like schools as a strategy for survival was part of minority religious life in the South long before the Church of God was organized; Roman Catholics and Jews had learned to do that generations earlier.

Catholics and Jews in the nineteenth century also had to combat a hostile religious and cultural environment in much of the South; so, too, did groups like the Seventh-day Adventists, whose practice of keeping Saturday as a sacred day and working on Sunday brought not only public ridicule but occasional arrests for violating local "blue laws." Yet anti-Catholicism and anti-Semitism were often more virulent in areas where there were the fewest Catholics and Jews. For Catholics, establishing parochial schools was one way to deal with hostility. By retreating into wholly Catholic enclaves, members would be more withdrawn from the larger culture and therefore able to maintain a Catholic identity. Hence institutions not only announced to the larger culture that a minority group was flourishing in the midst of a religious world dominated by evangelical Protestantism, they also provided a retreat from the hostility and suspicion that prevailed in the region. Certainly by the later twentieth century, Collegedale, Tennessee, had become an enclave where Seventh-day Adventist ways prevailed, and all of Bradley County, Tennessee, was something of a shelter for the Church of God (Cleveland, Tennessee) and the Church of God of Prophecy.

By the end of the first decade of the twentieth century, Jews had also employed similar strategies. Jewish federations and community councils existed in virtually every major Southern city. Such agencies fostered a cooperation among Orthodox, Conservative, and Reform Jews that facilitated survival in an alien environment. They also made Judaism part of public culture, even where anti-Semitic attitudes and practices excluded Jews from using social welfare organizations that served the larger community. These parallel structures meant that Jews could provide for their own welfare and could simultaneously create networks to cement a Jewish cultural identity, even when it was difficult to sustain a Jewish religious life organized around traditional ritual practice.

Another mechanism that has allowed minority religions to maintain a viable existence in the South has been to mirror some of the social attitudes of the dominant culture. Doing so at least creates the sense that a minority group can "fit in" to the larger culture and not undermine its operating values or challenge its biases. For example, in the antebellum period, few Catholics challenged the system of slavery. Some owned slaves, and many church leaders openly supported slavery and then the movement for secession when Southern states began to withdraw from the Union to form the Confederate States of America. In the civil rights era of the twentieth century, Southern Catholics continued to reflect regional racist values, despite church pronouncements condemning legalized discrimination, sometimes denying access to Catholic schools and hospitals to African Americans. Only when the church hierarchy insisted that the region's Catholic congregations and institutions adhere to the church's policies prohibiting discrimination did practice begin to change. Mirroring prevailing social attitudes made Catholics seem less different from the white evangelical majority and may have mitigated some residual anti-Catholic sentiment.

In the late twentieth century, Catholic teaching and much evangelical sentiment came together in a different way. The Roman Catholic Church had long officially opposed the practice of abortion; by the end of the twentieth century many evangelical Protestant leaders began to urge political action as a way to impress their positions on the larger culture.

Of course, some adherents of every minority religion were drawn to the dominant Protestantism and converted, often because of marriage to a Protestant. Others simply found it easier to convert than to live on the margins of the larger culture. Life on the margins was a constant struggle to sustain and transmit to succeeding generations a religious identity that was always suspect and misunderstood by those in positions of social, political, and economic power.

Yet marriage between members of a minority religious group and others has long been a problematic issue. If it facilitated survival by bringing members of the minority group into familial connections with persons from the larger culture, it also threatened survival because children from families where parents came from different religious traditions were often less likely to identify with the minority tradition. The latter is particularly the case if children of succeeding generations receive their education in public schools and have the majority of their contacts with individuals from other religious groups. As a rule, the first generation is more likely to insist on marriage within the group and frown on intermarriage; endogamy buttresses the bonds holding a minority community together and thereby increases its chances for avoiding extinction. However, when the minority religious group is very small, the pool of eligible marriage partners is also correspondingly small and marriage outside the group is more likely. The steadily increasing rate of intermarriage by the close of the twentieth century was spurred as well by the gradual easing of any social stigma attached to marriage across religious traditions in the larger society. If there was no social taboo against intermarriage, there was little religious communities could do to thwart the trend.

Some studies have shown, for example, that as late as 1970 in Southern Roman Catholic dioceses where Catholics accounted for no more than 2 percent of the total population, between half and three-quarters of Catholics who married had non-Catholic spouses. The Southern Jewish population, although likely to support Jewish institutions ranging from synagogues to community centers, where the Jewish population was minuscule, faced the same dilemma and generally experienced an even greater erosion of commitment among those in mixed marriages.

Intermarriage may have facilitated entree into the larger society, yet minority religious cultures often confronted some internal problems that complicated their claiming a stake in the public life of the region. For example, although Roman Catholics owed their earliest presence to Spanish and French settlements in the region, in time immigration brought great ethnic diversity to the Catholic population. Even if members of different ethnic groups all claimed allegiance to the one universal Catholic church, internally there were frequently ethnic rivalries and differences in religious styles that made it difficult for Catholicism to maintain a single voice as a minority. In more recent decades, the most obvious manifestations of this internal diversity have come with immigration from Central and South America and from the Caribbean.

In much of the South, by the beginning of the twenty-first century, urban parishes had a significant constituency for whom Spanish was the first language, and increasing numbers of congregations began offering at least one service on Sunday conducted in Spanish. But the difference between the faithful who speak Spanish and others in the parish is more than linguistic; there is a different style and ambience to Latin American Catholicism than there is to the various strands of European Catholicism that earlier Catholics brought with them into the South. Immigrants from Cuba who came to Florida beginning with Castro's coming to power not only added a distinct flavor to Catholic life there, but in their efforts to nourish an ethnic identity that was often intertwined with Catholic and Caribbean ways, also organized parishes and even a shrine in Miami dedicated to Our Lady of Charity that the historian Thomas Tweed has aptly dubbed "Our Lady of the Exile."[1] In this case, a statue of the Virgin was brought from Havana to Miami in 1961, a replica of a statue installed in a Havana shrine dedicated in 1927.

Catholics are not the only group that has had to deal with a growing Latino presence; nor are areas like Florida and Texas, with a long border shared with Mexico, the only places where a fresh style has enriched the region's religious culture. Many Latino immigrants are Protestant, often of a Pentecostal persuasion. They have in some cases formed their own congregations, but frequently have brought a vitality and diversity to established congregations associated with groups like the Church of God (Cleveland, Tennessee) and the Assemblies of God. Even mainline denominations, such as the United Methodist Church and the Episcopal Church, have begun funding missions to Spanish-speaking residents in the region's towns and cities. By the twenty-first century, Latino Americans were to be found throughout the South; for example, figures from the 2000 census showed that more than 40 percent of the residents of Whitfield County in northwest Georgia were of Latin-American heritage. Their impact on the region's public life extended well beyond the scores of Mexican restaurants that had broad appeal. The lower grades in the public schools in Whitfield County had a significant majority of students who came from Spanish-speaking families.

At the same time, however, by the last third of the twentieth century other stunning changes had come to the make-up of minority religions in the South. If in an earlier epoch Catholics and Jews had represented the groups with the greatest impact on public life, and if ethnic diversity within these communities had augmented the diversity they brought to Southern religious life, there was now a very different dimension to minority religious cultures. For the first time, Southern cities were boasting Hindu temples; Buddhist centers were appearing in places other than the usual college and university locales; and mosques were serving a rapidly growing number of Americans who identified with Islam, although only 0.9 percent of the Southern population in 2000 identified with one of the Asian traditions or with Islam. Here trends mirrored those of other regions, although the shift stood out all the more because these traditions were not simply variants of the dominant Christian heritage, but represented stark alternatives to the usual ways of being religious. As Christian congregations, both Protestant and Catholic, raced to extend their ministries to those whose first language was Spanish, they also realized that there were increasing numbers in their midst who spoke Korean, Vietnamese, and any number of other Asian languages. A few may already have identified with one of the Christian denominations, but many looked to different religious traditions to give meaning to their lives.

Much of this new diversity, particularly the stunning growth of Islam, Hinduism, and various expressions of Buddhism, received its impetus when Congress revamped immigration laws in 1965, the first significant overhaul in more than 40 years. Earlier quotas had favored immigration from northern and western Europe, thus assuring that the bulk of those entering the country would identify with some form of Christianity. After 1965, with ever larger numbers of immigrants coming from Asia and the Middle East, more and more immigrants identified with some form of Buddhism, Islam, or Hinduism. As well, a disproportionate number of new immigrants came to the South. For example, the Center for Immigration Studies reported that between 1990 and 1998, 25 counties in Georgia—more than in any other state—witnessed a 50 percent or greater rise in immigration. The largest numbers came from Mexico, India, Vietnam, and countries formerly part of the Soviet Union.

In 2000, a group of students at the University of North Carolina at Chapel Hill tracked more than 30 organized Buddhist centers flourishing in that state.[2] While some served an American convert clientele through meditation centers near universities or in larger urban areas, more and more served immigrant communities—Laotian, Thai, Vietnamese, and the like—from modest quarters such as former residences that were often unidentifiable to passersby as religious centers. Although the numbers belonging to these groups are still small, they exhibit a striking rate of increase. Those who draw primarily Asian-Americans to their activities are the most likely to go unnoticed.

Like ethnic parishes in Catholic circles generations earlier, they are not only religious centers helping sustain the faith brought from a land of origins, but they are also cultural centers committed to keeping alive the way of life that gave meaning to generations within the family heritage. This ethnic dimension also means that these centers are not likely to engage in even modest efforts to seek converts from among their Christian neighbors, who would not appreciate the cultural folkways that buttress the identity of first- and second-generation immigrants.

For the Buddhist tradition, this reticence to seek converts reflects something of a break with the past, for Buddhism in Asia historically has been a proselytizing religion. By contrast, centers that serve Vietnamese Americans, for example, are simply doing what immigrant religious communities have always done: helping adherents adjust to a cultural ethos dominated by evangelical Protestants who see Buddhists as potential converts to Christianity and keeping a religious and cultural identity viable. Those Buddhist centers that seem more intent on seeking converts tend to be those groups that already are made up of non-Asians. Even so, they tend to be less aggressive in the South, recognizing their minority status, as Roman Catholics and Jews recognized theirs generations earlier.

However, some who have converted to Buddhism have also cast Buddhist teaching in language more resonant with the surrounding Christian culture rather than in language more directly tied to Asian experience. For example, converts to Buddhism may be more inclined to speak of God in ways reminiscent of Protestant concepts in order to show parallels with a Buddhist approach, while Asian immigrant Buddhists would find such language baffling, if not inappropriate.

But the growing numbers of Buddhists in the South and the steadily increasing interest among European-Americans from the region in things Buddhist have also led to the establishment of retreat centers that appeal to both European-American and Asian-American practitioners. Among the more well-established such enterprises in the region is the Southern Dharma Retreat Center in Hot Springs, North Carolina, an hour's drive into the mountains from Asheville. This operation, with a Web site that provides links to many other Buddhist centers across the country, offers an array of programs reflecting several different Buddhist traditions and approaches; some even draw on other religious heritages, ranging from Christianity to Jainism, with the result that many who are not themselves practicing Buddhists come to the center to seek spiritual renewal.

If American converts to Buddhism have been less aggressive in proselytizing than one might expect, and if Asian immigrants have shied away from seeking converts to concentrate their energies on buttressing religious and cultural practices they brought with them from their homelands, Hindus living in the region come from a tradition that has never been inclined to proselytize.

At least from the time of the Harappan culture in the Indus River valley some 4,500 to 5,000 years ago, Hindu religious life has been inextricably linked to the culture of a particular place, the Indian subcontinent. The Hindu tradition for millennia has thus been intertwined with the culture of India. Consequently, Hindus did not need to seek converts. Even today, approximately 85 percent of the people in India identify themselves as Hindu. Although occasionally someone in India or elsewhere has converted to Hinduism over the years, the numbers are extraordinarily small. As with Judaism, Hinduism is a tradition into which one is born. It thus represents a way of life as much as a distinctive set of religious beliefs and practices. This profound interconnection between religion and culture by its very nature precludes the idea of actively working to gain converts.

This history of non-proselytizing means that the presence of Hindus in the public religious culture of the South at the dawn of the twenty-first century is even more likely to escape notice than the presence of other minority groups. But the American experience in general and the Southern context in particular have had an impact on the shape of Hindu expression in the region. Hindus are inveterate temple-builders, although Hindu devotion is based in the home, not in attending services at the temple. In India, because of the thousands of years of Hindu presence, temples seem to tourists to be omnipresent. Even so, for many in India, particularly men, going to the temple to make an offering or to receive a blessing with any regularity is far less vital than engaging in an act of devotion in one's home. Even modest homes have a space, ranging from a nook in a corner to an entire room, set apart for puja (worship). Because the temples seem always to have been there and signs of the plausibility of Hindu ways pervade all of public life in India, identification as a Hindu does not require the same commitment to temples and their work that it does in the United States, especially in the South, where there are few cultural props that buttress Hindu identity.

Like Buddhist centers that serve an immigrant constituency, Hindu temples have likewise become hubs for celebrating and sustaining Indian culture for families in a given area. Hindu immigrants are aware that Americanization may make it difficult for children born in the United States and educated in American schools to retain a distinctive Indian/Hindu cultural identity. Hence, those whose background and inclination would have made them less likely to be involved in temple life in India are more likely to be involved in the United States. Recognizing that the temple has become a symbolic center for both religious celebration and cultural affirmation, immigrant Hindu men have not only spearheaded either the construction of temples or the conversion of existing structures into temples, something that could be taken for granted in India, but they may well also invest more time and energy in supporting the priest and temple programs than they would in India.

Because the bulk of the Indian immigrant community in the South and elsewhere is still in the first and second generations, it remains to be seen whether the strategy of coming together to support and staff temples will serve to sustain both a Hindu and an Indian identity over the long haul. Regardless, it is clear that the minority status of Hinduism in the South has required Hindus to take a more public role in creating institutions that would promote such cultural and religious cohesion. Hence, whereas in India a temple may be dedicated only to one manifestation of the divine, usually one linked to Siva or Vishnu or their consorts, in the South (as in the United States in general) temples may house symbolic representations of more than one form of deity. In this way, temples draw a larger segment of the Indian-American community into their range of activities. Some temples in larger cities offer educational programs for children, where they can learn about both things Hindu and things Indian. In the Asian context, with subliminal supports to buttress Hindu identity pervading the larger culture, such programs are not needed.

As already noted, because Hindu devotion is traditionally home based rather than temple based, some analysts suggest that only a fraction of the Hindu immigrant population has associated itself with any of the growing number of temples across the South other than on those occasions marking important religious or cultural festivals. Some fear a steady erosion of a distinctive Hindu identity as succeeding generations become more Americanized and less conscious of distinctive Asian mores, even if those who are currently involved may evidence a greater degree of commitment to the institutions of immigrant Hinduism.

Here the Hindu immigrant experience in the South parallels the earlier experience of Jews who came into the region. At the same time, it will be interesting to see if Hindus in the South experience the same kind of intra-regional migration patterns as Southern Jews. In the nineteenth and earlier twentieth centuries, small

Jewish communities sprang up in many small cities and towns across the South—a function of the involvement of Jews in retailing. But the sons and daughters of Jewish store owners have, in the past couple of generations, increasingly left the small-town South. Southern Jews are now for the most part largely concentrated in Atlanta and a few other major urban centers. Hindus, too, are small-business operators, running motels and convenience stores across the South. Will their college-educated offspring likewise gravitate to urban centers? It seems likely that a critical mass of Hindus in such areas will serve as a barrier against complete assimilation.

The situation with Islam is at once both similar and more complex. It is similar because much of the growth of Islam in the South has also come in the years since 1965 when immigration laws were changed. But it is made more complex because by the mid-1960s, some Southerners of African-American descent were drawn to the Nation of Islam, or Black Muslims, a group with some ties to the larger Islamic tradition yet with distinctive qualities. It is made more complex also because other expressions of Islam, in the South as elsewhere, have had increasing appeal to African Americans in terms of converts.

Apart from African Americans, the growth of Islam in the South reflects the increasing presence of Muslim immigrants, not primarily converts. These immigrants come not only from Asian and Near Eastern countries. Especially since the 1970s, there has been as well a steady increase in Muslim immigrants from Africa, whose cultural heritage is rather different from that of the growing number of African-American converts to Islam. As well, most scholars of American Islam suggest that the Nation of Islam has lost some of its adherents since the mid-1960s, with many presumably affiliating with some other branch of Islam. Regardless, interaction between temples or mosques associated with the Nation of Islam and mosques associated with, for example, the Federation of Islamic Associations or the Islamic Society of North America has been minimal. Islam itself thus has many faces in the South.

Estimates of the number of Muslims vary widely, in part because some analysts believe that the majority of Muslims in the South and elsewhere are "unmosqued." That is, they are not affiliated with a mosque and therefore are not likely to attend weekly prayer services on Friday, although they may endeavor to participate in special festivals and other important occasions. Nevertheless, by the dawn of the twenty-first century virtually every Southern city of even modest size boasted two or three mosques identified with the Sunni tradition and perhaps one or more identified with the Nation of Islam.

Among world religions, Islam is growing at a rapid rate, thanks to its historic emphasis on proclaiming its teachings as the sole truth and aggressive tactics in pursuing potential converts. In the South, however, Muslims have been more muted in their endeavors to gain new adherents for the faith among those of European-American descent. On the one hand, practicing Muslims are aware that the dominant evangelical Protestant style of the surrounding culture is suspicious of Islam on religious and theological grounds, regarding the monotheistic claims of Islam as dangerous competition. The culture of the "Bible Belt" has seemed an antagonistic environment for building a strong and growing public presence for Islam. On the other hand, the popular image of Islam as being anti-American, a perception rooted in the Iran hostage crisis more than 20 years ago and fueled by the terrorist attacks of September 11, 2001, has led many Muslims, particularly those of Middle Eastern background, to fear reprisal should they endeavor to promote their faith aggressively. For many, issues of personal safety have muted the historic mandate to spread the truth of Allah.

As with other immigrant communities, though, Islam has gained some adherents when Muslim men have married women, some from evangelical Protestant Christian backgrounds, who have in turn become converts. Indeed, white Southerners who came into the ranks of Islam tended to be women who entered the faith because they married Muslim men. Even in the South, Muslim women could often be identified readily because of their wearing a distinctive head covering. Few, however, appear in the burqa that covers the entire body and is required in public for women in countries where the Shi'ite tradition of Islam predominates.

The burgeoning presence of Muslims, Hindus, and Buddhists in southern religious culture may represent the most visible feature of minority religious life in the twenty-first century. There are, however, at least two other dimensions of minority religious culture that merit discussion and have left their mark on the region's larger religious culture. One centers around the styles associated with the religious culture of the Appalachian mountain region. The other revolves around the large number of movements, small in the number of adherents when compared with evangelical Protestantism, that have distinctive religious ways that often reflect a particular ethnic heritage.

Perhaps the most widely known and most misunderstood religious style associated with Appalachian religious culture is the practice of serpent handling. First documented in the Chattanooga area early in the twentieth century, serpent handling is now found throughout the Southern Appalachian mountain region, although the number of practitioners remains small. Indeed, media attention to serpent handling, often the result of the death of someone bitten during worship, has no doubt made the practice appear more widespread than it actually is and has kept it in public view. Handlers base their beliefs on a passage in the Gospel of Mark: "And these signs shall follow them that believe....They shall take up serpents; and if they drink any deadly thing, it shall not hurt them; they shall lay hands on the sick, and they shall recover." (Mark 16:17-18, KJV)

Popular perception mistakenly assumes that practitioners are persons of lower income levels, lacking significant formal education. By the twenty-first century it was clear that most practitioners came from families in which handling had been part of religious life for three or more generations, regardless of socio-economic and educational background. It is also the case that most individuals born to families where handling is practiced do not themselves become handlers. Among these families there remains a powerful sense of the presence of the supernatural in daily life and an abiding conviction that the faithful were called to follow biblical injunctions, such as those in the passage from Mark cited above. The sense of the supernatural had deep roots in the mountain culture of Appalachia, where at one time life was lived close to the land and natural forces had a dynamism that surpassed anything humans could muster.

Attempts to outlaw serpent handling on the grounds that the practice undermined the general welfare have proved unsuccessful but have kept the practice in public consciousness. Practitioners neither seek converts nor call attention to their pursuit of a mountain holiness. Most would willingly forsake the public attention that comes when someone dies as a result of being bitten, for they see the larger society as an alien realm, by its very character hostile to the truths of faith. Yet the practice endures, bolstered in part by the relative geographical isolation of most congregations where handling is integral to worship and also by the conviction that only a few will ultimately heed the commands of the gospel regarding the signs of authentic faith.

At the same time, the great majority of those living in the mountains of Appalachian are not serpent handlers. Rather, their religious styles reflect both the strands of Holiness that remain an undercurrent among many Southern evangelical Protestants, with an emphasis on personal moral behavior, and also remnants of a Calvinism stretching back to the first Scots-Irish migrants into the mountains in the later eighteenth and early nineteenth centuries that emphasizes the overwhelming providential power of God in controlling human affairs.

Finally, there are countless groups, many with a distinctive ethnic cast, that augment the public presence of religion in the South. The Greek Orthodox Church, for example, traces its heritage in the South to the arrival of immigrants from the Mediterranean area in St. Augustine, Florida, in 1768. By the time of the major wave of Greek Orthodox immigration between 1890 and the outbreak of World War I, enclaves had also been established in other cities in Florida and also in places like New Orleans, Atlanta, and Charlotte. At the dawn of the twenty-first century, Florida was still home to nearly half the parishes in the Diocese of Atlanta, which embraces churches in North

Carolina, South Carolina, Georgia, Florida, Alabama, Mississippi, Louisiana, and part of Tennessee.[3]

In some ways, the story of the Greek Orthodox is similar to that of Judaism in the South, for both groups have confronted high levels of intermarriage that threaten to erode abiding commitment to a distinct religious tradition. Yet both have also flourished, in part by celebrating ethnic dimensions linked to their respective religious traditions. For example, in Greenville, South Carolina, an annual Greek festival, organized through the church, attracts hundreds of non-Greek and non-Orthodox Christians to its numerous cultural activities, thus serving as a public reminder of the religious diversity that prevails in the urban South. Such festivals can be found in Greek Orthodox communities throughout America.

More recently, immigrants from the Caribbean have brought with them the religion of Santeria, literally the "way of the Saints." Representing a fusion of styles associated with Roman Catholicism that came with the Conquistadors of the Age of Exploration and Discovery, tribal religions carried by Africans brought to the Caribbean as slaves, and indigenous religious ways, Santeria represents another minority religious culture for which media attention has made its public presence more prominent than numbers warrant. In the case of Santeria, the practice of animal sacrifice, particularly of chickens, as part of a religious ritual led to court cases to determine whether municipalities could outlaw the practice.

Some wanted it banned presumably because of health and sanitary concerns. Others believed the practice was protected by the First Amendment guarantee of free exercise of religion. Not until the U.S. Supreme Court ruled that in this case such sacrifice was a legitimate religious act were practitioners of Santeria free to pursue their religion without threat of persecution and legal action. Yet the practice itself cannot be separated from the intertwining of Catholic, African, and Caribbean cultures that immigrants brought with them. Ethnicity once again becomes a means of preserving a minority presence that flourishes on the margins of the dominant Southern evangelical Protestant culture.

One other group for whom ethnicity is vital, albeit in a rather different way, warrants mention. The Church of Jesus Christ of Latter-day Saints, better known as the Mormons, have had a presence in the South almost from the time Joseph Smith gathered his first followers in 1830, although in 2000 only 0.5 percent of Southerners identified themselves as Mormons. Prior to the Civil War, the Mormons experienced relatively modest success in efforts to bring their message of the post-resurrection appearance of Christ to the native peoples of the Americas. Yet they remained steadfast in their conviction that the faithful constituted a new people of God, an ethnic community based on belief and practice rather than on conditions of birth. Particularly because of their acceptance of the

Book of Mormon and other religious documents as sacred texts alongside the Bible, Mormons frequently experienced suspicion and hostility at the hands of evangelical Protestants who insisted that the Bible alone was the authoritative Word of God. As a result, many drawn to the Mormons joined fellow believers in Utah and elsewhere in the West where Mormon ways dominated public life much the way evangelical Protestantism seemed to dominate public life in the South.

However, in the decades since the close of World War II, the Mormons have experienced a resurgence in the South, paralleling a rapid rate of growth elsewhere in the United States. Proclaiming their truth through aggressive door-to-door evangelizing, presenting their views as consonant with the Protestant Christianity that has for generations set the tone for Southern religious life, and forming the tight-knit congregations that allow analysts to view them as functionally equivalent to an ethic community, the Mormons are establishing a solid niche in the public religious culture of the South. The increasing acceptance of Mormon ways may also reflect the Mormons' commitment to traditional nuclear families and generally con- servative political positions that are resonant with much of white Southern thinking.

The South may still be the Bible Belt in the popular mind, but it also has a long history of religious diversity. Minority religions have developed tactics for survival in the midst of a sometimes hostile culture surrounding them. Sometimes maintaining a public presence has resulted from adapting to the dominant style of the larger culture, as in the way nineteenth century Southern Catholics tended to mirror the support for maintaining chattel slavery common among most white evangelical Protestants. Sometimes the impact on public life has come through clustering in enclaves where a minority tradition becomes almost a majority, as the number of Churches of Christ adherents in parts of Texas and East Tennessee (often near colleges and schools) suggests. Other times, maintaining a sense of isolation from the larger culture, as with Appalachian serpent handlers, or emphasizing ties to particular ethnic communities, as with the Greek Orthodox, have buttressed efforts of minority groups not only to survive but to flourish. If evangelical Protestant ways have captured the popular imagination, under- currents of religious diversity have enhanced the influence of religion on the shared public life of those who live in the South.

At the same time, though, some sociologists have pointed out another trend. If a higher proportion of Southerners claims a formal religious identity, whether with one of the dominant Protestant groups or one of the countless minority movements, than do Americans in other regions, the proportion of Southerners classified as "unchurched" or without formal religious affiliation is approaching the national average. Although the public culture of the South still reflects a rich religious history with an evangelical Protestant stamp, the growing numbers of those who eschew a formal religious identity will add to the complex ways that the contours of public life disclose a profound religious presence.

Endnotes

1 See Thomas A. Tweed, *Our Lady of the Exile: Diaspora Religion at a Cuban Catholic Shrine in Miami* (New York: Oxford University Press, 1997).

2 Thomas A. Tweed and the Buddhism in North Carolina Project, *Buddhism and Barbecue: A Guide to Buddhist Temples in North Carolina* (Chapel Hill, NC: Buddhism in North Carolina Project, University of North Carolina, 2001).

3 Perhaps because in 2000, Greek Orthodox adherents accounted for only 0.3 percent of the Southern population, there is no full-length account of their distinct story as a minority religious community in the region.

Chapter Six

The Peripheral South: Florida and Appalachia

Samuel S. Hill

A folklorist colleague had spent many hours attending services at a Primitive Baptist church in southern Appalachia. He took pains to expend the time and energy to become acquainted with those attending in the interest of establishing genuine friendship. Intending from the beginning to film their services, he bided his time before requesting their permission to do so. When he did, the elder in charge, doubts about the trustworthiness of the visitor having been dispelled, responded with something like, "I reckon so," but went on to insist that no one who saw the videotape was ever to be pressured to agree with what they saw of the services conducted in the mountain church.

In reporting this story, the participant/observer-visitor could only declare that James Madison lives. These Appalachian folk of deep conviction were honoring the First Amendment to the letter—and better, in full spirit.

Several hundred miles closer to the Equator and much nearer sea level, in Florida, a prominent state political leader, upon learning in a conversation that I was a scholar interested in the religious life of the state, observed that "Florida is a hedonistic state, but it is far from unreligious."

Just a glance at the map enables one to realize that both the Appalachian region and the Sunshine State somehow have to be included in the South (in the language of this study, the South Atlantic). But they require treatment as "peripheral" to the region, even more culturally than topographically. In a study of religion in public life, as on so many other topics, "the South" stands out as a region, a fact reinforced by such fine definition as to suggest that the region can have a periphery. Other American regions are less definitively regional to start with, one consequence being that they can hardly be regarded as having peripheries. That designation really makes little sense when applied to, say, New England or the Midwest. What areas would qualify—or tolerate ascription--as peripheral to New England or the Midwest?

Some such reference to "outlying" appendages to Dixie has been common for some time. But in a recent study Earl and Merle Black, scholars of American political life, have applied the category to some of the region's northern, not Deep South (and not only the "border") states.[1] As we seek here to penetrate the relation of religion to the public life in the South Atlantic, the Appalachians and the state of Florida don't fit that placement very neatly—but they do deserve our attention and they demand treatment in sharp focus. They have more in common with the South than with any other region, to be sure, yet they hardly comprise a region, being about as different from each other as Oregon is from Massachusetts. Their being unclassifiable together or, also significantly, as part of the broader South, is the impetus for this chapter. In the process of doing so, we inevitably reflect on the traits of that much larger territory.

An inquiry into public life may be launched by referring to the political scene, noting that Appalachia has long been predominantly Republican while Florida has recently attained significant (not majority) affiliation with that party, most consistently within its native white male population. The positions of Appalachian Republicans and Florida Republicans have different historical roots and differ appreciably. What is of concern to many in one may not occupy much attention in the other. The Appalachian population may be said to owe its party preference to the area's historic value of "we'll mind our own business," of resisting outside intervention in their lives, private or public, grounded in what has been termed "Jeffersonian yeomanry." Indeed, one university in the areas presents as its mascot—or icon—the head of a mountaineer, with a corncob pipe in his mouth and chin whiskers—"Josef," meaning, "do it yosef." This value, usually associated with Republican Party philosophy, is embraced by many "old-timers" and is supplemented by the rather standard economic conservatism of the business community in the high country towns.

By contrast, the Florida Republican make-up owes a great deal to three sources, all of fairly recent origin:

- the migration of conservatives from historically GOP constituencies in northern states
- issues of foreign policy on the part of Caribbean migrants who have entered the state in the last three or four decades, especially anti-Castro Cuban-Americans
- the switching of many long-time state residents from Democratic to Republican Party.

Yet, taking superficial note of GOP strength within the two populations is only a way of starting to investigate religion in the public life of each and both. It is necessary to examine each population in some depth, then compare them and indicate something of the ways in which these "peripherals" differ from the South as a whole.

Appalachia

The Appalachian Regional Commission, a U.S.-government designated agency, covers a huge expanse that extends from western New York state southwest to northeastern Alabama. Glancing at a relief map of the eastern United States affords a pretty accurate picture. This chapter treats southwestern West Virginia, eastern Kentucky, southwest Virginia, northwest North Carolina, eastern Tennessee, and northern Georgia—the "southern highlands," often so called. This large area is sometimes further subdivided into central and southern Appalachia, and not without good reason. The human stock, economic resources, topography, and religious heritage all differ considerably between southwestern West Virginia and eastern Kentucky on one hand and southeast Tennessee and northern Georgia on the other.

The best-known and classic southern Appalachian religious image is the small mountain church, meeting in a plain building, likely Baptist or Holiness (not to be confused with Pentecostal); led by male elders who preach sermons directly inspired by the Spirit—without notes and usually without preparation; with lined-singing that generates haunting sounds; from which class distinction is absent, in which men and women often sit apart; and where worldly behavior and opinions are deplored in favor of the Bible's eternal truth and call to righteous living. The simplicity of the structure, people, and service impresses any visitor and produces a variety of responses. There is no mistaking this kind of event with any other church gathering in America.

Emma Bell Miles, who migrated to southeast Tennessee in the early twentieth century, captured this scene well when she pointed to two paradoxes, one involving narrow creeds and broad friendship, the other plainness commingled with beauty and grace. She wrote of the "bullheaded contrariness of the preaching and believing" and observed, startlingly, that prayer is infrequently offered for the people's temporal benefit.[2] Nothing ordinary about the church life is conveyed by this image; its like is nowhere else to be found, at least as a general phenomenon.

Grasping the attitude of the mountain church toward the action of engaging in organization sheds light on both the religious and the political perspectives of the group. This old indigenous form of congregational life, still frequently found in the southern highlands, prefers the local unit to any organized forms. Typically these churches are not denominationally affiliated. While the church names of many may be familiar—Baptist, Pentecostal, Holiness, Brethren—they do not imply affiliation with national or regional bodies. The title of one recent study of such groups—*Local Baptists, Local Politics*—is revealing; and the sentiment is not limited to that family of churches.

This spirit carries over to the political attitudes of people so minded about church life. The more connected a congregation is to a wider fellowship, the more likely it is to be directly involved in public politics. Those churches without affiliation are highly unlikely to engage, as churches, or even as individual members, in political causes, rallies, voting campaigns, and lobbying. Generally, they do not organize for social action.

Why? At base, this perspective rests in their localism with respect to both political and religious structures. The historian John Alexander Williams concludes that in the political arena county government is primary, well outweighing both state and regional considerations and identifications. This notion of public leadership amounts to a "federated oligarchy" in his terms.[3] If we follow Daniel Elazar's delineation of types of political culture, we find that life in Appalachia belongs to "traditionalist political culture." That is, its concern is to maintain existing social order, holding on to the incumbent leaders and values. Its public life does not fall into either the "moralistic political culture," seeking to enlist public interest or emphasizing citizen participation, or into "individualistic political culture," with its multiplicity of views.[4]

On the religious front, a church is not The Church in any sense, it is a congregation of people meeting to worship and learn how to live. Not suitably characterized as provincial, its mission has to do with preserving their communities as they are—or intend to be. Excessive worldliness is to be bridled, strong families are to be developed. In Clifford Grammich's terms, they aim to foster a single good, that of "the local church authority and community."[5] This is indeed a part of the "traditionalist political culture."

Many of these churches stand foursquare against the mission causes that animate so many denominations all around them, including those that dominate the broader South, namely, the evangelization of the world. That conviction has to do with their Calvinist theology—God will save those he has chosen to save in His own ways according to His sovereign schedule—but also it is bound up with their focused, prescribed understanding of the church's mission just stated, constraining worldly behavior and building strong families (which does not add up to full-throated Calvinism).

Grammich's work led him to conclude that, in national political terms, they are friendlier to the specific-goal dedication of populist movements than to Progressivism's commitment to general reforms. Williams bolsters this contention by referring to the planting of Kingsport, Tennessee, as a new town by

Eastman Kodak in the 1920s. Such "progressive planning ideals" were "the exception rather than the rule among Appalachia's new towns."[6]

This type of congregations is numerous in the southern highlands, especially in the rural areas and in small towns. Yet, famous as their reported type of mountaineer is—sometimes reduced to a stereotype, they belong to a society that may be said to contain three kinds of human culture. One such breakdown of the larger population lists them this way: town folk, big road folk, and hollow ("holler") folk. (Another cataloguing sees them as: town and city, substantial farmers, and branchwater mountaineers.) The "hollow folk," whose views of religion in public life we are now considering, have crafted a distinctive form of Christian ethical response to the world in which they live.

Loyal Jones, the Berea College scholar of mountain life, regards "lingering Calvinism" as the single most distinguishing trait of that people's philosophy of life. He notes five characteristics:
- humility and modesty
- independence
- personalism
- "familism"
- reluctance to confront others

People so formed are not forward or pushy, and they are given to downplaying their own ability and accomplishments. They resist being told what to do, acting out of their own convictions, subject to no other authority, including that of ministers. Their understanding of the Christian message is personal, not abstract but down-to-earth. The family is society's basic unit, including the extended family. While patriarchal, it recognizes women's influence, in fact it helps generate that influence. Finally, the weakness of others is treated with tolerance; the imperfections of all people are realized. This attitude extends to disinterest in proselytizing. A society—and culture—shaped by those qualities is dramatically set off from any general American profile.[7]

It is justifiable to think of this Appalachian religious culture as conservative, but use of that label requires that it be differentiated from any and all other expressions of conservatism in America, emphatically religious conservatism as that title is applied in contemporary American life. This is not the "Religious Right"—very far from it. Nor does it manifest any semblance of libertarianism. What is practiced is a religious ethic of personal righteousness and community uprightness.

We should observe that there is a sharp divergence from historic Calvinism as lived out in John Calvin's Geneva and colonial New England to this variety of that theological tradition. The classic "Christ the Transformer of Culture" model, which characterizes Calvinism most often, simply does not apply to these southern highlanders. They do not set out to transform the world, either society or church. Instead, godly animation is meant to lead to congregational, community, family, and personal integrity of behavior and to acceptance of others with respect and the absence of a judgmental spirit. In specific, the agenda does not include homosexuality and abortion; it does not even list "winning others to Christ" as the responsibility of Christians. Thus, this expression of religion in public life diverges from Calvin's Geneva, from the Christian Coalition, and from a Southern Baptist evangelistic crusade.

But the story is more textured than this, partly because the "hollow people" do not exhaust this region's population. A brief review of southern Appalachia's social history helps enlarge understanding. It has been noted that the region's party of choice has for some time been Republican. Yet West Virginia, the only state wholly classified as Appalachian, is heavily Democratic. Moreover, a major feature of Lyndon Johnson's Great Society was the war on poverty of the 1960s, whose premier battleground was southern Appalachia.

Turning back to the nineteenth century, it is important to remember how different the highlands' economy, and its concomitant social structure, was from that of the lowland and piedmont South. Plantations made up no part of the highland way of life. The earth served as the major resource for making a living, to be sure, but farming occurred on a small scale, raising food for family needs, not for the production of cash crops.

That earth was something else in addition, the home of natural resources to be extracted. Coal mining comprised much of the economic income of the region for a century from the mid-nineteenth century, and also contributed heavily to its social structure. Another earth-derived industry, timbering, ranked second in the mountain economy. It is worth noting that before 1900 Appalachia, especially western Pennsylvania and northern West Virginia, was the world's major producer of oil and gas. But resource extraction was not the only enterprise for this society and economy. Appalachian yeomanry resisted plantation capitalism, but it could not resist industrial capitalism. There were more "company towns" in Appalachia than anywhere in the nation.

Thus this sub-region derives from different historical sources and conditions than the heartland southern states that were, owing to their Democratic Party affiliation, properly dubbed "the solid South." Most of the mountain people allied with the Union in the Civil War, standing in marked contrast to the agricultural belt to the east and the west alike. African Americans were present in Appalachia, but in much smaller proportions than nearby states or even counties in the same state. Historical study reveals that, while the mountain whites were motivated more by pragmatic considerations than by idealism, they lived alongside black people with a relative lack of hostility.

Mountain Republicans generally maintained that black people had the basic right to vote, even if they were not really viewed as equals and were rarely permitted to run for office. While some lynching occurred in the mountain areas (reflecting a concern with social control), there was much support for universal suffrage. From these conditions there emerged a "coalition of blacks and mountain whites in the Republican Party." Gordon B. McKinney concludes that this coalition was "a powerful force" in five states: Kentucky, West Virginia, Tennessee, Virginia, and North Carolina. In 1900, blacks comprised 7.37 percent of the total population in the mountain counties of those five states.[8]

For their part, Earl and Merle Black declare that race has not ceased to be a factor that explains southern public life. The Solid South virtually owed its existence to the race factor—at least to its ramifications and implications. The decline of that South's Democratic Party over the past 40 years and the rise of the Republican Party are attributable in no small part to federal policies regarding race as promulgated during the Civil Rights era. Many Southerners reasoned that "they had not left their party, their party had left them," and were led to do something about that fact. This has been particularly true of native white men in the South. Within that portion of the electorate, 62 percent are "core Republicans," against only 18 percent who are "core Democrats." (Among migrant white men, 44 percent are core Republicans and 31 percent are core Democrats.) While the "race factor" is far from synonymous with racism, it retains a measure of influence over southern opinion.[9]

Highlighting the partisan distinctions between the Appalachian population from the Civil War forward with that of the broader South from the same era until the demise of the Solid South reminds us once more of the "peripheral" relation of that mountain culture, political and beyond. Moving to the recent past and the present, we see more apparent than real congruity between Republicanism within the mountain population and outside it.

True enough, a vote is a vote, and a party registration is a party registration. But the national Republican Party is obliged to expand, or adjust, its message to be effective with a variety of registrants. Native white men are more conservative on several moral issues than migrant men, by 50 percent to 10 percent. It is not much of a stretch to infer that the mountain voters have a good deal more in common with the "migrants" than with the "natives." Those issues include affirmative action, abortion, and attitudes toward homosexual people. There can be little doubt, however, that on one issue the natives and the mountaineers are as one, namely, regard for the Bible as literal truth. Indeed, Appalachian people score higher on that issue than native white men.

While identifying the voting patterns and moral positions of Appalachian residents is a tenuous process—they live in certain counties of the several states and sometimes in certain parts of those counties, there are exit poll data from Appalachian portions of Georgia, Kentucky, Tennessee, West Virginia, and North Carolina for the 2000 presidential election. The overall vote was 54.7 percent for Bush and 42.7 percent for Gore. Among evangelical voters, the spread was 75.1 percent to 22.4 percent. In the case of mainline Protestant voters, 50.2 percent cast their ballots for Gore and 49.3 percent for Bush.

Party affiliation places Republicans first among evangelicals with 50.1 percent. Overall, however, a larger percentage are Democratic than Republican by 40.8 percent to 36.7, which shows the variety of peoples living in that large span of territory from West Virginia to Georgia. Similar complexity appears in other aspects of the voting public, with one figure of special interest: When asked about "government activism," 48.6 percent of mainline Protestant voters prefer "less."[10]

Some may wonder then why, with liberal, Democratic Party social programs expending vast resources on Appalachia from the early 1960s for more than a decade, the region did not switch its loyalty to that party. The historian Richard B. Drake points to the popularity of the GOP from 1910 to 1925, and the heavy support it received in the election of 1932. Then the Great Depression made a political impact. For the next 40 years, the Democratic Party fared better. Its leadership, from presidents Franklin Roosevelt and Lyndon Johnson to several state governors and progressives such as W. D. Weatherford of Berea College and Blue Ridge Assembly fame, brought about developments and changes that increased Democratic strength.

There was quite a list of achievements. The Civil Conservation Corps, Works Progress Administration, National Youth Administration, Agricultural Adjustment Administration, National Industrial Recovery Act, and the Tennessee Valley Authority all came out of the New Deal. The nation's nuclear arms enterprise was centered in Oak Ridge, Tennessee, a town that lay on the western reaches of the mountain culture.

Labor unions, spiritually aligned with the Democrats, gained strength, especially the Congress of Industrial Organizations (CIO) and the United Mine Workers (UMW). Late in this season of federal activity, the identification of John Kennedy with West Virginia, and the economic/social philosophies of John Kenneth Galbraith, Michael Harrington, and the eastern Kentucky attorney Harry Caudill enjoyed a wide readership and direct application to the prevailing social conditions. Poverty joined racial discrimination as causes inspiring action from the outside (though it's sobering to remember that the nation's capital is located only a few dozen miles from the eastern stretches of Appalachia).

Despite this, Democratic Party strengthening did not amount to a takeover. The mountain peoples remained predominantly Republican. The "war on poverty" never gained much popularity within the area itself. President Nixon's "coming out" in 1979, following his resignation from office and several years of privacy, was staged dramatically and appropriately in eastern Kentucky's Leslie County. Then, the mountain precincts went heavily for Ronald Reagan in 1980. For the rest of the century, welfare state concerns retreated. Any suggestion that the Appalachian culture would alter its natural preference for government "that governs least" in the face of massive intervention by federal and state programs is simply wide of the facts. Its people persisted in wanting to be left alone.

How precisely this society's attitudes are correlated with the widely held Calvinistic theology of much of the population is impossible to determine. But surely religion is one of the "factors," along with the political, economic, racial, and social. At home, so to speak, beliefs and values associated with religious faith add significance. They loom as especially distinctive when compared with the prevailing popular evangelical faith of the majority churches often not so far away in the lowlands—"off," as the common mountain expression has it.

The large part of the evangelical Protestant community that is so dominant in the southern region is driven by the evangelistic mandate to convert the world, one sinner at a time. Appalachia throbs to a different cadence.[11] Old-line Calvinism trusts the Almighty to redeem those He has chosen to redeem, according to His own schedule and plan. No human action can turn this trick. Incidentally, more than a few of the faithful who attend services, some for many decades, are not members, and so have not been baptized, because they are awaiting the Lord's call to them. Living in such a state is no occasion for regret or fear, however; rather it is a mark of their conviction that the Lord is fully in charge and is to be trusted. They live with hope; better, they live in hope.

The huge number of churches across "the Southland" from Virginia to Texas that regard conversion as a (or even the) primary ministry affirm spiritual suste-nance, for certain; but they are not sustained by hope. While "hope" is certainly a category of Christian meaning in their lexicon, the defining impulse is urgency, resulting in some impatience to reach an attainable goal. There is a profound difference between Appalachian Calvinism and what may be termed a Southern conversionist evangelicalism.

The operative category beneath this difference is mystery. For mountain Calvinists, mystery pertains not merely to the fact of God's love for sinful humanity—"Why should He love me so?"—but extends even to how, when, and with whom He acts. Only God is in charge, only His acts are effective, only His schedule pertains. This means that people are left with hope and trust; that is *all* they have—not agency, not guarantees, not crusades to make things happen. But "all" in this case implies no deprivation whatsoever. When you have God, what else matters in the least? One can almost hear them reason: Does it make any sense for me to put trust in myself, my own actions, my own righteousness? Not a chance. Instead, one trusts, waits, has every confidence. Thus Mystery is the shape of reality and it is the occasion for full confidence. Their way of godliness does not generate activity in the interest of achievement.

Communication of this meaning of mystery cannot be expected to transpire between the mountain Calvinist people and the evangelism-impelled spirit and crusades of many churches in the broader South. For those thousands of churches and millions of adherents, hope belongs in a different frame of Christian meaning. While Appalachian Calvinists wait in hope, never anxious and always assured (whenever they are believing authentically), evangelistic Baptists, Methodists, Pentecostals, and "Jesus people" are geared to go, active and aggressive, mobilizing their mighty forces for the saving of every person everywhere.

Southern conversionist evangelicalism vibrates with urgency and impatience as it bends every effort to realize an achievable goal. Delay in attaining success is seen as failure. Life's supreme goal is to replace "lostness," that is, life without God and without hope, with assurance, the certainty that in the conversion experience one has passed "from death to life." This means that assurance has shifted from the general category of hope and trust to the claim of virtual certainty.

The contrast between the mystery-hope-trust nexus of the mountain folk and the aggressive, results-driven, achieving-the-goal pace of Southern conversionist evangelicalism could hardly be sharper. The great German sociologist Max Weber, who made one brief visit to the southern highlands in 1904, may well have been affected by what he glimpsed there. At any rate, he wrote powerfully of the demystification, the disenchantment, of the world that the modern Enlightenment wrought in philosophy and science—what might be called the mathematicization of Western culture. Viewed through these lenses, traditional Appalachian faith has opted for the classic walk of poets and adventurers, trusting trust and regarding God's government of the world as known to Him and not deducible by human categories. On this showing the conversionist evangelicals, best identified by the Southern Baptist Convention, has "bought into" modernity with great enthusiasm—and predictable success.

But mountain religion needs to be seen as something quite other than quaint. Its record stands a chance of living up to authenticity, of resisting capitulation to "the world" in favor of a worldview grounded in the conviction that God's Spirit "enchants" and "mystifies" life, material and human. No wonder the music one hears in the singing and, no less, in the preaching in mountain churches has it a haunting quality. As for the notorious snake (or, more properly, serpent) handling engaged in by perhaps 2,500 of the upland faithful, it shows the seemingly detached, even too-magisterial-to-be-engaged Calvinist high God of heaven hovering near enough through Word and sacramental presence to let thirsty human souls drink of His presence and power.[12] The deep longing for the slaking of that thirst takes extreme form with the handlers, but far more often shows through in Appalachia in prayer, worship, the eager reading of Holy Scripture, and the sweet fellowship believers share with one another.

Religious membership statistics tell only part of the Appalachian story. According to the North American Religion Atlas (NARA), in most of the mountain counties of the South the Southern Baptist Convention is the largest denomination, with the United Methodist Church also prominent. In addition, in several mountain counties more conservative denominations such as the Assemblies of God, the Pentecostal Holiness Church, and the Church of God (Cleveland, Tennessee) register a numerical predominance rarely matched in lowland counties. While this portrait of the religious demography of Appalachia is instructive, it misses a lot.

NARA relies for the most part on the membership statistics of national religious bodies, but many churches in Appalachia possess no larger organizational affiliation; moreover, there are many believers (in hope) in Appalachia who are not baptized members of any church. (Indeed, this may help explain why such a small proportion of Southerners self identify as religiously unaffiliated, relative to the number of Southerners who show up on the NARA data as not belonging to a religious organization.[13])

There really is a sense in which "figures do lie" when the goal is to account for religious life in Appalachia. Dramatic evidence of this can be seen by comparing West Virginia, the one state located entirely within Appalachia, with Mississippi, a Deep South state with no Appalachian counties. According to NARA, Mississippi has the lowest percentage of religiously unaffiliated (15.1 percent) in the South and West Virginia the highest (60 percent). In the American Religious Identification Survey (ARIS), which measures self identification, the number of Mississippians who say they have no religious affiliation is 7 percent—roughly half the NARA percentage (as in most of the rest of the country). But in West Virginia, ARIS found that only 13 percent of West Virginians reported no religious affiliation—not much more than one-fifth of the NARA percentage in the Mountain State. It can hardly be doubted that a disproportionately large number of West Virginians (and, by extension, Appalachian folk generally) go to churches that simply are not counted in the NARA database.

The implications of these findings and interpretations, taken together, show how relatively little may be learned about religion in public life within the Appalachian population by simple encounter with religious membership data. However, there is an intriguing dimension on the positive side. A substantial percentage of mountain people carry out their lives quite privately. Their contexts are the family, nuclear and extended, their local communities, and the community church. "Religion in public life" has greater pertinence to American cities and towns and to rural areas more integrated into the cultural mainstream than to the more introverted life framework of the southern highlands. By learning that this project's theme does not apply very directly to Appalachia we learn that religion in people's lives may occupy another province than involvement in public agencies and responsibilities.

Florida

There is no Florida that takes the form of any kind of public unity. That fact may tempt discouragement that the topic of religion in public life there is susceptible to investigation. The attempt by the political scientists Kenneth Wald and Richard Scher to explain that condition, fortunately, provides plenty of insight to give assurance that it is possible to acquire some understanding: they describe the state as "less a cohesive political community than a collection of media markets."[14]

Unlike California, Florida bears the marks of a strong regional imprint, the South, where evangelical Protestantism long ago broke the ground for high-intensity religious life. Unlike Iowa, where religious life is also pervasive and widely shared, in Florida the prominent forms are not quiet, rather they are aggressive.

Breaking that description down, it is possible to say that, in both political makeup and religious identification, the state has become highly diverse, now approximating the type of political culture that Daniel Elazar calls individualistic. When Elazar formulated this category in 1984, the two main examples he saw were Iowa and California—states where diversity was so prevalent that no general patterns could be established. Two decades later, the conclusion can be reached that Florida (and perhaps other states as well) has joined those two. Yet a welter of forces and influences seems to make Florida unique among all the states, no matter what their political type.

By this reasoning, the old pattern of moral traditionalism of the South, while it remains influential in Florida, is now having to share the public stage with the individualistic political culture. A confrontation results: between the moralists' concern to enlist citizens' general interest, thus to turn particular moral positions into public policy, and individualism's contrasting perspective, the virtual necessity of tolerance, of live and let live, leading to the logical conclusion that the moralists should tamp down their particularity. In the public life of Florida no change is automatic and no outcome is predictable.

Data certify that, first, diversity is higher in Florida than in the South generally and, second, that religious affiliation is lower there than in the South treated as a region. The second fact is not, however, to be taken as indicative of a state with a weak religious sector. Its vaunted hedonistic lifestyle—sun and sand, swimming and fishing—has not led to a secularist positioning, secularism having nothing like the hold that it has on the states of the West Coast. Florida is by no means an elongated version of Las Vegas, where "what happens here stays here."

This condition was true before the appearance of the Religious Right about 1980. While that movement's role in the state must be examined, it must also be noted up front that that coalition of forces has not wrested control of Florida's political, moral, or religious life. Just the same, there is no getting around the impact it has registered on the state's culture. Wald and Scher have called attention to its power: "[T]he movement has unleashed a spirit of religiosity that has permeated the fabric of politics in the state."[15] The political leader quoted at the beginning of this chapter is surely correct: "Florida may be hedonistic, but it is far from unreligious." The old sociological axiom that the ways of modern thinking inevitably lead to the displacement of traditional religion has no currency in Florida. There is not a state culture like it.

The Sunshine State lacks a "core culture." No particular place is the state culture's "capital city." The forces that blow through the state seem consistently to be centrifugal. No one portion of the state dominates, nor any of the large metropolitan clusters, politically or in point of taste or style. Unlike the situation in many states, where one newspaper sets the tone and influences public opinion, no such newspaper exists in Florida. Instead, there are several influential papers based in the larger cities, more of them liberal-leaning than clearly conservative. Neither political party holds a lock on the population. Party registration stands close to 50-50. The governorship lately has seemed almost to rotate between the parties. The United States Senate seats belong to state leaders who may be Republican and may be Democratic; at this writing they were split. It is the case that the Congressional delegation and the make-up of the state legislature have become solidly Republican and are apt to remain that way for some time. Presidential elections, however, are up for grabs.

All things considered, Florida is more conservative than liberal, with the GOP slightly in the lead. But candidates enter races cocksure of winning at their peril, with of course exceptions in districts that are comfortably associated with one of the parties. The slightly larger Republican Party faces division within its ranks, with economic and pragmatic conservatives (among them Governor Jeb Bush) proving to be the more effective long term than moral conservatives. Democrats also struggle to achieve party unity. The company of true liberals is small and ineffective on any statewide basis (although it makes a difference in some communities).

The African-American vote in Florida is overwhelmingly Democratic. In the 2000 presidential election the totals showed 95.3 percent of blacks voting for Gore, 4.7 percent for Bush. This surpasses the 91 percent to 8 percent margin in the South at large. In the governor's race in 2002, however, the Democratic

Party had to contend with a candidate of and from the black electorate who ran to protest his people's interests being given slight concern in the party's nomination process and formation of its agenda.

A clue to understanding Florida in comparison with the rest of the South can be gleaned from the 2000 election exit poll on the Latino Catholic vote. In the "South" region that includes Florida, and where no other state boasts a sizable Cuban-American population, 39.6 percent of the Latino Catholic vote went to Al Gore in the presidential election. But in Florida Gore received only 29.2 percent. The story is quite different in the Southern Crossroads region, which includes Texas and where "Latino" points mostly to Mexican-Americans. There Gore received 55.6 percent of the Latino Catholic vote. Almost certainly, religious identity here takes second place to the political-moral culture of peoples' country of origin and, perhaps more significantly, the migrants' reasons for leaving the home country. Religion may be an "independent variable" (this writer judges that it is), but it is not separable from other considerations and commitments on the part of the faithful.

Religious membership statistics for Florida are well worth noting on two counts in particular: the percentage of the total population that reports religious membership of any kind and the particular affiliation of those who do belong. Concerning the former, Florida's 49.9 percent is the lowest among all the states of the South except West Virginia (40 percent)—and, as noted above, the West Virginia percentage must be taken as indicative less of an absence of religious affiliation than of a lack of reporting by religious bodies.[16] This veers sharply away from the reported membership in most other states in the region; for example: Alabama at 77 percent, Tennessee at 65.1 percent; Georgia at 62.5 percent, and North Carolina at 60.7 percent. Throughout several of the 50 states, figures have a tendency to reflect the presence (or absence) of what may be thought of as a quasi-established church; that is, one dominant body into which much of the population has been born across several generations and is unlikely to abandon (whatever the degree of individuals' loyalty and involvement may be). Thus, Utah has an emphatically Mormon establishment; most southeastern states are more or less Southern Baptist; the upper plains states have a strongly Lutheran cast; and many states, especially in New England and the Mid-Atlantic, are overwhelmingly Roman Catholic.

Before the 1920s, Florida was religiously and culturally of the South, consequently Baptist, Methodist, and Presbyterian. (Nearly all of the state's population over that long period resided in the northern tier of counties.) The Florida of today is a product of major additions to, and therefore radical shifts from, a once unmistakably regional culture. This permits us to observe that the state has moved from showing a hegemonic face and becoming increasingly diverse in the decades after World War II.

The NARA data, compiled at the turn of the millennium, show a mélange. The two denominations with the largest memberships are Roman Catholic and Southern Baptist, claiming 16.2 percent and 8.1 percent of the total population respectively. Historically the United Methodist figures are 2.9 percent, trailing the Jewish total that is estimated at 3.9 percent (largely concentrated in the cities along the east coast from Jacksonville to Miami). The combined total for historically African-American Protestant denominations—Baptist, Methodist, and Pentecostal—is estimated at 7 percent. Only four other groups exceed fractional status, the Assemblies of God, a Pentecostal denomination, and two "mainline" bodies, the Episcopal Church and the Presbyterian Church, USA.

The strength of the Catholics and the Southern Baptists is no surprise. For one thing, these are the nation's two largest religious bodies. In that respect Florida might be considered microcosmic—although the strength of the first is national and the second regional. But two items are pertinent. One is the regionalist identification of the state until the 1920s when non-southerners began to move in as automobiles and roads changed everything, followed by larger numbers since World War II. Also, the dominating strength of the Catholic Church in much of the area from which immigrants have moved into the Sunshine State, from the colder climates of northern states and from the chilly religious and political/economic conditions in several Caribbean and Central American nations.

Both of these religious constituencies are conservative. Religious dynamics being as complex as they are, however, we must understand that conservatism takes many forms. It is no secret that these two groups have more often been at odds than they have been friendly and respectful toward each other. Sometimes one has to wonder how two traditions that are so definitive about their own specific body of teachings—often showing tendencies toward exclusivism, with each inclined to insist on its claim to possess *the* truth—can share space under the Christian umbrella. (In practice, of course, the two usually have not found commodious room for each other.) Then, taking into account the large number of other forms of conservative Christianity, from Pentecostal groups to urban mega-churches, to strong dissident cells within traditional mainline Protestant churches, to newly formed breakaway bodies from those bodies, the observer may be tempted to assume that the force of Christian conservatism is irresistible.

As has been noted, Florida is a moderately conservative state politically. The Republican Party holds a slight edge in registration among the state's voters. And, emphatically, there is only a meager tradition of doctrinaire liberalism or radicalism within that population. Transitory Americans seeking a progressive political climate have been attracted to northern California, Oregon, and some areas of New England, but rarely to any sunbelt state, most especially Florida. Conventional wisdom has it that people move to Florida to get away from responsibility—the description of the state as (partly) hedonistic addresses that condition. To the degree to which that is true, the size of the retiree segment is illuminating. In 2002, 17.6 percent of the Sunshine State's residents were 65 years of age or older (many who had retired to Florida from elsewhere), the nation's highest rate by 2 percent. Add to that the love of outdoor sports and there would seem to be a recipe for a conservative drift.

It might be assumed that the Religious Right has particular appeal to the religious folk of Florida. The Wald-Scher study concludes that its influence is surely present, but is less than a dominant force in the state's political life. It is easy to forget that one may be a conservative Christian and not affiliate with today's Religious Right.

Examples include Roman Catholics, that large company of Southern Baptists who take their bearings principally from their own denomination's stands, and Mormons. The unique blend of conservative and liberal found consistently in the African-American community must never be overlooked; that is, in social policy it is liberal, on moral matters traditionally conservative. But we know that in the voting booth the former consistently trumps the latter. Moreover, about one-third of the GOP primary voters in Florida belong to groups that have not been so hospitable to the Religious Right—Roman Catholics or Jews in particular. The study comes to the view that "Florida's Republican electorate is less socially conservative than in other southern states."[17]

The power of the Religious Right in the Sunshine State was greater in the 1980s than it was around 2000. Moreover, its influence all along has been keener in local elections than in those for state and national offices. School-board issues stand as a prominent target of its activity. While Religious Right conservatives have had their days in the sun (so to speak), the Republican Party leadership has more often been propelled by economic and pragmatic considerations. Party leaders of the latter sort have sometimes referred to their Religious Right allies as "a necessary annoyance." The governorship and the leadership of the state senate, in particular, and sometimes of the house, have belonged to the economic conservative camp.

Florida's unique position is highlighted by three major barriers to conquest by Religious Right strength. One has to do with the differences between the house and the senate; while the house has often focused on moral issues—school prayers, gay rights, school vouchers, and abortion—the senate was not much interested in devoting time and passion to those types of concerns. Term limits for elected officials is the second. In a state with so many new citizens, so little tradition, and such enormous diversity of people and positions, the challenge of identifying, recruiting, and grooming candidates is huge and takes time. The third barrier is the state judiciary. Ballot language may be approved or disapproved by the state Supreme Court, and a number of the moral causes and proposals promoted by the religious conservatives falter there.

However sympathetic individual justices may be, they may have to judge that the "movement's goals are incompatible with the rule of law."[18] A case in point is the court's September 2004 ruling that declared unconstitutional a law giving the governor the right to prevent the withdrawal of life-sustaining measure from a patient determined by doctors to be in a persistent vegetative state.[19]

Those religious conservatives who are driven to place their moral concerns before the public in order to cleanse and uplift the general society do bring thoughtful work to the formulation of their agendas and development of advocacy strategies. But they do not exhaust the company of religious conservatives, of whom many (just as in Appalachia) do not seek to transform the society at large, usually concentrating their moral programs on church, family, and local life.

A 1997 study, *The Bully Pulpit: the Politics of Protestant Clergy*, sheds light on the widely varying positions of ordained leadership across the nation toward public involvement. Among clergy who fall anywhere on the conservative side of center in their social theology, a large percentage emphatically promote what is called a "Civic Gospel." That term refers to holding such beliefs as: The United States was founded as a Christian nation; nations will prosper if they are faithful to God; it is hard to be a true Christian and a political liberal; and, free enterprise is the only Christian political system. But among those whose stance on social theology is left of center (near or far), the commitment is to a "communitarian" orientation. These leaders stress the "horizontal" aspect of religion effectively summarized as "community building among interdependent individuals."[20]

When it comes to political agenda, the study found conservative clergy focusing on such "moral issues" as abortion, divorce, sex education, school prayer, limited government, and low taxes. By sharp contrast, liberal clergy, caught up with "social reform," devote their energies toward charity to those in need, guidance and counseling, facilitating self-help in local communities, and opposing injustice and oppression. As part of carrying out their nationwide study, the five political scientists who produced *The Bully Pulpit* saw wisdom in identifying several demographic characteristics of clergy surveyed: education, type of family from which they came, whether they grew up in urban or rural places, age, marital status, and so on. Their work prompted reflection on the salience of including region of residence in the demographic profile. The data led them to identify people from only one region, namely, the South. Rather dramatically, the outcome was that 57.9 percent of those who belong to the wide sector of conservatives reported a southern residence (which, of course, includes Florida).

Another way to characterize the various moral causes and positions, for laity as well as clergy, is to think of them as "message markets." Among the messages, or causes, that are sellable, that have broad appeal in our time, are several that afford depiction of the sides taken: Israel/Armageddon; anti-abortion; rational purity, that is, the inviolable requirement of absolute orthodoxy; belief in the power of evil, and the literal existence of a personal Devil; the call for America to be a Christian nation; legislation legalizing prayer in public schools; and asserting that political conservatism is the godly way. The cataloguing that captures the representative concerns and agendas of liberals includes: tolerance of all people; striving to achieve the success of civil rights; and environmental ethics.

Whatever items are prominent on that list now, they differ from the concerns of a generation or two ago—and doubtless from what will be regarded as compelling in the future. In the evangelical South, today's public agenda differs from those agendas of the recent past. It is staggering to realize how recessive the interest in Prohibition has become. Through the 1960s, passing laws to prohibit the manufacture, sale, and consumption of alcoholic beverages was the ranking moral concern, with energy expended on behalf of that cause attaining phenomenal proportions. Consumers and sellers had to (and did) devise all sorts of shenanigans to circumvent such legal strictures as the anti-liquor forces were able to legislate at state, county, and community levels.

Tellingly, those laws against drinking have all but totally disappeared (a development that has contributed to the national rise of Mothers Against Drunk Driving [MADD]). Some joke that what many once did in private they now are content to do in public. Chuckle as we may, we must not overlook the fact that a large (if indeterminate) percentage of the South's people remain teetotalers. Nor is the argument adequate that that battle has been abandoned because theirs has been recognized to be a lost cause. More is going on here than surrender or compromise or concealment.

Beyond question, the fear of the deterioration of the family structure on which the society has been founded is a major driving force of the public concern of today's religious conservatives, a supposition evident in the prominence of marriage, family, and sexuality issues on their list of evil forces and influences pervading our society now. Beneath this cluster of concerns, of course, lies the question of authority. By what standards are responsible people called to live? Or are there none? Is it up to every person to devise his or her own way? Are all moral practices and ethical teachings relative, dictated by personal preference or the prevailing cultural context? For people such as these, the answer is an emphatic "no." This generation's abominable sin is held to be relativism. Here we encounter another instance of the ascendancy of the individualistic camp in social/political thinking, this time more directly associated with ethical decisions than with political culture. The conservative religious/political forces in Florida are fighting a far more serious and broad-based battle than their predecessor moralists. To their eyes, nothing less is at stake than the foundations of ethical living and the basic structures of civilized society.

Appalachia, Flordia, and the Broader South

These two "peripheral" religious/political cultures exist, are significant, and by definition stand outside the central stream of Southern society and culture. Perhaps they can be thought of as marginal members of the same neighborhood. While it is reasonable to repeat that neither Florida nor Appalachia is typically southern, they are nearer to being that than to anything else; in fact, both of these cultural areas share much with the larger regional culture. So, by implication, it is possible to gain insight into that broader South by setting these two "peripherals" alongside it.

One fruitful way of approaching this topic is to ask about dominant, often normative, religious patterns. Appalachia embodies one: the Holiness and Baptist churches. These are characteristically small and independent, having little or no affiliation with a larger organized body. Hence they are local in both their mission and their organization. That localism carries over into their political life as well, with attention to social leadership outside the boundaries of county and immediate area sparse indeed. It follows rather logically they are usually Republican. The "do it yosef" motto captures their spirit. They live by the conviction that the scope of organized government is properly a limited one. Thus their issues are their own, those that grow out of their personal and local values and concerns, not typically those promoted by a national party.

Florida, by contrast, owns neither dominant nor normative religious/political patterns. Although for a long time it was an extension of southern culture, the Sunshine State has over the past half-century become a state without a core culture, and that condition also prevails in the religious life of its people: Generalizations simply do not apply. The fact that the white population is now slightly more Republican than Democratic is the result of more factors than continuity with southern regional behavior.

What of the broader South? For close to two centuries, a regional version of evangelical Protestantism prevailed as the pacesetter for the religious life of the people. There were other expressions, of course, both from traditional Christianity and from new, often indigenous, sources. But Baptist people and Baptist-like beliefs and practices constituted normalcy—"what every schoolchild" grew up knowing to be the correct teachings of the Bible and the church. This program might be referred to as the culture of southern conversionist evangelicalism.

There is little doubt that such a perspective is still present, even prominent, with its mandate to bring to a conversion experience that transforms and saves from "lostness" each and every person in the world. That is the case despite the inroads of previously minority or unknown traditions such as Catholicism, "nonwestern religions," and some groups that are more liberal and some more conservative.

Indeed, the disruption of this long-definitive interpretation of Christianity correlates with recent "new departures." Holding the line against liberalism, fighting the war against corrosive forces, staying true to the old-time faith has become a preoccupation with powerful segments of the ruling elite, emphatically in the Southern Baptist Convention and the still young Presbyterian Church in America (PCA). In the former case, sides have been taken, the "fundamentalists" *against* the "moderates" in what has proven to be a veritable battle to the death. Among Presbyterians, this institutional division manifesting little goodwill gave birth to the PCA over against the historic body of regional Presbyterians, which in 1983 merged with the formerly northern branch of the tradition to form the Presbyterian Church USA—an action that pushed Southern conservatives to form their own orthodox body.

Correlated with these conditions, the long-standing dominance (and of course the cultural normativity) of the Democratic Party (the "Solid South") among the ruling white population has been overturned. Now that population, especially the male population, is heavily Republican. Thus, in both religious and political life, one position reigned unchallenged for many decades, but has been replaced by the opposite commitment. Among white people, that is. The African-American sector is a culture in its own right. The contemporary alignment simply shifts from their having a small place or none at all in the political scheme of things to occupying a forceful position in the region's public life, however on the other side of the political fence from the white population.

In addition to the dominance/normativity issue, this treatment of Appalachia, Florida, and the broader South brings to the fore something of the differing per-sonalities of the three cultural places. Tersely stated, they are variously old, new, and ongoing. The religious/cultural life of Appalachia reflects the emergence long ago of distinctly local ways of thinking, practicing, and organizing. It really is astonishing how much consistency this kind of Protestant Christian life has shown in holding fast to the old-time religion. Taste for adjusting or keeping up is in small supply at best. These people and churches prize anchorage, sturdy faithfulness, and living as a set-apart community of Christian disciples.

Florida shows an entirely different face. The forms of religious life that flourish there tend to be glamorous, fresh, exciting, and entertaining, featuring music and preaching that are attuned to the still young electronic age. Preachers typically walk about with microphones in hand or over their heads. Music makes use of electric guitars and small combos, with gospel music replacing classical hymnody, words to the singing projected on to a screen above the pulpit. The most successful ministers are gifted as entertainers, and more than a few of them are television celebrities. More than a few of the congregations they lead qualify as megachurches, both in size and in manner of operation.

Best of all, these kinds of churches, present in cities and towns, offer "full service." People come to worship, of course, and unvaryingly to study the Bible. But to these traditional functions are added social gatherings, athletic contests, fellowship occasions, mission projects, and much more. The church offers the premium value of *belonging,* opportunity to get acquainted, to develop friendships. It also conducts classes and activities for children and whole families, events for having fun, all of these providing a sense of identity and involvement. This program of events and opportunities occurs in the setting of a state to which many have recently moved. There a high percentage of residents know few people in population centers that do not live off a cultural capital found in established communities "back home," with familiar patterns of interaction.

These full-service churches serve multiple purposes, in other words, often lovingly and with engaging flair. When research is done on the membership and activities of these communities of faith in Florida, it is likely to show that many of the participants are new to church life, and that more belong to denominations that are different from those they knew in their past. This has been a trend across the nation, but its prevalence is greatest in places with little tradition and many new residents, Florida and California at the top of that list.

Religious life in the broader South is scarcely stagnant. Just the same, long-honored ways and patterns stand strong, rendering less necessary and inviting adjustments and adaptations. What has changed is the relinquishing of dominant standing by the traditional denominations—Baptist, Methodist, and Presbyterian. Near-automatic cultural respect to those bodies and deference to them has diminished substantially. Congregations and denominations now must hustle to attract and retain members and positions of influence in cities and towns. Groups once thought to be the preserve of the lower classes have leaped those borders and have become the spiritual home to people across the spectrum. Pentecostal churches flourish. Independent congregations abound, most of them some kind of Baptist. Roman Catholics make up a larger proportion of the population, principally through migration from northern and western cultures—along with immigrants from south of the border and the gulf straits. Not to mention the unaccustomed presence of Hindus, Buddhists, and Muslims.

Despite all this, the religious life in communities from Virginia to Georgia shows a reasonable constancy. That constancy continues to be at sharp variance from the Appalachian patterns that remain distinctive; and as well, from the kinetic, innovative church life of Florida. Overlapping is present, but we do well to treat Appalachia and Florida as distinctive religious subcultures in the South, America's most churched and religiously expressive region.

Endnotes

1 Earl Black and Merle Black, *The Rise of Southern Republicans* (Cambridge, MA: Harvard University Press, 2002).

2 Emma Bell Miles, *The Spirit of the Mountains* (Knoxville: University of Tennessee Press, 1975), 144.

3 John Alexander Williams, *Appalachia: A History* (Chapel Hill: University of North Carolina Press, 2002), 136-139.

4 Daniel J. Elazar, *American Federalism.* 2nd ed. (New York: Thomas Y. Crowell, 1972).

5 Clifford A. Grammich, Jr., *Local Baptists, Local Politics* (Knoxville: University of Tennessee Press, 1999), 183.

6 Williams, *op. cit.,* 238.

7 Loyal Jones, *Faith and Meaning in the Southern Uplands* (Urbana and Chicago: University of Illinois Press, 2001), 203-06.

8 Gordon B. McKinney, "Southern Mountain Republicans and the Negro, 1865-1900," in *Appalachians and Race*, ed. John C. Inscoe (Lexington: University Press of Kentucky, 2001), 205-06.

9 Black and Black, *op. cit.,* 241-47.

10 Voter News Service General Election Exit Polls, 2002. Hereafter "VNS."

11 The following discussion relies on Samuel S. Hill, "The Virtue of Hope," in *Christianity in Appalachia*, ed. Bill J. Leonard (Knoxville: University of Tennessee Press, 1999), 297-311.

12 For more on serpent-handling in the South, see chapter by Charles Lippy in this volume.

13 The ARIS telephone survey found that only 11 percent of Southerners identify themselves as unaffiliated—roughly a quarter of the percentage that fail to show up on NARA's reported membership rolls (40.3 percent). Throughout the rest of the country, the proportion of self-identified unaffiliated is twice that size, i.e., one-half the percentage of those not counted in the denominational reports.

14 Kenneth D. Wald and Richard K. Scher, "'A Necessary Annoyance'? The Christian Right and the Development of Republican Party Politics in Florida," in *The Christian Right in American Politics*, ed. John C. Green et al. (Washington, D.C.: Georgetown University Press, 2003), 85.

15 *Ibid.*, 97.

16 Still, it should be noted that, according to ARIS, only 12 percent of Floridians claim no religious affiliation.

17 Wald and Scher, *op. cit.*, 83.

18 *Ibid.*, 95.

19 For a discussion of the politics of this case, see Conclusion.

20 James L. Guth, et al., *The Bully Pulpit: The Politics of Protestant Clergy* (Lawrence: University Press of Kansas, 1997), 64, 60.

CHAPTER SEVEN

THE CIVIL RELIGIONS OF THE SOUTH

Andrew M. Manis

Civil religion may be understood as a cultural blending of religious and patriotic ideas that invests a nation or a region with a sense of sacredness. Nations frequently have varieties of civil religion, and since the South has been the American nation's most religiously and patriotically distinct region, the most distinct varieties of America's civil religion have grown up there.

As Charles Wilson argues in *Baptized in Blood: The Religion of the Lost Cause, 1865-1920*, in the aftermath of the Civil War white Southerners explained their defeat by means of a southern civil religion that venerated the symbols, ideals, and saints of the war they had lost. Along with this "lost cause" ideology, a discussion of southern civil religion must also include a range of regional and racial considerations. Recognizing that African Americans have as much claim to southernness as do whites, I have elsewhere argued that the South has produced competing civil religions, best seen in the Civil Rights Movement. This chapter extends that discussion in light of America's current war on terrorism.[1]

Civil Religions, Civil War, Civil Rights

The first important manifestation of southern civil religion was probably the region's defense of slavery from which Southerners developed fuller arguments about their region's distinctiveness as compared to the North. Later these impulses coalesced into a "Confederate nationalism" that propelled the South into secession and the Civil War.[2] After the Civil War, the sacred objects, rituals, and monuments of the southern civil religion came to be focused on the saints in gray.

Out of the crucible of the war, southern civil religion became the means by which the white South confessed its faith that God had chosen it as the representative of pure Christianity and Americanism. It also articulated white Southerners' confidence that defeat had not signaled God's abandonment. Having undergone divine chastisement—being "baptized in blood"—the South had been purged and prepared for a greater destiny. From this abbreviated system of belief, southern civil religion developed every other constituent part that sociologists of religion believe is necessary in a full-fledged religion.

Beyond its beliefs, for example, the religion of the Lost Cause developed a trinity of Confederate saints—General Robert E. Lee, General Thomas "Stonewall" Jackson, and President Jefferson Davis—often depicted in iconic photographs in the region's schools, homes, and Protestant churches. The Confederate battle flag, of course, constituted the southern civil religion's most sacred object. Religions require a hymnody, which the southern civil religion provided in "Dixie." Confederate monuments dotted the southern landscape as sacred spaces, while devotees developed rituals to help commemorate Confederate Memorial Day and the birthdays of Lee and Jackson. Other rituals came to be used for conducting funerals and reunions of Confederate veterans, and for dedicating Confederate memorials. Sermons and political speeches lauded the values of the Confederacy, while the Lost Cause spun off organizations functioning like Confederate monastic orders for both men and women: The United Confederate Veterans, the United Daughters of the Confederacy, the Sons of Confederate Veterans.[3]

The "splendid little" Spanish-American War and the Great War in Europe to "make the world safe for democracy" brought southern and northern soldiers together to fight side by side, effecting a reunion of South and North. Wilson argues that this regional reconciliation weakened the Lost Cause version of southern civil religion, but sowed the seeds for the growth of "new dreams of southern destiny." Between the 1920s and the 1950s, the Southern Literary Renaissance produced writers like W. J. Cash, Allen Tate, William Faulkner, Robert Penn Warren, Walker Percy, and James McBride Dabbs, all of whom speculated about southern distinctiveness and destiny. Of these, Dabbs most self-consciously tapped the southern religious heritage to "preach" a southern civil religion by which black and white southerners would learn to live together. A harmoniously biracial South would become "God's Project," destined to "show the way to the rest of the world."[4]

In this formulation Dabbs, perhaps unwittingly, reflected an understanding of American destiny articulated by African Americans as early as the nineteenth century. African-American leaders like Frederick Douglass described dual nationalisms where black leaders saw their role as a divine call to purge and redeem the nation, and thus help it to fulfill its destiny as a beacon to the oppressed.[5] The African Methodist Episcopal (AME) Church, especially, reflected a civil religion that included dual destinies for both the nation and its people. Black Americans were divinely called to push America toward its national destiny. The editor of the AME's official organ, the *Christian Recorder,* believed that the separation of the races kept the United States from becoming "the great field of training for... solving the great problem of a universal brotherhood, the unity of the race of mankind, and the eternal principles of intellectual, moral, and spiritual development." By forcing America to come to terms with racial difference, by pushing white America toward acceptance of racial equality, African Americans helped fulfill both the nation's and their own destinies.[6]

By the post-World War II era southern blacks coming home from having fought Nazi racial ideology in Europe were no longer willing to tolerate a similar ideology at home. Truman's progressive civil rights policy, which included desegregating the armed forces, coupled with the Supreme Court's 1944 *Smith v. Allwright* ruling ending the white primary and the 1954 *Brown v. Board of Education* decision ending school segregation, all convinced southern blacks that God was making "a way out of no way." The Civil Rights Movement, especially as led by Martin Luther King Jr., updated black America's dual civil religion. In language of the American dream King articulated the hopes of black Southerners that America would live up to its calling to embody and exemplify to the world an ideal brotherhood. America had a special role in creating the brotherhood, noted the Birmingham civil rights minister Fred Shuttlesworth, for "once we got all the melting pot together here, and the hardest bit was to assimilate the blacks into it, then we could be an example for the world."[7]

Thus the Civil Rights Movement can be understood as a revitalization of a black civil religion, which heightened both the providential understanding of American history and the particular role of black America within that history. In this civil religion black Southerners understood the end of segregation as the fulfillment of their long-cherished hopes for America. King saw the movement as an attempt to call America back to its essential meaning. The black community would provide "a new expression of the American dream that need not be realized at the expense of other men around the world, but a dream of opportunity and life that can be shared with the rest of the world." Commenting on the practice of segregation, Nannie H. Burroughs, president of the National Baptist Women's Convention, argued that efforts to "build a democracy out of race attitudes left over from slavery" would render America unable to realize its original dream.[8]

This version of civil religion highlighted the idea of pluralism to argue that desegregation fulfilled the American purpose. As a microcosm of the world's diversity, America was called by God to be an exemplar nation, revealing how the rest of the world might live together as a family of nations. From this perspective, blacks viewed desegregation as a further step toward the actualization of the hoped-for state in which America might come to terms with its own pluralism. Fred Shuttlesworth stressed that America's living with its pluralism required the desegregation of the races: "I say America either means integration or we might as well dismantle our concept [of America]. We might as well send the Germans back to Germany, and the Italians back to Italy, and everybody back where they came from, and give the country back to the Indians. America means integration or it means nothing."[9]

Black assertiveness, however, sparked a revival of the civil religion of the Lost Cause. Answering what they considered an onslaught of radicalism, segregationists used their own historical interpretations to turn the South into a battleground of a civil religious holy war. For them, the specter of desegregation meant a disappointment of the hope that the South would remain "white man's country." In a popular diatribe embodying the conservative white South's "massive resistance" to *Brown*, Georgia's governor, Herman Talmadge, fused the patriotic symbols of southernness and Americanness. Admonishing fellow Southerners to preserve the southern way of life, he appealed to the sacred memory of the saints of American civil religion: "It will take courage...of the kind our forefathers showed when they signed the Declaration of Independence, the kind of courage they showed at Valley Forge,...at Gettysburg, and during the Reconstruction Era after the War Between the States."[10]

Ironically, by the Civil Rights era, conservative white politicians *and pulpiteers had* transformed the tragic elements of the Lost Cause into a triumphalistic civil religion, enunciated by southern pulpiteers as well as politicians. One Southern Baptist pastor saw his denomination as strategically positioned within the divine purpose, warning that the "future of our denomination, our nation, and perhaps the world depends on our stewardship of the gospel now." U.S. Senator James O. Eastland, a Methodist from Mississippi, sounded a similar note: "The future greatness of America depends on racial purity and maintenance of Anglo-Saxon institutions, which still flourish in full flower in the South."[11]

This version of civil religion warned of the threat of racial amalgamation, recently made more serious by the integrationists. The Mississippi jurist Tom Brady warned that Communists understood that "a mongrelized race is an ignorant, weak, and easily conquered race." Brady judged that the cultures of Egypt, India, Burma, Siam, Greece, Rome, Spain, and Central America had all been destroyed by "negroid amalgamation." To these white Southerners desegregation symbolized an absolute threat. As Robert Patterson, the founder of the Citizens' Councils, put it: "We just felt like integration would utterly destroy everything that we valued."[12]

Most white Southerners of that divisive era still favored segregation, but tried to avoid both the integrationist civil religion of the NAACP and the segregationist civil religion of the Citizens' Councils. Patterson epitomized the sense of foreboding generated by the conflict: "Integration represents darkness, regimentation, totalitarianism, Communism, and destruction. Segregation represents the freedom to choose one's associates, Americanism, state sovereignty, and the survival of the white race. These two ideologies are now engaged in mortal conflict and only one can survive....There is no middle ground."[13] For this reason, the journalist Robert Sherrill argued that in their conflict over civil rights "southerners are not just waging a political and economic war against change, but a religious war."[14]

Thus, in the Civil Rights era two civil religions, two definitions of national reality, competed for the civil allegiance of the bystanders in the middle. One version of civil religion pulled them in a more southerly direction, toward the status quo and the segregationist tradition. The other pulled them toward a millennial America where "all men are created equal." The frequency with which these middle-of-the-roaders said integration was inevitable but cautioned, "Not yet," testified to their dilemma. Forced by social circumstance and the historical process to choose between two versions of sacred reality, these Southerners answered first with indecision and finally with immobilized silence.

By the mid-1960s, the more inclusive civil religion won the day—but only temporarily and partially. Television scenes from Birmingham and Selma converted a president and the Congress, resulting in the landmark Civil Rights Act of 1964 and the 1965 Voting Rights Act. Such success was quickly mimicked by other liberation movements and the protests against the Vietnam War. The losers in the civil religious wars of the 1960s now had more to disturb them than just racial diversity. In response, like the southern fundamentalists who lost the public relations war surrounding the 1925 Scopes "Monkey" Trial, they licked their wounds, began building their own institutions, and bided their time until the opportune moment. They would re-emerge in a broader civil religious conflict that is now called the "culture wars."

Culture Wars: Nationalizing Southern Discontent

Historically, there have been two different models suggesting how society and religion ought to relate to each other in America. In the "custodial model" (colonial New England being the most salient example), civil authorities serve as the custodians of society's spiritual as well as physical well being. Against this stood the "pluralist" model of dissenters like Roger Williams, who believed that religion was a matter of private concern, of individual conscience, and none of the government's business.[15]

Ever since New England Puritanism was compromised by revivalism, Unitarianism, and floods of Catholic immigrants, the evangelical South has been the chief representative of the custodial model. After the First and Second Great Awakenings in the eighteenth century, evangelical Protestants (mainly Baptists, Methodists, and Presbyterians) gradually moved into numerical and cultural dominance in the antebellum South. As custodians of antebellum southern church and culture, ministers and theologians produced biblical defenses of slavery that eventually melded into religious justifications of the Confederacy. These southern divines, however, did more than merely defend their society against northern abolitionism. As Eugene D. Genovese has argued, they also saw their society as the bulwark against apostasy and secularism. By the outbreak of the Civil War, orthodox ministers feared a Yankee victory would lead to theological liberalism and a rejection of Christian orthodoxy.[16] During the Civil War, a Greensboro minister representatively declared, "A pure Christianity is wrapped up in this revolution, and Providence is using the South for the grand work of its preservation and extension."[17] Just before the war, South Carolina's *Southern Presbyterian* detected "a religious character to the present struggle. Anti-Slavery is essentially infidel. It wars upon the Bible, on the Church of Christ, on the truth of God, on the souls of men."[18]

In the South's defense of both theological and racial orthodoxy, both before and after the Civil War, the region saw itself as called by God to spread what a Southern Baptist Home Mission Board official in the early 1900s called "the Anglo-Saxon evangelical faith."[19] The poverty of the post-Civil War South led later floods of immigrants to America largely to bypass the South, making it possible for the region's Protestant homogeneity to persist well into the twentieth century. As late as 1966, nine of 10 southerners identified themselves as Protestants, and 77 percent did so in 1988.[20] Thus, by the mid-twentieth century, the South was *par excellence* the region where calls for a "Christian America" were welcome and where religious and cultural dissent was not. In the South moral custodians were largely free to envision a happily homogeneous, WASPish Southland and nation.

During and after World War II the South, whose insularity had previously protected it from serious incursions of pluralism, slowly began to be challenged in ways strong enough to threaten its racial and religious status quo. A war against Nazi racial ideology made the "American dilemma" even more obvious to blacks and liberal whites. President Harry Truman's desegregation of the armed forces and postwar civil rights policies, coupled with Branch Rickey's and Jackie Robinson's noble efforts to integrate the national pastime, emboldened African Americans, putting the forces of change at the ready. All that was necessary to put these forces in motion was a catalyst. The storm gathered as Thurgood Marshall and the NAACP challenged public school segregation, and the *Brown* decision touched off a torrent of racial transformation in the South and the nation.

In addition to altered race relations, the post-World War II South also underwent alarming demographic and cultural changes for many devout Southerners and set the stage for cultural conflict. In this period, the South became more

urban, with the percentage of Southerners living in cities increasing from 37 percent to 67 percent between 1940 and 1980. During the same period, urbanization
of the non-South increased by only 11 percent—from 66 to 77 percent.[21] The
Sunbelt phenomenon also brought an influx of non-Southerners into the South.
Twenty percent of residents of the South in 1980 were born outside the region,
up from only 8 percent in 1950.[22]

Higher education increased in the South, as it did nationwide after 1950. In
1950 only 6.2 percent of Americans over 25 had attended four years of college;
in 1991 the proportion was 21.4 percent, with the percentage among southerners
only slightly lower. All these social factors weakened the South's cultural and
religious homogeneity. The percentage of Protestants fell from 90 to 77 percent
between 1966 and 1988, while nationwide the percentage of Protestants fell only
two points, from 60 percent to 58 percent.[23]

Linking these regional changes with the perception of moral crisis in America in
the same period helps one see why many Americans, and especially Southerners,
felt that everything nailed down was coming up. The Civil Rights Movement,
the protests over the Vietnam War, the removal of public school prayer, *Roe v.
Wade*, Watergate, the secularizing tendencies of television, the growing violence
in American life, and efforts toward gay rights all created among conservative
Americans a discontent with pluralism. Having rejoined the national mainstream
after World War II, the South found its religious adjustment to modern America
very uncomfortable. With its custodial tradition still healthy, the region responded
with the resurgence of the religious right in the 1980s.

"If Mama ain't happy," so the saying goes, "ain't nobody happy." Herein lies
a new, regional version: If the Southland ain't happy, the nation ain't happy.
While the Religious Right included many from across America, its leading voices
speak with southern accents—Jerry Falwell, Pat Robertson, Oral Roberts, James
Robison, Jimmy Swaggart, as well as the Southern Baptist leaders Adrian Rogers,
Paul Pressler, and Charles Stanley.

Despite the importance of these cultural and religious transformations, the racial
changes remained central. The religious historian William R. Hutchison has recently
argued that *Brown* bolstered the pluralist impulse in America more significantly than
any public policy change in the twentieth century. Against this trend there stood a
"counterpluralist" impulse that found its most powerful expression in the Religious
Right. Predominantly white and Protestant, these counterpluralists, Hutchison
observed, were not only troubled by the proliferation of minorities and new religions,
but fearful and angry that they were losing control of their "own country."[24]

By the late 1970s the South's civil religious conflict over civil rights was
beginning to be nationalized into a more contemporary *American* conflict. The
melting pot, a metaphor so dear to Fred Shuttlesworth and others of an earlier

era, had not worked for African Americans. As the sociologist Todd Gitlin has aptly put it, "boiling as it was, the pot was not thought to be capable of melting just anyone."[25] Inclusion had always assumed white skin, but those tending the pot were now being forced grudgingly to include African Americans in the Great American Recipe. Unwilling again to secede from the union, many southern whites had to "grin and bear it," accepting the federal government's dictates through clenched teeth. The region's cities and states gradually desegregated their public facilities, now with a bit more "deliberate speed" than in the days of massive resistance, and began to protect black voting rights. Before long the South accepted integrated schools and the larger cities saw the election of a growing number of black mayors and legislators.

Meanwhile, southern blacks celebrated their progress and pushed for further victories. Celebrations of the progress and admonitions to further activism came to be regularly expressed in the African-American civil religion that grew out of the black freedom struggle. Temples and monuments of this civil religion can be found in the civil rights museums of Birmingham, Selma, and Memphis. An emotionally powerful sculpture outside Montgomery's Southern Poverty Law Center quotes King and the Hebrew prophet Amos to memorialize all of the martyrs killed in service to the movement. In Atlanta the King Center for Nonviolent Social Change "keeps the Dream alive" and ushers silent pilgrims to King's grave, perhaps this civil religion's "holy of holies."

Across America as well as the South, every third Monday in January the Martin Luther King holiday functions as the black civil religion's High Holy Day, with a few white politicians and presidents along to pay their respects. Public observances of the holiday in churches and civic arenas welcome predominantly African-American congregations to hear recitations of the Dream Speech and the singing of freedom songs. Black preachers or politicians deliver stem-winding sermons or speeches invoking the memory and spirit of civil religious saints— King, Rosa Parks, John Lewis—and despite his lack of real participation in the actual movement Malcolm X. At the end the sprinkling of whites in the audiences join the now-traditional cross-armed handclasp and try valiantly to sway rhythmically in the ritual singing of "We Shall Overcome." In each venue this black civil religion exults in the past and presses on into the future, again in ritual benediction: "Thank God we ain't where we use to be, but we got a long way to where America ought to be."

Black elected officials like Birmingham's first black mayor, Richard Arrington, have played a significant role in leading their cities to fund the building of these civil rights museums. Other black politicians helped lobby Congress to create the King national holiday in 1983 and have faithfully participated in local commemorations each year since the holiday went into effect. Besides aiding in the efforts to celebrate the symbols of the Civil Rights Movement, the rise of African-American elected officials has also created some problems. Among whites their emergence stimulated "white flight" from the central cities to the suburbs. Among African Americans it set up a contest between the elected leaders and the preacher-activists, both of whom used this civil religion to claim status as the rightful national spokespersons for black interests.[26]

This African-American form of civil religion was most clearly reflected in the 1984 and 1988 presidential campaigns of the Reverend Jesse Jackson, who was thereby able to trump the claims of elected politicians and win what the historian James M. Washington called "the presidency of black America." Washington also noted that by being audacious enough to campaign "as if his race did not disqualify him from becoming president of the United States," his very presence in the race served both to threaten white supremacy and to assert African-American pride.[27] At Jackson rallies many likely agreed with one elderly black man in attendance who commented, "I haven't felt this proud since Joe Louis."[28]

Aiming his appeal to the "black masses" from rallies in African-American churches, the Jackson campaign won some 3 million votes in 13 primaries in 1984. Chief among Jackson's accomplishments were his efforts to stimulate voter registration and actual voting among blacks, especially in the South. Total black voter registration increased in 1984 by 14.5 percent over the previous presidential election, sparked at least in part to Jackson's candidacy. In addition, the percentage of the black voting-age population who actually voted in 1984 increased 5.3 percent over that recorded in 1980.[29] Jackson took 21 percent of the votes in six southern primaries, but was able to gain only 2 percent of white votes in Alabama, 6 percent in Georgia, and 8 percent in North Carolina. Overall his appeal garnered him some 450 delegates to the Democratic National Convention.[30]

Four years later Jackson improved his performance in the primaries, finishing ahead of Al Gore and the eventual nominee, Michael Dukakis, to win in Alabama, Georgia, Louisiana, Mississippi, and Virginia. Taking second place in Florida, Missouri, North Carolina, Tennessee, Texas, and four other non-southern states, he ended the primaries with almost 7 million votes (29 percent of all votes cast, including 10 to 25 percent of the white vote) and some 1,200-convention delegates.[31]

Jackson's message in both campaigns exhibited a fascinating mixture of traditional black Baptist spirituality and civil religion. Revival-like rallies and altar calls beckoned respondents to give up drugs and/or register to vote. Pastors and churches of the National Baptist Convention USA provided a powerful network of supporters across the nation. As always, church choirs led the congregations in spirited participation in both standard hymns and the cherished freedom songs—

civil rights mass meetings *redivivus* but with more purely political objectives. On the eve of one Tuesday primary day, Jackson mixed civil and denominational religiosity, assuring the congregation: "We can transform the crucifixion and on Tuesday roll the stone away and on Wednesday morning have a resurrection: new life, new possibilities, new South, new America."[32]

In his historic address to the Democratic National Committee, Jackson clearly enunciated what may be considered the *sine qua non* of any civil religion, namely a concept of America's divine calling. "We are not a perfect people," he admonished. "Yet we are called to a perfect mission...to feed the hungry, to clothe the naked, to house the homeless, to teach the illiterate, to provide jobs for the jobless, and to choose the human race over the nuclear race.... My constituency is the damned, disinherited, disrespected, and the despised." By speaking of America's calling to a "perfect mission," Jackson identified the American people as Church, which the biblical word *ecclesia* defines as "called out ones." Further, he envisioned these "chosen people" as called to feed the hungry and clothe the naked, activities that characterize God's People and are the standard by which divine judgment will measure them (Matt. 25: 34-36). At the same time, however, Jackson added to the divine agenda the more politically progressive elements of fighting illiteracy, joblessness, and the nuclear arms race.

Jackson's America was, however, the sort that presented a multicultural challenge to southern traditionalists. Announcing that his constituency is "the damned, the disinherited, the disrespected, and the despised," he continued:

> Our flag is red, white, and blue, but our nation is rainbow—red, yellow, brown, black, and white—we're all precious in God's sight. America is not like a blanket—one piece of unbroken cloth, the same color, the same texture, the same size. America is more like a quilt— many patches, many pieces, many colors, many sizes, all woven and held together by a common thread. The white, the Hispanic, the black, the Arab, the Jew, the woman, the Native American, the small farmer, the businessperson, the environmentalist, the peace activist, the young, the old, the lesbian, the gay, and the disabled make up the American quilt.[33]

Rejecting the melting pot metaphor, oft-cited even by African-American ministers of previous generations, Jackson elsewhere employed a more pluralistic analogy that included both separation and assimilation:

> Melting pot means you pour everything into one and you melt it, and then nothing is nothing and everything is everything. I'm not with

that. I'm with the vegetable soup, where you a have common base, but the peas, beans, potatoes, and meat all maintain their identity. When it starts simmering and you start drawing some flavor from the meat, the beans, and the potatoes, then all of us contribute to the base. We contribute to the commonwealth, but we do not lose our identity."[34]

Such a vision of America, inclusive even of morally "damned" or "despised" lesbians and gays, has of course been viewed by the Religious Right as an enemy ideology in the culture wars. Ironically, the 1988 presidential primaries saw a symbolic contest of religious visions between Jackson's crusade and that of the television evangelist Marion G. "Pat" Robertson. Though not as successful as Jackson in attracting voters, Robertson also used churches and pastors as his base and enjoyed some success early in the primary season, particularly in caucus states where success depends on energizing an enthusiastic cadre of activists. After upsetting George Bush in the Iowa caucuses, Robertson was hurt by verbal gaffes on a variety of issues. Like Jackson, Robertson expected the South, where unlike Jackson he could appeal to conservative white evangelicals, to give his campaign a boost. Two-thirds of voters in every southern state told pollsters they disapproved of Robertson, who alienated large numbers of Falwell-type fundamentalists with his charismatic theology. On Super Tuesday, Robertson failed to meet expectations, garnering only 13 percent of the total vote. By mid-May he was forced to suspend his campaign, which had won fewer than 50 delegates and reduced him to a non-factor at the Republican National Convention. In stark contrast to Jackson's America, Robertson based his campaign on an appeal to an embattled "culture of traditionalist Protestantism" embittered by liberals who had cast America adrift by loosing it from its "Judeo-Christian" moorings.[35]

Although the two Baptist preachers from the South never campaigned against each other directly, their presence in the primaries continued the civil religious conflict of the Civil Rights era and was a harbinger of what, two years later, the sociologist James Davison Hunter would call the "culture wars." Like many subsequent analyses of these culture wars, Hunter gives the issue of race too little attention. In reality, the South has become the primary theater of the wars, and *the heart* of the current *Kulturkampf* is a conflict between a homogeneous civil religion of exclusion and a pluralistic civil religion. Moreover, this particular phase of civil religious conflict began in the civil rights era and continues into this new millennium.

Armed with this civil religion of inclusion the Civil Rights Movement eventually won its primary victories on the streets of Alabama, first in Birmingham and then in Selma. Then came the commitment of the federal government to its goals in the Civil Rights Act of 1964 (resulting from the Birmingham protests), the Voting Rights Act of 1965, (resulting from the Selma to Montgomery March), and the Great Society programs (resulting from the assassination of John Kennedy and election of Lyndon Johnson). But the victory would be short-lived, and political genius that he was, Johnson had an inkling of what was to come. On the very night that he signed the Civil Rights Act of 1964, LBJ explained to his press secretary, Bill Moyers, his reason for feeling downcast rather than elated, "Because, Bill, I think we just delivered the South to the Republican Party for a long time to come."[36]

Johnson could hardly have been more prescient, both as to the white South's defection and the duration of it. Today we stand almost 40 years since Johnson's comments and a return of a Prodigal White South to the Democratic party is nowhere in sight. Johnson's political instincts rightly told him that casting his party's lot with the agenda of black America would alienate his fellow white Southerners. Indeed, many Southerners viewed Johnson, a Texan, as a traitor to the South because of his racial liberalism, and though he won a landslide victory over Barry Goldwater in 1964, he lost the Deep South. One could hardly have been lonelier, or more in danger of being beaten up, than the rare white southern school child unwise enough to gloat to his classmates on the day after the election that his parents' candidate had won and theirs had not. Not long after the election, there appeared in Birmingham, Alabama, and doubtless other southern venues, license plates with a cartoon of a Democratic donkey with a Johnsonesque face, passing gas, and a caption that read, "LBJ Has Spoken."[37]

More significantly, since then the Democrats have lost not only most of the white South, but they have also consistently lost the majority of white male votes in the entire nation. As the former columnist Tom Wicker has noted, "The Democratic Party after 1964 lost a critical and growing share of the white vote, owing to the party's supposed devotion to black interests." Indeed, the last Democratic presidential candidate to win a majority of the nation's white males was Johnson in 1964.[38] The disaffection of whites from the Democratic agenda of the Great Society, increasingly perceived as the black agenda, was remarkably rapid. Non-southern white hostility to black advances can be seen in opinion polling data. When Johnson took office in 1963 a Harris poll found that only 31 percent of Americans polled believed that the federal government was pushing integration "too fast." Only five years later the figure had risen to 51 percent. A 1976 Gallup poll indicated the percentage was an even higher 72 percent.[39]

Thus a national reversal began within three years of the high water marks of the Civil Rights Movement. In addition to the Democrats' "capture" by the civil rights agenda and its commitment to the Great Society, middle-class white voters, especially in the South, were angered by the Watts riots of 1965, Martin Luther King's denunciation of the Vietnam War in 1967, and the civil disturbances after King's assassination in 1968. This helps explain their disaffection with black interests and their move away from the Democratic Party.[40]

Two questions thus arise. First, to whom did middle- and working-class white voters angry at civil rights agitators and the counterculture go in the 1968 presidential election? Second, how then was this white backlash against the gains of the Civil Rights Movement connected to the broader array of social issues that make up the culture war of recent days? The answer to both questions is the same: George Wallace. The historian Dan T. Carter, first among a number of historians, has made a solid case for the "fighting judge" and later governor of Alabama as the antecedent of "the politics of rage."

Through the 1980s and 1990s, the issues Wallace articulated and the enemies he excoriated "moved from the fringes of our society to center stage." Wallace did not create the conservative groundswell of the culture war. However, Carter argues, "he anticipated most of its themes." Wallace himself noted as much when he pointed out that, "They all talking like me. Nixon, Reagan, Clinton. Welfare reform. Crime. Big government. Taxes on the middle class. They all saying now what I was saying then."[41] By thinking of his 1968 third-party run for the presidency, Wallace had broadened his criticism beyond the traditional racial politics of his "schoolhouse door" phase to a wider range of social battles that were later joined by the Moral Majority and the Christian Coalition. Yet beneath it all lingered the slightly domesticated racism that had earlier demanded "Segregation today, segregation tomorrow, segregation forever."

Carter points out that Wallace knew that a substantial percentage of the American electorate despised the civil rights agitators and antiwar demonstrators as symptoms of a fundamental decline in the traditional cultural compass of God, family, and country. This decline was reflected in rising crime rates, the legalization of abortion, the rise of out-of-wedlock pregnancies, the increase in divorce rates, and the proliferation of "obscene" literature and films. Always moving beneath the surface was the fear that blacks were moving beyond their safely encapsulated ghettoes into "our" streets, "our" schools, "our" neighborhoods.[42]

Thus fears of black criminality and associations with the disorder of the 1960s counterculture were not only central to Wallace's message, but were "the warp and woof" of the new social agenda of the conservative counterrevolution.[43] The Wallace message and his enlarged following outside the South suggested, of course, the prevalence of racism outside the South, and in the process came to the attention of Richard Nixon. As early as 1966, Nixon had decided to run for the presidency, and during a fund-raising trip to South Carolina he told Harry

Dent, aide to Strom Thurmond and chief architect of Nixon's southern strategy, that getting the Wallace vote in the South was the key to victory. In the 1968 campaign, Nixon taped a "law and order" political advertisement in which he echoed Wallace's themes. John Erlichman later told of his boss's effusive praise of the commercial, exulting, "It's all about law and order and the damn Negro-Puerto Rican groups out there."[44]

After the 1968 election, which Nixon barely won and during which Nixon was the second choice of more than 70 percent of Wallace voters, Nixon vowed to stick with his southern strategy and do his best to keep the Wallace vote in his 1972 re-election bid. He certainly reflected the spirit, even if he avoided the exact phraseology of the famous Wallace line, spoken after a race-baiting opponent defeated him in the 1958 governor's race, that he intended never to be "out-niggered again." Soon, Nixon's domestic policies reflected Wallace's call for law and order and criticism of busing to achieve racial balance in the schools. Carter sums it up nicely: "When George Wallace had played his fiddle, the President of the United States had danced Jim Crow."[45]

Since then, at least in the voices that have occupied the Oval Office, the Republican Party has largely been George Wallace without the southern accent. As the dean of southern historians, C. Vann Woodward, put it, "[S]outhern white Democrats have been Republicanized and northern white Republicans have been southernized."[46] Ronald Reagan echoed Wallace themes with a friendlier face. As a rising Republican spokesman for General Electric, and later as Governor of California, he opposed the Civil Rights Act of 1964. After his presidential nomination in 1980, he began his general election campaign announcing his commitment to states' rights in Neshoba County, Mississippi, where three civil rights workers were murdered in 1964. By the end of the Reagan administration the Religious Right had been emboldened enough for Robertson to challenge Vice President George Bush for the 1988 nomination. Robertson, one critic suggested, amounted to a "rambling, shined-up George Wallace with a spiritual overlay."[47]

Similar themes were a regular part of Republican strategies throughout the first Bush administration and in Newt Gingrich's tenure as Speaker of the House. As recently as his 2000 presidential campaign, Patrick Buchanan promised that his new Reform Party would "defend America's history, heritage and heroes against the Visigoths and Vandals of multiculturalism." His radio ads emphasized the culture war, claiming "It's time to take our country back from those who are tearing it down." He added: "In the culture war, Al Gore is the enemy and George W. Bush won't fight."[48]

Having thus reacted against the pluralistic images of America and the racial gains of the civil rights era, the wider American nation has increasingly mythologized the nation in ways similar to the homogeneous civil religionists of the white South. The issue of racial and cultural diversity remains at the heart of the culture war. Michael Lind has correctly perceived that, since Nixon and Reagan, the Republican Party has moved from relatively progressive racial policy to using race as a wedge. He adds: "The politics of 'culture war'...is, like so much else in the GOP, a transplant from the poisoned soil of the Bourbon South." Not coincidentally, in presidential elections white Republicanism in the South has risen sharply from 40 percent in 1968 to as high as 67 percent in 1988 and 72 percent in 1984. Several political scientists have thus argued that the rise of two-party politics in the South has made the culture wars possible and assures that "culture wars between the Democratic and Republican Parties appear increasingly significant in southern political life."[49]

For contemporary southerners, perhaps the most hotly contested battleground of the culture wars remains how to deal with the region's Confederate past. Writing about the South's continuing battles over the Civil War, the historian David Goldfield sees these issues as crucial both to the region and the nation: "What southern society will become in this new century, especially given the growing economic and political importance of the region, and what America will become as well, will depend largely on how southerners reconstruct their past."[50]

No segment of this larger concern is more controversial than debates about the Confederate flag. This issue relates directly to the most wrenching culture war of nineteenth-century America, the Civil War, and touches upon symbolic meanings of both America and the Confederate South. Because it does, the battle elevates the emotional temperature wherever and whenever it is joined. The matter also generates powerful feelings because it divides Southerners racially—those who cling to the flag are almost exclusively white, while virtually all African Americans oppose its use, many actively.

Another important reason why this issue stirs up powerful emotions on both sides is precisely because it has to do with a flag. Flags are among the most sacred objects of any civil religion. For those who fly them, a flag embodies the mythic meanings and the sacredness of the nation they love, as well as the values for which the flag stands. To destroy a flag is not mere vandalism; it is a violation. It is a profanation of that which citizens believe to be sacred about their nation. For this reason more than any other, Americans refer to flag burning as "desecration."

Since the 1990s the flag issue has arisen several times in a variety of southern venues. Early in the Clinton administration, controversies over the flag developed in Georgia, Mississippi, and Virginia.

In Mississippi, the debate raged over use of the Confederate flag at University of Mississippi football games, when the 700 black undergraduates refused to sit in the student section because white students were there waving the controversial emblem. Related to this, three black members of the Ole Miss band put down their instruments, stood, and folded their arms to protest the playing of "Dixie."[51]

That same year, the city of Danville, Virginia, became embroiled in the debate when the board of trustees of the city's Museum of Fine Arts and History voted to stop flying the flag from atop its building, which in fact is the historic "Last Capital of the Confederacy." (During the last week of the Civil War, as the Yankees closed in on Richmond, the Confederate government was moved west to Danville.) "We Southern Americans are a little pissed off," protested a member of the Sons of Confederate Veterans, apparently speaking for many who expressed themselves in a slightly more genteel manner. Over the next few days, the *Danville Register and Bee* was flooded with over 7,000 phone calls, 95 percent of which indicated opposition to removing the flag. The paper also ran page upon page of letters to the editor reflecting similar feelings. Linwood Wright, president of the museum's board of trustees, also received a flurry of calls, some of which he described as "venomous."[52]

Some of the arguments for flying the flag rehashed old historians' debates by which many white Southerners assuaged their guilt by denying that the flag or the Confederacy represent slavery. They largely argued that the flag represented the Confederacy as a period of American history that, though tragic, could not be changed and should not be whitewashed. They denied that the flag represented slavery, but stood rather for states' rights and the valor with which their great-great grandfathers fought and died. No one questions the courage of Confederate soldiers as they fought for principles in which they believed. But clearly, they believed in slavery even if they were a part of the percent of antebellum southern whites who did not own slaves. White Southerners have had a long tradition of avoiding the fact that the Civil War was *primarily*, though not exclusively, about the problem of slavery in a land that claimed that "all men are created equal."

Those who argue that the Confederate flag does not imply slavery or racism would do well to note a March 1861 speech in which the Vice-President of the Confederacy, Alexander Stephens, asserted that, unlike the "Old" Union, the Confederacy did not stand for the equality of the races. Rather, he continued: "Our new Government is founded upon exactly the opposite ideas; its foundations are laid, its cornerstone rests, upon the great truth that the Negro is not equal to the white man, that slavery—subordination to the superior race—is his natural and normal condition."[53] And Stephens was hardly alone. States' rights was a means to the end of preserving slavery and was therefore a subsidiary rather than the primary cause. So if the Confederacy's noble cause was to preserve slavery, it is difficult to deny that its flag at least indirectly symbolizes slavery and the racism upon which it was based. *That* is part of the southern heritage, and arguing that the flag does not symbolize that is precisely to gloss over and rewrite southern history.

But other arguments set forth in the Danville debate reflect connections with the current culture war, as many of its hot-button issues showed up in the tangential arguments of flag defenders. Political correctness, often the scourge of many of today's cultural conservatives, was seen as inspiring the decision to remove the flag. One Danvillian wrote, "Flying the flag…may not be politically correct, but it is historically correct." Another writer attributed the black response to the flag to being too easily offended. "It is precisely this type of thinking," he wrote, "which has driven God and prayer from our classrooms." Similarly, still another reader took aim at Danville city council member Joyce Glaise, who had applauded the museum's decision. Comparing Glaise to America's most hated atheist, Madeline Murray O'Hair, the letter complained: "We're already had one woman single-handedly try to bring down the morals of our nation by having prayer removed from our schools. Now you want to remove another vital part of our heritage. *No way!*"

Many writers called on the city to wave the Confederate flag as proudly as they would the American flag. Finally, reflecting the nostalgia for the good old days, one writer commented, "I think most of the people who live here liked our town the way it used to be."[54] Whether these citizens preferred Danville "the way it used to be" before the Civil War, or simply before the Civil Rights Movement, is unclear, but there is little doubt that their arguments for the Confederate flag match up with many of the concerns of conservative culture warriors.

During the 2000 elections, the flag was raised as a campaign issue in both the South Carolina state and presidential primaries. In May the state legislature approved a bill moving the flag from atop the statehouse to a Civil War monument on the capitol grounds. The measure was passed as a response to a five-month tourism boycott of South Carolina by the NAACP, an action that cost the state more than $20 million in revenue from conventions and conferences. The decision also led to protests among flag supporters. As the NAACP boycott got under way, so did the presidential primary season. Covering the early primaries, reporters asked questions that forced candidates to take sides on the issue. Arizona Senator John McCain acknowledged its divisiveness, but said, "I believe it's a symbol of heritage." The primary victor, George W. Bush, tread lightly, saying it was a matter for the people of South Carolina to decide. The Democratic candidate, Al Gore, supported the removal of the flag from the state capitol and criticized Bush for ducking the issue.

In Georgia the flag became a cause celebre twice in recent years. In 1992 the popular governor Zell Miller ran afoul of the electorate and almost cost himself a second term, because of his plan to change the state flag, which incorporated the

Confederate emblem. That version of the Georgia flag had been adopted only in 1956, Miller pointed out, as a protest against integration. He called it "the fighting flag of those who wanted to preserve a segregated South."

By the time he gave his State of the State speech in 1993, Miller knew he did not have the votes to change the flag. Yet he addressed the issue directly, and in terms reminiscent of both the Civil War and the contemporary culture wars. He identified the Confederate flag with "the dark side of the Confederacy—the desire to deprive some Americans of the equal rights that are the birthright of all Americans, and yes, the determination to destroy the United States if necessary to achieve that goal.... Yet we maintain as a symbol of our state a flag that challenges the very existence of the United States of America."[55] The governor lost that fight by a large margin. But he correctly predicted that the issue would not die and that the Rebel-dominated flag of Georgia would not last too far into the future.

In 2001, reacting to threats of a similar NAACP boycott against Georgia and led by Governor Roy Barnes, the Georgia General Assembly voted to change the state flag to a new design that made the Confederate emblem much less prominent. Southern heritage groups almost immediately declared war on Barnes, pledging to unseat him in his 2002 re-election campaign and distributing bumper stickers sporting the Rebel flag and the slogans, "Keep the Flag. Change the Governor" and "Boot Barnes." A Democratic-turned-Republican state legislator, Sonny Perdue, later launched a gubernatorial campaign promising to give the citizens of Georgia a referendum on the state flag. In one of the biggest upset victories in recent memory, Perdue defeated Barnes to become the first Republican governor of the state since Reconstruction. Most observers of Georgia politics agreed that tinkering with the state banner had cost Barnes his job and that Perdue had entered the Governor's Mansion wrapped in the Confederate flag.

Perdue then steered away from the issue, avoiding comment on the flag until his second day in office, when he told an interviewer that he saw a referendum as "the only way Georgia can move on." Black state legislators scoffed at the idea that a referendum would heal the divide, most warning that the return of the Confederate emblem would be accompanied by renewed tension, economic boycotts, and a public relations black eye for the state. While certain white Georgians view the flag as symbolic of southern valor and heritage and most blacks see it as the emblem of slavery, the governor avoided going on record. "I'm not going there," he insisted, "I'm not going to impugn the referendum process." Nevertheless, he tipped his hand at his inauguration by banning Confederate flags at the ceremony. To protest the move, three small planes circled the air space over the capitol with banners imploring, "Let Us Vote.

You Promised."

An *Atlanta Journal-Constitution* poll in early January 2003 revealed that two-thirds of Georgians wanted a referendum on the flag, with more than 50 percent viewing the emblem as a symbol of southern heritage and a third seeing it as a symbol of "oppression and racial division." Armed with this knowledge, Perdue pushed through the General Assembly a nonbinding referendum, which would still require legislative approval, for March 2004. Coupled with the referendum, however, was the adoption of another new Georgia flag, this one based on the old Confederate Stars and Bars, but without the controversial St. Andrew's Cross.

Perdue proposed a two-part referendum, the first aimed at getting voters' approval for the 2003 design. Absent that, a second referendum would ask voters to choose between the pre-1956 design, which was similar to the most recent design, and the more controversial version, which bore the St. Andrew's Cross and was adopted in 1956 as Georgia's expression of "massive resistance" to desegregation. When black state legislators opposed any vote including the Rebel Cross and civil rights organizations threatened boycotts in response to any such referendum, the two-referendum plan lost support. On the last day of the longest session of the Georgia legislature since 1889, the second referendum was dropped, making the first a choice between the 2001 flag put through by Barnes and the 2003 design. Speaking for the Sons of Confederate Veterans, Dan Coleman expressed disappointment and warned, "I imagine that everybody will want to become politically active again."[56]

It is no coincidence that the culture wars and the recent battles over the Confederate flag arose in the same decade. Racial and cultural difference in America has become an undeniable reality as blacks and other previously marginalized Americans have demanded an equal place at the table. For white Southerners change comes slowly. A 1970 survey by the National Opinion Research Center showed that 55 percent of white Southerners agreed strongly that blacks should not push for inclusion where they are not wanted; 26.5 percent agreed slightly. In 2000, 19 percent agreed strongly and 30 percent agreed slightly. Rural areas of the South have seen the least change and the most support for Confederate symbols. In Columbia, South Carolina, Chris Sullivan, editor of *Southern Partisan*, spoke to this issue, complaining that the South is becoming too much like the rest of the country and citing immigration and commercial development as the main culprits. Most Southerners are adjusting to such changes, but Charles R. Wilson has noted that "an intensely committed ideological group" has viewed the politics of the post-Reagan era as "a kind of last stand." They have enlisted in the culture wars with a rebel yell.[57]

The Culture Wars Go International

Commenting on the end of the Cold War, the sociologist Todd Gitlin has asked a pertinent question: "Without the enemy, what united the states?"[58] Turning inward in the 1990s ultra-conservatives could now focus attention on their historic domestic enemies, liberalism and liberals. Beginning in the 1980 election, "liberal" increasingly became a "four-letter word" and the culture warriors were drawing a line in the sand against those they so labeled. America's most dangerous enemies, the culture warriors argued, were the indigenous "Blame America First" crowd. Until September 11, 2001.

But two days after the terrorist attacks on the World Trade Center and the Pentagon, the South's two foremost culture warriors were making connections between "enemies foreign and domestic." On the *700 Club* broadcast, Jerry Falwell told Pat Robertson: "I really believe that the pagans, and the abortionists, and the feminists, and the gays and the lesbians who are actively trying to make that an alternative lifestyle, the ACLU, People for the American Way—all of them who have tried to secularize America—I point the finger in their face and say, 'You helped this happen." Robertson "totally concurred" with his guest, opining: "It [terrorism] is happening because God Almighty is lifting his protection from us. We have a court that has essentially stuck its finger in God's eye.... We have insulted God at the highest level of our government. Then we say, 'Why does this happen?'"[59]

If not "everything," September 11 changed quite a bit in America. Attacked by foreign enemies on U.S. soil for the first time since the War of 1812 (the attack on Pearl Harbor took place before Hawaii became a state), Americans in all regions have brought out their flags and supported a retaliatory "War on Terrorism" with firm, almost enthusiastic resolve. Falwell's and Robertson's comments relating the actions of Islamic *jihadis* to God's judgment against the Religious Right's pluralistic enemies made a clear connection between the culture wars and the struggle against terrorism. Indeed, September 11 sparked a significant change, an internationalization, of America's ongoing culture wars.

Despite President Bush's admonitions not to make this struggle into a war against Islam, the president's own dualistic language in describing the effort gave some of his southern fundamentalist followers license to inveigh against Islam as a religion of violence. Indeed, the president's early, knee-jerk reaction to the attacks was precisely to call America's retaliatory efforts a "crusade." The Freudian slip was quickly reversed by White House public relations experts and the president later termed Islam a "religion of peace." Still, in almost biblical cadences, Bush regularly portrayed the War on Terrorism as a struggle between good and evil.

In early 2003, on the eve of launching a war against Iraq, Mr. Bush told religious broadcasters in Nashville that America was called to bring liberty to "every human being in the world." In Saddam Hussein, he warned, the United States was "encountering evil," adding, "If anyone can be at peace, I am at peace about this."[60] Many news accounts tell of the president's sense of destiny. He reportedly once told Richard Land, the conservative ethics guru of the Southern Baptist Convention, that he believed God wanted him to be president. After September 11 Mr. Bush occasionally spoke of "being chosen by the grace of God to lead at that moment."[61]

Gradually the restraint toward Islam prescribed by the president was undermined by his own rhetoric and was all but jettisoned by some of his most loyal followers. By the summer of 2003, just after the president landed in a flight suit on the USS Abraham Lincoln to announce the Iraq mission accomplished, prominent leaders of the Religious Right and the Southern Baptist Convention (SBC) began to take direct aim at Islam. The former SBC president, Jerry Vines, described the Prophet Muhammad as a "demon-possessed pedophile." He added: "Allah is not Jehovah either. Jehovah's not going to turn you into a terrorist that'll try to bomb people and take the lives of thousands and thousands of people." When asked, the current SBC president, Jack Graham, told reporters he agreed with Vines.

In addition to these incidents, the syndicated conservative columnist Ann Coulter called on Muslims to find "some sort of hobby other than slaughtering infidels." Just after September 11, Coulter advised, "We should invade their countries, kill their leaders, and convert them to Christianity." Franklin Graham, heir of the Billy Graham Evangelistic Association, told one talk-show host that Islam was an inherently violent religion. The Family Policy Network launched a suit to stop the University of North Carolina from requiring freshmen to read a book on the Quran, an assignment the Fox News superstar Bill O'Reilly compared to teaching Hitler's *Mein Kampf*. The SBC's Richard Land said he did not disapprove of the president's efforts to distinguish terrorism from Islam. "But I'm afraid," he added, "that his comment that Islam is a religion of peace is more a wish than a fact."[62]

But the most celebrated (or condemned) instance of the war on terrorism as an internationalized culture war was the comments of Lt. Gen. William G. Boykin. Before his assignment as Deputy Undersecretary of Defense for Intelligence, Boykin had served as commanding general of the U.S. Army's John F. Kennedy Special Warfare Center and School in Fort Bragg, North Carolina. He had led the "Blackhawk Down" mission in Somalia and told his experiences to evangelical church groups. In June 2003, he told the Good Shepherd Community Church in Sandy, Oregon, that Osama Bin Laden, Saddam Hussein, and Kim Jung Il hate America "because we're a Christian nation. We are hated because we are a nation of believers." These enemies, he claimed, "will only be defeated if we come against them in the name of Jesus." Defending the Iraq War as a "spiritual battle," he told the Oregon congregation, "Satan wants to destroy this nation, he wants to destroy us as a nation, and he wants to destroy us as a Christian army."

A native of Wilson, North Carolina, Boykin graduated from Virginia Polytechnic Institute and the first three stops in his military career were in southern venues, Fort Hood, Texas, Fort Campbell, Kentucky, and Fort Stewart, Georgia. Embodying the military-religious traditions of the Old South, the general's highly decorated career made him seem like a latter-day "Stonewall" Jackson. He served his country in the infamous 1980 hostage rescue mission in Iran, Grenada, the drug wars in Columbia, and in Somalia. Often appearing in uniform, he also boasted of being "a warrior in the kingdom of God" and praised the leadership of President Bush, who prays in the Oval Office and "was appointed by God" to his office. At a Southern Baptist church in Daytona, Florida, Boykin narrated his encounter with the Somalian warlord Osman Atto. Relating Atto's boast of Allah's protection, Boykin told the congregation, "I knew that my God was bigger than his. I knew that my God was a real God and his was an idol."[63] He also told audiences that Bin Laden was not America's real enemy. "It's the enemy you can't see," he warned, "It's a war against the forces of darkness. The battle won't be won with guns. It will be won on our knees."[64]

In a sermon to the First Baptist Church of Broken Arrow, Oklahoma, Boykin's comments connected the war on terrorism and American support of Israel to interpretations with which culture warriors' typically argue for America's Judeo-Christian foundations. Citing John Adams list of Hebrew contributions to American government and both Thomas Jefferson and Benjamin Franklin's recommended national symbols with an Exodus motif, he explained the current U.S. commitment to Israel. "We will never abandon Israel," he asserted, "We will never walk away from our commitment to Israel because our roots are there. Our religion came from Judaism, and therefore these radicals will hate us forever."[65]

After the *Los Angeles Times* broke the Boykin story on October 15, 2003, several national newspapers, including the *Times*, the *New York Times*, and the *Washington Post* called on the president and Secretary of Defense Donald Rumsfeld to fire or at least chastise Boykin. At the same time spokespersons of the Religious Right came to Boykin's defense. The Family Research Council president, Tony Perkins, impugned Boykin's detractors as attacking his rights of free speech. The columnist Cal Thomas, formerly a Moral Majority colleague of Jerry Falwell, wrote an op-ed piece in Boykin's defense. The Reverend Bobby Welch, pastor of the Daytona church, issued a sharp statement of support, saying, "I despise the unthinkable and asinine fact that some take cheap backstabbing shots at a real God-fearing American hero who continually risks his life to protect all of us."[66]

As the controversy escalated, Rumsfeld announced an investigation of the general's public comments, and Virginia's Republican Senator John Warner and Michigan's Democratic Senator Carl Levin, speaking for the Senate Armed Services Committee, asked Rumsfeld to reassign Boykin while the investigation went forward. Finally, after several days of official silence, President Bush issued a mild rebuke of General Boykin, saying that Boykin's views did not reflect either the president's or the government's opinion of the war on terrorism. Likewise, Rumsfeld refused to discipline the general or criticize him publicly.

The South has been at the center of the culture wars, and true to its history of strong support for the military, the region has led the nation in support for the Iraq theater of the war on terrorism. Polls in the *Atlanta Journal-Constitution* have shown high levels of support not only during the successful first phase of the war but also during the summer of 2003, when the U.S. efforts to win the peace faced a rising number of guerilla attacks. At the beginning of the Iraq War, in March 2003, A Zogby poll showed that 69 percent of Southerners supported the war. Five months later, during the growing guerilla phase of the hostilities, a *Newsweek* poll showed that across the nation 59 percent of Americans would still support the war if could do it over again. In the South, however, that number was 63 percent. Nor had support for the president wavered. Linda Butler Johnson, county leader of the Charleston, South Carolina, Republican Party, said, "I've had more e-mails and calls requesting Bush-Cheney bumper stickers and pins in the past two weeks than I've had in the last three months." In a Zogby poll, 57 percent of Georgia respondents approved of the president's handling of the Iraq War, compared with 37 percent who disapproved. Ralph Reed, Southeastern chairman of the Bush '04 campaign and former chairman of the Georgia GOP, said, "Even when other parts of the country have wavered, the South has traditionally been the most patriotic region."[67]

In spite of this strong support for the Iraq War, there is evidence that the culture war divisions correspond with disagreements about the war on terrorism. Perhaps this is most obvious in the ways America's popular recording artists, particularly in country music, memorialized September 11 and entered the debate over the war. When Nashville and the country music world—traditionally the home of patriotism and piety—finds itself divided in its responses to September 11, one knows that either "country ain't country anymore" or that the culture war divisions are deeper than we imagined. That 9/11 would spark a large number of musical reactions in Nashville was predictable, but not the diversity of opinion.

The first to raise controversy was Toby Keith's ode to both September 11 and to his military father. The song received a big public relations boost when Peter Jennings refused to use a Keith performance of the song on a national broadcast. When an interviewer asked Keith's opinion of Jennings' decision, the singer wryly asked, "He's from Canada, isn't he?" Released just as the United States began its retaliatory strikes against Afghanistan, "The Angry American" ("Courtesy of the Red, White, and Blue") lighting up the unnamed Taliban's "world like the Fourth of July as soon as we could see clearly through our big black eye." Uncle Sam put "your name at the top of his list," while "the Statue of Liberty started shaking her fist" and "Mother Freedom start[s] ringing her bell." Together, they all deliver the biggest applause line in the final stanza: "You'll be sorry you messed with the US of A. We'll put a boot in your ass, it's the American Way."

As phase two of the war on terrorism began in Iraq, with much more dissent than been had accompanied the fighting in Afghanistan, Darryl Worley's "Do You Remember?" so closely linked the invasion of Iraq with September 11 it could have been written by the Bush administration. "I hear people saying we don't need this war," Worley begins, "I say there's some things worth fighting for." To those who worry about a possible quagmire in Iraq, "before you start preaching," he asks "Have you forgotten how it felt that day to see your homeland under fire…. And you say we shouldn't worry 'bout Bin Laden—Have you forgotten?" When critics accuse the United States of "looking for a fight," the militant troubadour agrees, "After 9/11 man I'd have to say that's right."

On the other side of the divide, possibly the biggest controversy since 9/11 was the comment of the Dixie Chicks' lead singer, Natalie Maines, who told an audience in London, "Just so you know, we are embarrassed that the president of the United States is from [our state of] Texas." Maines had earlier criticized Keith's song, creating a stir among country music fans who wrote *Country Music Weekly* with harsh letters condemning the Chicks. That furor paled in comparison, however, to the one touched off by the anti-Bush statement. In retaliation Clear Channel radio banned its nationwide network of stations from playing the group's music and angry fans destroyed their copies of Chicks' CDs. Eventually, the Dixie Chicks appeared on ABC television to be lectured by Diane Sawyer and to explain themselves and apologize to the president. Part of their half-hearted apology included an apologia that included a quote from Teddy Roosevelt: "To announce that there must be no criticism of the President, or that we are to stand by the President, right or wrong, is not only unpatriotic and servile, but is morally treasonable to the American public."[68]

Somewhat outside the country-music genre, the singer-songwriter Don Henley could not resist a political comment or two in the Eagles' new recordings. A feisty Texan of liberal persuasion, Henley has leveled strong critiques of American culture before in songs like "Dirty Laundry" and "Workin' It."

He responded to September 11 with "Hole in the World," in which a "cloud of fear and sorrow" was largely caused by "all this fighting over who will be anointed." Explaining the reference, he condemned the clearly civil religious notion of American exceptionalism: "I'm tired of this country acting like God is an American. God doesn't have favorites. I'm tired of the President wrapping himself in the flag and scripture and justifying his actions that way. The song talks about who is the anointed, and that's really the basis for what the song is about. We need a little more humility in this country. We're looked upon around the world as being a very bloated, egotistical nation."

Henley also seems to predict difficulty for the United States in extracting itself from Iraq in "Long Road out of Eden." Noting that Eden was likely located in present-day Iraq, Henley notes the irony that "the petroleum we're fighting over comes from lush vegetation that was once in that area. So when you're driving around in your SUV, you're actually burning the Garden of Eden." He added sardonically: "We're not going to try to get too terribly political. Lord knows rock stars shouldn't get political. No opinions, please, from musicians. At this stage of the game, what's the point? Until the hysteria dies down and the jingoism and xenophobia all die down, there's not much point in saying anything."[69]

Thus, in the three years since September 11, the most patriotic and pious—and southern—genre of American popular music has, like the nation at large, been divided by the war on terrorism. Looking perhaps for solace, and seeking to stay above the fray, the country artist Alan Jackson won a Grammy by offering the mournful benediction, "Where Were You When the World Stopped Turning." Confessing that he was not "a real political man" who did not "know the difference in Iraq and Iran," the Georgian simply knows Jesus and that "faith, hope, and love are some good things he gave us/And the greatest of these is love." The nation and the region will need some of all three before these culture wars are over.

Endnotes

1   Charles Reagan Wilson, *Baptized in Blood: The Religion of the Lost Cause, 1865-1920* (Athens: University of Georgia Press, 1980); Andrew M. Manis, *Southern Civil Religions in Conflict: Black and White Baptists and Civil Rights, 1947-1957* (Athens: University of Georgia Press, 1987); see also my revised and expanded edition, published with a new subtitle, *Southern Civil Religions in Conflict: Civil Rights and the Culture* (Macon: Mercer University Press, 2001).

2   Drew Gilpin Faust, *The Creation of Confederate Nationalism: Ideology and Identity in the Civil War South* (Baton Rouge: Louisiana State University Press, 1990).

3 Wilson, *Baptized in Blood,* passim.

4 Charles Reagan Wilson, " 'God's Project': The Southern Civil Religion, 1920-1980," in Rowland A. Sherrill, ed. *Religion and the Life of the Nation: American Recoveries* (Urbana: University of Illinois Press, 1990), 66-79; James McBride Dabbs, *Who Speaks For the South* (New York: Funk and Wagnalls, 1964), 368, 371-7.

5 Leonard I. Sweet, *Black Images of America, 1784-1870* (New York: W. W. Norton Co., 1976) 175.

6 *Christian Recorder,* February 14, 1863; See also Clarence E. Walker, *A Rock in a Weary Land: The African Methodist Episcopal Church During the Civil War and Reconstruction* (Baton Rouge: Louisiana State University Press, 1982), 41-42. Walker specifically argues that the AME's philosophy of racial uplift was part of its civil religion.

7 Shuttlesworth, interview with author, March 10, 1984. See also Andrew M. Manis, *A Fire You Can't Put Out: The Civil Rights Life of Birmingham's Reverend Fred Shuttlesworth* (Tuscaloosa: University of Alabama Press, 1999).

8 King "A Testament of Hope," *Playboy,* January 1969, 234, quoted in Smith and Zepp, *Search for the Beloved Community,* 127; Nannie H. Burroughs, President's Address, Women's Convention Auxiliary to the National Baptist Convention, *Annual of the National Baptist Convention,* 1954, 411.

9 Shuttlesworth, interview with author, March 10, 1984.

10 Herman Talmadge, *You and Segregation* (Birmingham: Vulcan Press, 1955), 76.

11 A. L. Strozier, "The Battle of the Giants," *Alabama Baptist 120* (July 14, 1955): 8 and 16; From the *Congressional Record,* 83d Cong., 2d sess., May 27, 1954, 7257, quoted by Bartley, *Rise of Massive Resistance,* 118-19.

12 Tom Brady, *Black Monday* (Winona MS.: Association of Citizens Councils, 1955), 67, 6; Patterson quoted in John Bartlow Martin, *The Deep South Says "Never"* (New York: Ballantine Books, 1957), 3.

13 Quoted in George B. Kelsey, *Racism and the Christian Understanding of Man* (New York: Charles Scribners' Sons, 1965), 105.

14 Robert Sherrill, Go*thic Politics in the Deep South* (New York: Grossman Publishers, 1968), 217.

15 These models of relations between church and state are suggested by Grant Wacker in his helpful essay, "Uneasy in Zion: Postmodern Society," in George Marsden, ed., *Evangelicalism and Modern America* (Grand Rapids: William B. Eerdmans Publishing Company, 1984) 28.

16 On anti-abolitionism as a defense of Christian orthodoxy, see Eugene D. Genovese, *A Consuming Fire: The Fall of the Confederacy in the Mind of the White Christian South* (Athens: University of Georgia Press, 1998) 87; See also his foreword to James O. Farmer Jr., *The Metaphysical Confederacy: James Henley Thornwell and the Synthesis of Southern Values* (Macon: Mercer University Press, 1999) xi.

17 J. Henry Smith, *A Sermon Delivered at Greensboro, N.C.*, 11, quoted in Drew Gilpin Faust, *The Creation of Confederate Nationalism* (Baton Rouge: Louisiana State University Press, 1988) 28.

18 *Southern Presbyterian,* December 15, 1860, quoted in Mitchell Snay, *Gospel of Disunion: Religion and Separation in the Antebellum South* (Chapel Hill: University of North Carolina Press, 1993) 59. See especially 59-67, for Snay's cogent analysis of the interrelationships between the biblical defense of slavery, the critique of abolitionism, and the defense of religious orthodoxy.

19 Quoted in Nancy Tatom Ammerman, *Baptist Battles: Social Change and Religious Conflict in the Southern Baptist Convention* (New Brunswick: Rutgers University Press, 1990) 39.

20 John Shelton Reed, *The Enduring South* (Chapel Hill: University of North Carolina Press, 1983) 57; George Gallup, Jr. and Jim Castelli, *The People's Religion* (New York: Macmillan, 1989) 86.

21 Carl Abbott, "Urban Growth," in Charles Reagan Wilson and William E. Ferris, eds., *Encyclopedia of Southern Culture* (Chapel Hill: University of North Carolina Press, 1989) 1444-1445.

22 Earl and Merle Black, *Politics and Society in the South* (Cambridge: Harvard University Press, 1988) 16.

23 Figures come from United States Census, 1990; John Shelton Reed, *The Enduring South: Subcultural Persistence in Mass Society* (Chapel Hill: University of North Carolina Press, 1972), 57-58; George Gallup, Jr. and Jim Castelli, *The People's Religion* (New York : Macmillan, 1989), 86.

24 William R. Hutchison, *Religious Pluralism in America* (New Haven: Yale University Press, 2003), 221-2, 226.

25 Todd Gitlin, *The Twilight of Common Dreams: Why America Is Wracked by Culture Wars* (New York: Henry Holt and Company, 1995), 59.

26 Adolph L. Reed, Jr. *The Jesse Jackson Phenomenon* (New Haven: Yale University Press, 1986), 1-10.

27 James Melvin Washington, "Jesse Jackson and the Symbolic Politics of Black Christendom," *Annals of the American Academy of Political and Social Sciences* 480 (July 1985): 97, 102.

28 Comment overheard by the author while attending a Jackson rally in Louisville, Kentucky.

29 *Ibid.*, 11-21.

30 Earl Black and Merle Black, *The Vital South: How Presidents Are Elected* (Cambridge: Harvard University Press, 1991), 257-8; Mfanya Donald Tryman, "Jesse Jackson's Campaigns for the Presidency: A Comparison of the 1984 and 1988 Democratic Primaries," in Huey L. Perry and Wayne Parent, eds. *Blacks and the American Political System* (Gainesville: University Press of Florida, 1995), 60; Thomas H. Landess and Richard M. Quinn, *Jesse Jackson and the Politics of Race* (Ottawa, IL: Jameson Books, 1985), 227.

31 *Vital South,* 267; Tryman, 57; Kenneth D. Wald, "Ministering to the Nation: The Campaigns of Jesse Jackson and Pat Robertson," in Emmett H. Buell, Jr. and Lee Sigelman, eds., *Nominating the President.* (Knoxville: University of Tennessee Press, 1991), 126-7.

32 Wald, 136.

33 Quotes from Jackson's convention speech are taken from Dierdre Mullane, ed. *Crossing the Danger Water: Three Hundred Years of African-American Writing* (New York: Anchor Books, 1993), 734-6.

34 Roger D. Hatch, *Beyond Opportunity: Jesse Jackson's Vision for America* (Philadelphia: Fortress Press, 1988), 94, 95.

35 *Vital South,* 286; Wald, 123-4, 142. Wald rightly sees both Jackson and Robertson as civil religionists. Using a well-worn distinction, he calls Robertson's version "priestly," while Jackson's is a "prophetic" civil religion.

36 Bill Moyers, "What a Real President Was Like," *Washington Post,* November 13, 1988.

37 On Johnson as traitor to the South, see Charles and Barbara Whalen, *The Longest Debate* (New York: New American Library, 1986).

38 Wicker, 38.

39 Louis Harris and William Brink, *Black and White: a Study of U. S. Racial Attitudes Today* (New York: Simon and Schuster, 1964) 100-117; George H. Gallup, *The Gallup Poll: 1935- 1971* (3 vols.; New York: Random House, 1972, III, 1933, 19041-43, 2011, 2021, 2128. See also Wicker, 8.

40 Oran Smith, *The Rise of Baptist Republicanism* (New York: New York University Press, 1997) 89; Earl and Merle Black, *Politics and Society in the South* (Cambridge: Harvard University Press, 1987) 218-219; *Vital South,* 292-276; Wicker, 6, 13, 38.

41 Dan T. Carter, *The Politics of Rage,* 472, 474; Wallace quoted in Applebome, 90. This connection between Wallace and late twentieth century rightwing politics is also noted by Earl and Merle Black, *Vital South,* 247-8, and James C. Cobb, *Redefining Southern Culture,* 89-90.

42 Dan T. Carter, *From George Wallace to Newt Gingrich: Race in the Conservative Counterrevolution, 1963-1994* (Baton Rouge: Louisiana State University Press, 1996) 14-15. Hereinafter cited as *FGWTNG.*

43 Carter, *From George Wallace to Newt Gingrich,* 42.

44 Carter, FGWTNG, 30-31, citing John Erlichman, *Witness to Power: the Nixon Years* (New York: Simon and Schuster, 1982) 223.

45 Carter, FGWTNG, 18, citing Gallup poll data; *Politics of Rage,* 471.

46 From a publisher's blurb for Carter, FGWTNG.

47 Wald, 132.

48 Pat Buchanan August 13, 2000, Reform Party Convention, Long Beach; Bob Kemper, "Buchanan Maps Last-Minute Ad Blitz," *Chicago Tribune,* October 31, 2000. Both sources accessed on the Buchanan campaign's Web site.

49 Michael Lind, "The Southern Coup," *New Republic,* 19 June 1995, 26, 29; Earl and Merle Black, *Vital South,* 295; Tod A. Baker, Robert P. Steed, and Laurence W. Moreland, "Culture Wars and Religion in the South: The Changing Character of the Party Struggle," in *Party Activists in Southern Politics: Mirrors and Makers of Change* (Knoxville: University of Tennessee Press, 1998), 35-6.

50 David Goldfield, *Still Fighting the Civil War* (Baton Rouge: Louisiana State University Press, 2002), 318.

51 Douglas Lederman, Old Times Not Forgotten," *Chronicle of Higher Education,* October 20, 1993, A51-52.

52 *Danville Register and Bee,* June 8, 1993; June 12, 1993.

53 Quoted in Emory M. Thomas, *The Confederate Nation: 1861-1865* (New York: Harper and Row, Publishers, 1979) 10.

54 *Danville Register and Bee,* June 5, 1993; June 9, 1993; *Danville Register and Bee,* June 10, 1993.

55 Miller quoted in Richard Hyatt, *Zell: The Governor Who Gave Georgia HOPE* (Macon: Mercer University Press, 1997) 325-326, 335-336.

56 *New York Times,* April 27, 2003.

57 *Steve Lopez,* "Ghosts of the South," *Inside Politics,* April 23, 2001.

58 Gitlin, 81.

59 Falwell and Robertson's statements are included in Edwin S. Gaustad and

Mark Noll, eds. *A Documentary History of Religion in America. Third Edition* (Grand Rapids: William B. Eerdmans Publishing Company, 2003), 704.

60 "Bush and God," *Newsweek*, March 7, 2003. Accessed at www.newsweek.com.

61 Jim Wallis, "Dangerous Religion: George W. Bush's Theology of Empire," *Sojourners*, http://www.sojo.net/index? action=magazine.article&issue=soj0 309&article=030910.

62 Deborah Caldwell, "How Islam Bashing Got Cool," *Religious Studies News* 18 (October 2003): 13, 27.

63 *Los Angeles Times*, October 16, 2003, www.latimes.com; "Background of General William Boykin," October 17, 2003, www.msnbc.com.

64 www.lifeway.com/ft_o402c.asp.

65 *Los Angeles Times,* October 15, 2003, http://www.msnbc.com.

66 *NYT*, October 22, 2003; Associated Baptist Press Release, October 21, 2003.

67 *Atlanta Journal-Constitution*, March 30, 2003, A1; *Atlanta Journal-Constitution*, August 24, 2003, A1.

68 Bernard Zuel, "Rock Requiems," *Sydney Morning Herald,* August 10, 2002, http://www.smh.com.au/articles/2002/08/09/1028158015112.html; Jason Schneider, "Steve Earle: Voice of Reason Or Treason?" *Exclaim*, October 3, 2002, http://www.exclaim.ca/index.asp?layid=22&csid1=1063.

69 *Fort Worth Star-Telegram*, June 15, 2003, http://www.dfw.com/mld/startelegram/living/6088510.html; *Rocky Mountain News*, June 23, 2003, http://rockymountainnews.com/drmn/music/article/0,1299,DRMN_54_2055932,00.html; *Rochester Democrat and Chronicle*, July 22, 2003, http://www.democratandchronicle.com/entertainment/night/after/ent_1242.shtml.

CONCLUSION

MOBILIZED FOR THE NEW MILLENNIUM

Charles R. Wilson

Evangelical Protestants have long dominated the American South, but they have not been a static group. Their aggressive missionary and crusading spirit has taken different forms in different eras. The earliest southern evangelicals were socially marginal and radical in their embrace of antislavery egalitarianism. Nineteenth-century Baptists, Methodists, and Presbyterians embodied the evangelical success story, working in regionally organized, congregationally oriented denominations, imposing a moral code on the region, and defending regional institutions from outside attack. By the mid-twentieth century, Methodists and Presbyterians were not fully within the evangelical fold, although a shared theological and moral conservatism often made them close to Baptists on issues of public life. Pentecostals and the burgeoning nondenominational church movement expressed the evangelical fervor anew, binding the working class to the middle class on some religious issues, despite differing economic situations.

Black Protestants have worshiped in their own evangelical denominations, sharing much in the way of Biblicism and moral conservatism with white Protestants; but living in the South's race-conscious, white-dominated society has given them a separate religious identity, and a separate religious politics. White and black evangelicals have historically responded to the South's changing socio-economic context to reassert the centrality of faith, and they continue to do so today.

The role of religion in the public life of the South has evolved as a result of growing secularism, expressed in the power of media in communications centers distant from the region to inculcate moral ideals different from the region's churches. Manifestations include the growing alienation from modern life, a sensibility shared widely in Western culture but taking peculiar root in a region whose moral and spiritual life long reflected a backward-looking vision of the good life; suspicion of centralized authority, which also draws on a long regional tradition and on hostility, in particular, toward a federal government perhaps symbolized here by "activist" judges; and the prosperity of the churches themselves, which has made possible resources for organizing and participating in local, state, regional, and national life as never before.

The southern faithful long balanced a concern for public morality within an overarching emphasis on the primacy of individual conversion followed by pious behavior. In the face of recent social changes in the region, southern churches, religious leaders, and lay people have tilted in favor of greater public regulation of moral behavior.

Few changes in the South are likely to be of more long-term significance than the arrival of Latinos in notable numbers. While Latinos have long been a presence in Florida, along the Gulf South, and in Texas, the 2000 Census reported that six of the seven states that had a more than 200 percent increase in their Latino population since 1990 are in the South (North Carolina, South Carolina, Georgia, Alabama, Tennessee, and Arkansas).

Some are transmigrants who maintain close ties to their places of origin and do not come to settle long term. Others have brought their families and are making new homes, with religion a key to their adaptation in this new South. Georgia and North Carolina have four of the six Catholic dioceses in the nation with the fastest growing Latino membership, and those dioceses are receiving a dramatic imprint of Latino faith. Pentecostal churches have had success in converting Latinos to their faith, and have also seen burgeoning growth in Latin America itself. The arrival of Latinos has created opportunities for evangelical missionary work but also injected a dynamic new group that clearly does not always share the outlooks of traditional white evangelicalism or black Protestantism.

But if Latino population growth promises a reconfigured social context for the development of religion in the South, a less noticed demographic development reaffirms that African Americans remain the central minority group in the region. The 2000 Census reported that the non-Latino black population of the South grew in the 1990s by 3.5 million—an astonishing 58 percent of the increase in the nation's African-American population. Much of the increase resulted from a return migration of blacks to the South—a population shift that began in the 1970s, when 1.9 million blacks came to the region, and continued in the 1980s, with 1.7 million black returnees.

The 2000 number points to a dramatic black population surge into the South, reinforcing the demographer William H. Frey's assessment that it remains "primarily a white-black region." For while Latinos were notable in coming to many southern states, 71 percent of Latino populatin growth in the 1990s still took place in Florida and Texas. The other 15 states classified as southern by the census (the

South and Southern Crossroads regions for the purpose of this series) gained 2.4 million blacks during the last decade, compared with 1.4 million Latinos, who came into states whose black populations were already substantially higher than their Latino numbers. It's worth noting, as well, that African Americans in the South retain high racial identification, as seen by those responding to the 2000 Census opportunity to check more than one racial category. The states with the highest "black only" response were all not only in the South but in the Deep South: Mississippi (99.3 percent), Alabama (99 percent), South Carolina (98.8 percent), Georgia (98.4 percent), and—in the Southern Crossroads—Louisiana (99 percent).[1]

Despite dramatic changes in the social context of religion in the South, the region's public life will likely retain, in religious terms, the strong imprint of the interaction of white evangelical Protestants and black Protestants. The former witness for social morality while the latter testify for social justice. While both groups have achieved notable successes in the public arena over the past half century, it is clear that, since the end of the Civil Rights Movement, white evangelical Protestants have been in the ascendant.

President George W. Bush stands as the avatar of the new sensibility of religious-cultural activism in the white evangelical belt that includes both the South and Southern Crossroads. This sensibility draws from strong religious inheritances from the past and yet since the 1970s has operated in a re-configured and changed South. Secularism and a diversity of faiths have come to the South, yet, as John C. Green notes, "traditional Southern religion has become even more distinctive in the context of growing diversity."[2]

Bush was elected in 2000 thanks to southern votes, including a sweep of the 11 Confederate states, which gave him more than half of the electoral votes he needed. States bordering the region, and with pronounced southern cultural influences, gave him another quarter of his votes. Observant evangelical Protestants were the core of the old white Protestant alliance, and they are the driving constituency of the Religious Right.

Bush fulfilled the southern strategy of resurrecting that alliance, combining the votes of observant evangelicals in the South with support of other white Protestants. Observant evangelical Protestants gave Bush 45 percent of all southern votes, making them by far his most significant voting group. Deep South white Protestants voted more strongly for Bush than those in the Upper South, reinforcing the profile previously noted of geographic differences within the South. Al Gore's vote also had a religious component, as he combined the overwhelming support of black Protestants, who represented 34 percent of his ballots, with votes from Latino Catholics and members of other faiths, drawing from the changed southern society. Bush's victory was a narrow one, but that made the large observant evangelical Protestant voting group important to the Republican victory.

John C. Green's analysis of the 2002 campaign in the South revealed that a key to the Republican victories that year was the mobilization by churches of the region's white evangelical Protestants. Comparing votes for members of the House of Representatives in the South and the rest of the nation, Green found that white Protestants generally voted Republican, with white evangelicals who attended church often giving 75 percent of their votes to Republican candidates. Republicans also attracted white Catholics, while the Democrats won votes from other religious minorities in the region, including black Protestants, Latino Catholics, Jews, and those regarding themselves as secular. The evangelical Protestant vote provided a late surge in close races in the South, with high-commitment evangelicals (those who attend church once a week or more) the key. Their 51 percent turnout was the highest percentage for any religious group in the South and, as Green says, it was "markedly greater than the same group displayed in the rest of the country."

The South itself in 2002 was a hothouse of religious political activity, with white mainline Protestants, high-commitment Catholics, black Protestants, and secular voters all voting at higher rates than their counterparts in other areas of the nation. However, low-commitment evangelicals in the South did not vote at such high rates and were less likely than high-commitment evangelicals to vote Republican. The key factor explaining the high-commitment political participation was, Green concluded, "church-based mobilization by the religious right: registering voters, passing out voter guides, and getting out the vote within Baptist, Pentecostal, and nondenominational churches." Regular church attendance exposes congregants to these cues. It appears that "white evangelical churches have now become the GOP's institutional power base from Virginia to Texas."[3]

The 2004 presidential campaign confirmed the importance of evangelical voters in Republican Party dominance in the South. About 20 percent of voters across the nation identify themselves as evangelical Protestants, and they voted for President Bush by a four-to-one margin. About a fifth of the nation's voters saw moral values as the most important campaign issue, and of those, about 70 percent voted Republican. The margins were even higher in the South. In Tennessee and Arkansas, for example, a third of those casting ballots listed moral values as the deciding issue for them, with 90 percent of those voting for Bush. The evangelical interpretation of the results was clear. Richard Land, president of the Southern Baptists' Ethics and Religious Liberty Commission, concluded that Kerry's vision was for a secular government, with his Roman Catholicism not affecting his public policy. As Land put it, "The president said, 'I'm a man of faith and my faith will impact my public policy' and...the American people took Bush's vision over Kerry's."[4]

The 2004 campaign was further confirmation that the Republicans had put together again the old southern white Protestant alliance of observant evangelical voters and conservative economic Republicans for a majority coalition. Ralph Reed, the former executive director of the Christian Coalition, was in charge of President Bush's campaign in the Southeast, and the president's re-election suggested new influence for Reed's strategy of combining the passion of the Religious Right with a certain political pragmatism that moved the Religious Right toward cooperation with Republicans who might not share all the moral concerns of evangelicals but would work with them.

Southern religious people had long looked to the "good man" as the defining quality in a political candidate, above and beyond ideology. George W. Bush seems to have carved out that role for himself. As Green notes, to rank and file evangelicals in the South, "this is a man who speaks the language of religious conservatives very well, talks about his own conversion experience, and talks about this in a deep and personal way." Most tellingly, "he is one of them."[5]

White evangelicals in the South have mobilized politically to seek public support for a worldview still rooted in the nineteenth century. They seek recognition of the legitimacy of their vision of a Christian civilization. They believe that moral absolutes exist and any honest individual can discern them. Society should affirm these moral absolutes in law and the government should actively work to preserve them. As Grant Wacker has noted, they believe that "in a Christian civilization government, no less than church or family, is squarely responsible for the cultivation of moral fiber."[6] The media, public educational institutions, and the federal courts are the enemies of this vision; their influence must be subdued so the tenets of the vision of a Christian civilization, which had once dominated the South's public life, can now be at the center not only of regional but also of national culture. Southern evangelicals see a "southern strategy" that is focused not just on the South itself but involves the South's (redeemer) role in shaping the nation.

Evangelical Protestantism will surely take on new authority in southern public life, but its success in achieving the vision of a Christian civilization will depend on its negotiating the complex terrain of contemporary southern society. "Moral values" as a term may have been captured by the social morality of the Religious Right, but social justice remains a prominent force in the South. Black Protestants continue to use their churches as an organizational base, supporting liberal candidates, and they are particularly vital to the efforts of black elected officials.

Visits of candidates to African-American churches are more common than in white Protestant churches, and black ministers more likely to discuss politics from the pulpit. If black churches mobilize for social justice causes, they often do so by reaching out to others. The "beloved community" defined by Martin Luther King Jr. and forged during the Civil Rights Movement continues as an ideal for black churches and many people of good will in the South. When the incidence of church burnings rose in the region in the mid-1990s, black and white Protestants often made new community-based alliances in rebuilding churches and trust across racial and denominational boundaries. Religiously based racial reconcili- ation efforts, environmental justice campaigns drawing from biblical discourse, church-based economic development programs, and interdenominational self- help projects all reflect this social gospel impulse.

In 2002 Alabama saw a particularly dramatic example of efforts to mobilize a social justice campaign, in this case one that drew, ironically if unsuccess- fully, from conservative Christian impulses. Governor Robert Riley tried to persuade Alabama voters to approve by referendum a $1.2 billion tax increase to correct a state tax structure that he had concluded exploited the poor. "Jesus says one of our missions is to take care of the least among us," Riley said.[7] Riley knew his Bible well, and voters could recall that he had been elected as a Bible-quoting Religious Right supporter as well as a conventional low- tax conservative Republican. A state financial crisis, as well as conscience, impelled him to propose the controversial tax increase.

Riley had been converted to his tax reform proposal through the writings of Susan Pace Hamill, a University of Alabama law professor and Methodist, who drew from Christian ethics in condemning a regressive state tax struc- ture that milked Alabama's poorest people at an 11 percent rate, compared to 4 percent for the wealthiest. "According to our Christian ethics," Riley said during his campaign for reform, "we're supposed to love God, love each other, and help take care of the poor." He insisted that it was "immoral to charge somebody making $5,000 an income tax."[8]

Riley's efforts, however, were for naught. His conservative Protestant credentials and his arguments won the support of the national Christian Coalition, but the organization's state chapter condemned the tax increase. Mainline Protestant groups supported Riley, but pastors of independent evangelical churches did not endorse his campaign, pleading that churches should stay out of politics. The traditional doctrine of the "spirituality of the church" was brought out of mothballs to oppose tax reform; it's likely that these same ministers would have seen matters differently on a "moral values" issue like abortion. Black religious leaders, perhaps distrustful of Riley's conservative record, kept their distance from the initiative, which also contributed to its failure.

Among the complex ways that conservative white evangelicals and liberal black Protestants can come together around moral and social issues was President Bush's faith-based initiative, which sought to make government funding available for churches active in community projects but reluctant to suppress the evangelistic dimension of their social ministries. Although many black ministers and activists were skeptical of the Republican Party and saw the effort as one designed to silence prophetic voices from the black community, others saw government support as providing essential resources. Megachurches are part of the changing South for both white and black churchgoers, but they are particularly significant in this context for African Americans. Black pastors at such churches as Atlanta's World Changers Ministries have congregations of 20,000 people or so who gather in buildings that could be sports arenas and hear preaching about God's plans for the worldly success of believers. To the faithful here, the issues are not the old ones of social and political engagement but individual conversion, pious behavior, and respectability. These "prosperity ministries" stress that if the individual rises, the broader African-American community will also rise. Faith-based initiatives can promote that goal.

Another issue of black-white religious cooperation in the South has been opposition to same-sex marriage. White evangelical Protestants have long had opposition to the public legitimation of homosexuality on their political agenda, but the 2004 decision of the Massachusetts Supreme Court recognizing marriages of gay and lesbian couples energized black opponents as well. Advocates of same-sex marriage sometimes describe support for it as a continuation of the civil rights struggle, but this rhetoric bothered some black ministers, with opposition often coming from black ministers outside the historically black denominations in various non-denominational and "community" churches, many of them megachurches.

In Georgia, black church leaders held rallies, met with the press, and effectively lobbied black legislators in support of an amendment to the state constitution banning gay marriage. In Mississippi, the black congressman Bennie Thompson initially opposed a similar state amendment but changed his mind and endorsed it under pressure from black ministers. In the 2004 elections, state amendments banning gay and lesbian marriage passed in every southern state (as well as elsewhere in the nation) where they were on the ballot. In a column, the editor of the editorial page of the *Atlanta Journal-Constitution*, Cynthia Tucker, lamented that this was "a triumph for bigotry based on the Bible" and compared the restriction on gay rights to the defense of slavery. "And they weren't just white voters," Tucker wrote. "Homophobia oozes across lines of color, linking black America with white in a common contempt masquerading as morality."[9]

If white evangelicals have found common ground with black Protestants on faith-based social services, they have also linked with Catholics in opposition to abortion and in other "right to life" issues. One case in point involved Terri Schiavo, a Florida woman who had been kept alive under the guardianship of her husband Michael after doctors pronounced her to be in a "permanent vegetative state" in 1990. In 2003, a Florida court—in response to his petition and after a long legal battle with her Roman Catholic parents—ordered the removal of her feeding tube, which would have led to her death within a few weeks. Florida Governor Jeb Bush and the state legislature, under new pressure from evangelical activists like Operation Rescue's founder, Randall Terry, then passed a law permitting the governor to intervene to prevent the feeding tube's removal. Those supporting Michael Schiavo saw the case as a private matter of a husband making a difficult decision based on his wife telling him before she fell ill that she would not want to remain in a vegetative state if any such catastrophe befell her. The syndicated columnist Leonard Pitts complained of the "galling hypocrisy" in the case, as some conservatives "jettison the conservative credo that government should interfere as little as possible in the lives and decisions of the people."[10] Advocates for keeping Schiavo alive, including both evangelicals and Roman Catholics, believed that removing the tube would violate their commitment to the sacredness of life.

Beyond such thorny policy issues, white evangelicals have sought to extend their ambitions to dominate the public sphere through symbolic struggles to define region and nation as embodying sacred expectations. The Confederate battle flag, with its St. Andrews Cross on a red background, was one of those prime southern symbols that celebrated not just the Confederacy but the entire southern way of life. It emerged first in battle, as a dramatic visual image around which troops could rally, and then became an emblem of the South's Lost Cause after the Civil War, as part of a civil religious complex that sacralized the Confederacy. Over the years, the Ku Klux Klan displayed the flag as part of its vigilante activities, and it was a prominent icon for opponents of the Civil Rights Movement.

It was incorporated into the Mississippi flag in the 1890s and the Georgia flag in the 1950s, both eras of rising white racial consciousness. Since the 1970s, blacks and their white allies have challenged the appropriateness of such flags, and since the mid-1990s both states have struggled to resolve the issue. In 2001 Mississippians voted to keep the flag by a vote of 65 percent to 35 percent, while in Georgia a new state flag was devised. South Carolina had long flown the flag over its state Capitol building, and after much haggling, the flag was removed from the Capitol in the summer of 2000 but still displayed on the Capitol grounds.

Civil religious symbols and rituals are supposed to give glimpses of some ultimate purpose for a society. But the South of the new millennium was not the post-Civil War South that had given birth to the Religion of the Lost Cause. The flag could not provide the unity that is needed for such symbols because it did not symbolize a positive cause for black Southerners, who are now among the cultural—as well as political—powerbrokers of the region. In Mississippi, the leaders of the Episcopal, Methodist, and Catholic churches all endorsed a new flag, as did Donald Wildmon, the prominent Religious Right leader. Voters in the state nonetheless seemed more interested in ensuring that recollection of, if not the ultimate purpose for, the Lost Cause survived. The passion and divisiveness of the debates on the Confederate flag show the difficulties of moving away from older civil religious meanings in the South.

The passion and divisiveness over the display of the Ten Commandments in the South show how region, nation, and religion have become intertwined in what might be considered the South's new civil religion. This symbol focuses broader meanings about how evangelical Protestants, and their allies, believe the South must embody Christian moral expectations not just privately but in the region's public spaces. In July 2002, Roy Moore, the newly elected chief justice of the Alabama Supreme Court, directed workers in placing a 5,280-pound granite monument he had designed, displaying the Ten Commandments and quotations from the Bible and the Founding Fathers of the American republic, in the rotunda of the state judicial building in Montgomery. This act drew upon popular fervor for the state to acknowledge open religiosity, and it created a memorable firestorm in the history of civil religion in the South.

Moore had claimed the Ten Commandments as his cause from his days as a state judge in Etowah County. He hung a hand-carved plaque of the Commandments in his courtroom and later won election to the Supreme Court as the "Ten Commandments judge." He himself embodied the cause in his personal life. Images of George Washington and Abraham Lincoln, it turned out, hung at his home, alongside those of Moses and Jesus. Raised in the Appalachian foothills, Moore attended a Southern Baptist Convention congregation in Gadsden, Alabama, and was given to quoting long passages from the Bible. A graduate of West Point, he went to Vietnam as commander of a military police company whose men called him Captain America for his super patriotism.

One of his fellow church members in Gadsden characterized Moore as "a patriot, someone like George Washington, Benjamin Franklin, or Thomas Jefferson." A poem he wrote during the Clinton administration expressed the evangelical sense of a spoiled America in need of redemption: "America the Beautiful, or so you used to be. Land of the Pilgrims' pride; I'm glad they'll never see. Babies piled in Dumpsters, Abortion on Demand, Oh' sweet land of liberty, your house is on the sand...."[11] In a place where citizens often complain of activist judges, this most activist of jurists emerged as a civil religious saint.

In 2003, a federal district court, and later the federal circuit court of appeals in Atlanta, ordered removal of the granite monument, pronouncing it a violation of the First Amendment's prohibition on government establishment of religion. The court compared Moore to "those Southern governors who attempted to defy federal court orders during an earlier era"—the civil rights era, with Alabama governor George Wallace in the forefront with his proclamations of states rights.[12] The state, regional, and national press made similar linkages, strengthening the sense that evangelical Protestant moral-religious crusading had replaced race as a defining public issue in the contemporary South. Ninety percent of Alabamians, according to one poll, favored keeping the monument in place.

The Ten Commandments story was not just peculiar to Alabama. After the federal judges ordered removal of the monument from the Montgomery judicial building, Democrat Ronnie Musgrove and Republican Haley Barbour, locked in a tough campaign for the Mississippi gubernatorial office, both offered to bring the monument to the state for display in the state Capitol building or the Governor's Mansion. Shortly after, in September 2003, the "Spirit of Montgomery Tour," on the road in seven southern states, arrived in Atlanta to find the governor and other Georgia politicians and civic leaders rallying around a plastic foam replica of Moore's Ten Commandments monument. Many people in the crowd carried signs with messages such as "Thou Shalt Not Put God's Law in a Closet" and "No King But Jesus."

At an earlier rally, in August 2003, to protest removal of the monument from its place, the Associated Press' Bob Johnson reported, "Demonstrators kept vigil Saturday outside the Alabama Judicial Building, singing, preaching and praying for a way to prevent removal" of the monument.[13] The words evoked bluegrass on the public square and black church demonstrators in the Civil Rights Movement.

The transformation of white evangelical churches into organs of political mobilization for the GOP has been based on observation of black church mobilization, with symbolic rallies only a part of the effort. Southern evangelical politicos have drawn from the black churches (and perhaps taken to a new level) not just the practice of doing politics on the ground— drawing from regional and national symbolism and ritual—but also establishing networks that reach across the country. This is an example of the hybridized black-white culture of the South, in which both sides do not exactly acknowledge their debts to each other but claim authority to do it because other churches have done so. There seems little question that the biracial religious South will continue to provide the context for on-going civil religious understandings of the relationship between the region and the nation for some time to come.

Endnotes

1 William H. Frey, "Migration to the South Brings U.S. Blacks Full Circle," *Population Today* (May-June 2001), 1, 4.

2 John C. Green, "Believers for Bush, Godly for Gore: Religion and the 2000 Election in the South," in Robert P. Steed and Laurence W. Moreland, eds., *The 2000 Presidential Election in the South: Partisanship and Southern Party Systems in the 21st Century* (Westport, CT: Praeger, 2001), 12.

3 John C. Green, "The Undetected Tide," *Religion in the News* (Spring 2003).

4 Kevin Eckstrom and Michele M. Melendez, "Values-driven Voters 'Ushered President Down Aisle,'" *Atlanta Journal-Constitution*, November 6, 2004.

5 Mark Rozell, "Evangelicals: Inside the Beltway," *Religion in the News* (Spring 2003).

6 Grant Wacker, "Searching for Norman Rockwell: Popular Evangelicalism in Contemporary America," in Leonard I. Sweet, ed., *The Evangelical Tradition in America* (Macon, GA: Mercer University Press, 1984), 300.

7 Lisa San Pascual, "The Social Gospel Lays an Egg in Alabama," *Religion in the News* (Spring 2003).

8 *Ibid.*

9 Cynthia Tucker, "Bible Verses Used as 'Bible Versus,'" *Atlanta Journal-Constitution*, November 11, 2004.

10 Leonard Pitts, "Time to Let Patient Die in Peace," *New Orleans Times-Picayune*, October 4, 2004.

11 Mark Bixler, "Supporters See Chief Moore as Moral Voice in Decaying Society," *Atlanta Journal-Constitution*, August 24, 2003.

12 Adam Liptak, "Court Orders Removal of Monument to Ten Commandments," *New York Times*, July 2, 2003.

13 Bob Johnson, "Vigil Prays for Monument to Stay in Rotunda," *Memphis Commercial-Appeal*, August 24, 2003.

APPENDIX

I n order to provide the best possible empirical basis for understanding the place of religion in each of the religions of the United States, the Religion by Region project contracted to obtain data from three sources: the North American Religion Atlas (NARA); the 2001 American Religious Identification Survey (ARIS); and the 1992, 1996, and 2000 National Surveys of Religion and Politics (NSRP).

NARA For the Project, the Polis Center of Indiana University-Purdue University at Indianapolis created an interactive Web site that made it possible to map general demographic and religious data at the national, regional, state-by-state, and county-by-county level. The demographic data were taken from the 2000 Census. The primary source for the religious data (congregations, members, and adherents) was the 2000 Religious Congregations and Membership Survey (RCMC) compiled by the Glenmary Research Center. Because a number of religious groups did not participate in the 2000 RCMS—including most historically African-American Protestant denominations—this dataset was supplemented with data from other sources *for adherents only*. The latter included projections from 1990 RCMC reports, ARIS, and several custom estimates. For a fuller methodological account, go to *http://www.religionatlas.org*.

ARIS The American Religious Identification Survey (ARIS 2001), carried out under the auspices of the Graduate Center of the City University of New York by Barry A. Kosmin, Egon Mayer, and Ariela Keysar, replicates the methodology of the National Survey of Religious Identification (NSRI 1990). As in 1990 the ARIS sample is based on a series of national random digit dialing (RDD) surveys, utilizing ICR, International Communication Research Group in Media, Pennsylvania, national telephone omnibus services. In all, 50,284 U.S. households were successfully interviewed. Within a household, an adult respondent was chosen using the "last birthday method" of random selection. One of the distinguishing features of both ARIS 2001 and NSRI 1990 is that respondents were asked to describe themselves in terms of religion with an open-ended question: "What is your religion, if any?[1]" ARIS 2001 enhanced the topics covered by adding questions concerning religious beliefs and membership as well as religious switching and religious identification of spouses/partners. The ARIS findings have a high level of statistical significance for most large religious groups and key geographical units, such as states. ARIS 2001 detailed methodology can be found in the report on the American Religious Identification Survey 2001at *www.gc.cuny.edu/studies/aris_index.htm.*

NSRP The National Surveys of Religion and Politics were conducted in 1992, 1996, and 2000 at the Bliss Center at the University of Akron under the direction of John C. Green, supported by grants from the Pew Charitable Trusts.

Together, these three surveys include more than 14,000 cases. Eight items were asked in all three surveys (partisanship, ideology, abortion, gay rights, help for minorities, environmental protection, welfare spending, and national health insurance). The responses on these items were pooled for all three years to produce enough cases for an analysis by region. These data must be viewed with some caution because they represent opinion over an entire decade rather than at one point in time. A more detailed account of how these data were compiled may be obtained from the Bliss Institute.

Endnote

1. In the 1990 NSRI survey, the question wording was: "What is your religion?" In the 2001 ARIS survey, the phrase, "...if any" was added to the question. A subsequent validity check based on cross-samples of 3,000 respondents carried out by ICR in 2002 found no statistical difference in the pattern of responses according to the two wordings.

BIBLIOGRAPHY

Ammerman, Nancy Tatom. *Baptist Battles: Social Change and Religious Conflict in the Southern Baptist Convention*. New Brunswick, N.J.: Rutgers University Press, 1990.

Anderson, Jon W. and William Friend, eds. *The Culture of Bible Belt Catholics*. New York: Paulist Press, 1995.

Evans, Eli N. *The Provincials: A Personal History of Jews in the South*. New York: Atheneum, 1973.

Flynt, J. Wayne. *Alabama Baptists: Southern Baptists in the Heart of Dixie*. Tuscaloosa: University of Alabama Press, 1998.

Glass, William R. *Strangers in Zion: Fundamentalists in the South, 1900-1950*. Macon, Ga.: Mercer University Press, 2001.

Hankins, Barry. *Uneasy in Babylon: Southern Baptist Conservatives and American Culture*. Tuscaloosa: University of Alabama Press, 1996.

Harvey, Paul. *Redeeming the South: Religious Cultures and Racial Identities among Southern Baptists, 1865-1925*. Chapel Hill: University of North Carolina Press, 1997.

Heyrman, Christine Leigh. *Southern Cross: The Beginnings of the Bible Belt*. New York: Alfred A. Knopf, 1997.

Hill, Samuel S. and Charles H. Lippy, eds. *Encyclopedia of Religion in the South*, 2nd edition. Macon: Ga.: Mercer University Press, 2004.

Leonard, Bill J. *Christianity in Appalachia*. Knoxville: University of Tennessee Press, 1995.

Manis, Andrew. *Southern Civil Religions in Conflict: Civil Rights and the Culture*. Macon, Ga.: Mercer University Press, 2001.

McCauley, Deborah Vansau. *Appalachian Mountain Religion: A History*. Urbana: University of Illinois Press, 1995.

Montgomery, William E. *Under Their Own Vine and Fig Tree: The African-American Church in the South, 1865-1900*. Baton Rouge: Louisiana State University Press, 1993.

Ownby, Ted. *Subduing Satan: Religion, Recreation, and Manhood in the Rural South, 1865-1920*. Chapel Hill: University of North Carolina Press, 1990.

Tweed, Thomas. "Our Lady of Guadeloupe Visits the Confederate Memorial: Latino and Asian Religions in the South." *Southern Cultures*, Vol. 8 (2002), 72-93.

Wilson, Charles Reagan. *Baptized in Blood: The Religion of the Lost Cause, 1865-1920*. Athens: University of Georgia Press, 1980.

INDEX

CONTRIBUTORS

Paul Harvey is assistant professor at the University of Colorado at Colorado Springs. He is the author of *Redeeming the South: Religious Cultures and Racial Identities among Southern Baptists, 1865-1925* (1997) and coeditor of *Themes in Religion and American Culture* (2004).

Samuel S. Hill is professor emeritus of religion at the University of Florida and author of such works as *Southern Churches in Crisis* (1966), *The New Religious-Political Right in America* (1982), and *One Name But Several Faces: Variety in Popular Christian Denominations in Southern History* (1996). He was editor of the *Encyclopedia of Religion in the South* (1984), a second edition of which will appear in 2005.

Charles H. Lippy is Martin Distinguished Professor of Religion and Philosophy at the University of Tennessee at Chattanooga. He is author of, among other works, *Popular Religiosity in the United States* (1994) and *Pluralism Comes of Age: American Religious Culture in the Twentieth Century* (2000). He was coeditor of the *Encyclopedia of the American Religious Experience: Studies of Traditions and Movements* (1988) and is coeditor of the new edition of the *Encyclopedia of Religion in the South.*

Cynthia Lynn Lyerly is associate professor of history at Boston College. She is the author of *Methodism and the Southern Mind*, 1770-1810 (1990) and is currently at work on a study of the writer Thomas Dixon's works.

Andrew M. Manis is professor of history at Macon State College in Macon, Georgia. He is the author of *Southern Civil Religions in Conflict: Civil Rights and the Culture Wars* (2002), *A Fire You Can't Put Out: The Civil Rights Life of Birmingham's Reverend Fred Shuttlesworth* (1999), and *Macon Black and White: An Unutterable Separation in the American Century* (2004).

William E. Montgomery teaches at Austin Community College and is the author of *Under Their Own Vine and Fig Tree: The African American Church in the South, 1865-1900* (1993).

Ted Ownby is professor of history and Southern Studies at the University of Mississippi. He is author of *Subduing Satan: Religion, Recreation, and Manhood in the Rural South, 1865-1920* (1990) and *American Dreams in Mississippi: Consumers, Poverty, and Culture, 1830-1998* (1999). He is currently editing the *Mississippi Encyclopedia* and working on a study of family in the South.

Mark Silk, coeditor of this volume, is associate professor of religion in public life and founding director of the Leonard E. Greenberg Center for the Study of Religion in Public Life at Trinity College in Hartford, Connecticut. A former newspaper reporter and member of the editorial board at the *Atlanta Journal-Constitution*, he is the author of *Spiritual Politics: Religion and Politics in America since World Are II* (1988) and *Unsecular Media: Making News of Religion in America*. He is editor of *Religion in the News*, a magazine published by the Greenberg Center that examines how journalists handle religious subject matter.

Charles Reagan Wilson is professor of history and Southern Studies and director of the Center for the Study of Southern Culture at the University of Mississippi. He is the author of *Baptized in Blood: The Religion of the Lost Cause, 1865-1920* (1980) and *Judgment and Grace in Dixie: Southern Faiths from Faulkner to Elvis* (1995). He is coeditor of the *Encyclopedia of Southern Culture* (1989).